Learning Legal Technology

Learning Legal Technology

A Primer for the Modern Lawyer

Nicholas A. Pleasant
Research & Systems Librarian
Belmont University

CAROLINA ACADEMIC PRESS
Durham, North Carolina

Library of Congress Cataloging-in-Publication Data

Names: Pleasant, Nicholas A., author.
Title: Learning legal technology : a primer for the modern lawyer / Nicholas A. Pleasant.
Description: Durham, North Carolina : Carolina Academic Press, LLC, 2025. | Includes bibliographical references and index.
Identifiers: LCCN 2025027303 | ISBN 9781531027902 (paperback) | ISBN 9781531027919 (ebook)
Subjects: LCSH: Computers--Law and legislation--United States. | Technology and law--United States. | Technological innovations--Law and legislation--United States. | Practice of law--Technological innovations--United States.
Classification: LCC KF390.5.C6 P67 2025 | DDC 343.7309/99--dc23/eng/20250607
LC record available at https://lccn.loc.gov/2025027303

Carolina Academic Press
700 Kent Street
Durham, North Carolina 27701
(919) 489-7486
www.cap-press.com

Printed in the United States of America

To Jennifer and my 4Ls
without whom this book would have been finished much sooner,
but so would I.

Also, to friends and family lost along the way,
Johnnie Pleasant (grandfather), Rob Farmer (mentor), and
Caleb Blewett (friend).

Contents

Preface

The legal profession stands, as it frequently does, at the crossroads of tradition and innovation. With the rapid integration of technology into every facet of society, attorneys and law students find themselves grappling with tools and concepts once thought exclusive to IT specialists. This book aims to demystify legal technology and provide readers with a practical foundation for understanding and leveraging these tools effectively in their practice.

My journey in writing this book stems from a desire to bridge the knowledge gap between the legal and technological worlds. Over the years, I have observed the challenges many legal professionals face in adapting to new tools and platforms. The journey began in 2020 when I was approached to teach a course on legal technology, a subject that has always fascinated me. I should clarify that by legal technology, I do not mean the law governing the use of technology, but instead focusing on the technological tools being employed in practice. After agreeing to teach the class, I began the process of seeking out textbook options to review in preparation, only to discover that no text existed at the time that met my vision for the class—a high-level survey course that provided students with exposure to the breadth of technology being used in the legal field without going so far in-depth as to discourage students from participating.

Lacking a pre-organized textbook, however, was probably a greater boon than I credited it at the time. I surveyed and categorized my class into major fields that students would most likely encounter in practice but might not gain exposure to in law school. This included eDiscovery platforms, case management software, legal research databases, and the growing importance of data analytics in shaping litigation strategies. Each topic required me to delve deep into cross-disciplinary research, seeking to create an appropriate blend of legal and technological knowledge for my students. Every lecture took days of preparation, and the research conducted for the section on cybersecurity was so robust that it provided me with enough background to sit for and complete the International Information System Security Certification Consortium's entry-level Certified in Cybersecurity exam.

This experience underscored the pressing need for a resource that could streamline this process for others. As I developed my lectures, I began to recognize patterns and core themes that could form the backbone of a book. This book is the next logical step in that process. My colleague Laura Randazzo suggested, after observing me laboriously slog through my research, that with the amount of work I had done, I could probably write a book on the topic. Her encouragement, coupled with the overwhelmingly positive feedback from my students, was the push I needed to begin this project. This book is designed to meet the challenges facing law students and practitioners head-on, offering clear, relatable explanations and actionable insights. Whether you're a seasoned attorney navigating the complexities of eDiscovery or a law student preparing your first-year brief, the goal is to empower you with the confidence and competence to embrace technology.

Throughout the chapters, you will find analogies and scenarios that bring technical concepts to life, making them approachable and relevant. For example, in the chapter on eDiscovery, I use the analogy of fishing to explain the concept of data collection and filtering: casting a wide net to capture potentially relevant information and then sorting through the catch to identify what is truly important. Similarly, the chapter on the Parts and Processes of a computer compares a computer to a legal office and analogizes the processes to those familiar to the reader, thereby giving a common ground to establish initial understanding. These analogies aim to make the abstract tangible and the intimidating manageable.

Chapter 1, "Computer Parts and Processes: Introduction and Basics," introduces the fundamental components of computers and their relevance to legal technology. Using relatable analogies, it explains key concepts like CPU, RAM, and peripherals in a relatable way. It continues to explore the ethical duties of technological competence for attorneys under the ABA's Model Rules of Professional Conduct, emphasizing the need for a basic understanding of technology in modern legal practice. Additionally, it provides an overview of how network communications and the internet function, providing insight into how they impact tasks like eDiscovery and data security.

Chapter 2, "Document Manipulation," provides a comprehensive guide to many of the more essential document manipulation tools and techniques for legal professionals. It covers Microsoft Word's advanced formatting features, such as styles, table of contents, and the table of authorities, as well as collaboration tools like track changes and comments. It also explores document security, metadata removal, and formatting specifics. Additionally, it highlights Adobe Acrobat's functionalities for OCR, redaction, Bates numbering, and securing documents. These tools collectively enhance efficiency, accuracy, and professionalism in legal document preparation and management.

Chapter 3, "Cybersecurity: Protecting Your Firm and Your Client," explores the critical importance of cybersecurity in the legal profession, focusing on protecting sensitive client information and maintaining compliance with ethical and legal standards. It introduces key concepts such as the CIA Triad (confidentiality, integrity, and availability), common cyber threats like ransomware and phishing, and the principles of compartmentalization and layered defense. The chapter also outlines best practices for employing physical, logical, and administrative controls to mitigate risks, ensuring client data remains secure in an increasingly digital and interconnected legal environment.

Chapter 4, "Cryptography, Blockchain, and Smart Contracts," explores the evolution and applications of cryptography, blockchain technology, and smart contracts in the legal field. It begins with an overview of cryptographic principles, including encryption methods and their role in securing communications. The chapter then delves into blockchain's decentralized, tamper-resistant ledger, highlighting its uses in evidence chain of custody, intellectual property protection, and real estate registries. Finally, it discusses smart contracts as self-executing agreements that enhance efficiency and reliability.

Chapter 5, "Artificial Intelligence," provides an overview of artificial intelligence (AI) and its transformative impact on the legal field. It explains key AI concepts, including machine learning, deep learning, and the distinctions between traditional and generative AI. The chapter explores practical applications of AI in legal research, eDiscovery, document automation, due diligence, and legal analytics, highlighting how these tools enhance efficiency and accuracy. Ethical considerations, such as the risks of biased training data, confidentiality, and the importance of human oversight, are also discussed.

Chapter 6, "EDiscovery: Practices and Tools," examines the process of identifying, preserving, and reviewing electronically stored information for legal proceedings. It highlights key concepts such as proportionality, relevance, and the litigation hold, while outlining the Electronic Discovery Reference Model as a framework for managing ESI. The chapter explores the evolution of eDiscovery tools, including technology-assisted review with features like predictive coding, natural language processing, and email threading, which streamline data review and improve efficiency. Emphasis is placed on balancing technology with human oversight to ensure ethical and effective discovery practices.

Chapter 7, "Courtroom Technology," explores the critical role of technology in modern courtroom practice. It emphasizes the importance of thorough preparation, including conducting a tech inventory in preparation for appearance in a given courtroom. Being familiar only with one's own equipment is insufficient when dealing with an integrated presentation system. A prepared attorney must familiarize themselves with how their equipment is going to interact with any given system prior to the day of presentation.

In a broader sense, this book reflects my belief in the evolving nature of the legal profession and its professionals. We are no longer confined to understanding just the statutes, case law, and doctrines that underpin our practice; we must also embrace the technologies shaping how legal services are delivered. AI tools like predictive coding in document review or algorithms used to assess sentencing risk can streamline processes, but if the underlying data has not been effectively reviewed and sanitized, repetitive or biased data can skew results. Similarly, the increasing prevalence of blockchain technology and its implications for contract law, intellectual property, and real estate requires that attorneys build fluency in these areas.

It is equally important to recognize that technology is not a panacea. While it brings unprecedented efficiency and innovation, it also introduces challenges such as data privacy concerns, cybersecurity risks, and ethical questions regarding the use of automation in decision-making. This book addresses these complexities head-on, providing readers with the tools to navigate them thoughtfully and responsibly.

One of the recurring themes in this book is the importance of adaptability. The legal profession is steeped in tradition, but those who thrive in the modern landscape are those who can adapt to change. Technology is not going away; if anything, its role in the legal profession will only continue to expand. From virtual courtrooms to blockchain-based smart contracts, the future of law is being shaped by innovations that were once the stuff of science fiction. Embracing these changes requires not only technical proficiency but also a willingness to reimagine how we practice law.

For example, consider the rise of virtual law firms. These firms leverage technology to provide legal services without the overhead of physical office space. While this model offers significant cost savings and flexibility, it also presents unique challenges in areas such as client communication, confidentiality, and the management of remote teams. Similarly, the use of data analytics in litigation strategy allows attorneys to predict case outcomes with greater accuracy, but it also requires a fundamental shift in how we approach legal decision-making.

This book also explores the human side of technology. How do we, as legal professionals, maintain our ethical compass in a world increasingly driven by algorithms? How do we ensure that the efficiencies gained through automation do not come at the expense of client relationships or the quality of our work? These are not just technical questions; they are questions of professional identity and values. By examining these issues, this book seeks to equip readers with the tools to navigate the intersection of law and technology with integrity and purpose.

Ultimately, I view this book as part of a larger conversation about the role of technology in modern legal practice. It is a conversation that is not confined to classrooms or boardrooms but one that touches every facet of our profession, from the ways we interact with clients to the strategies we employ in the courtroom. It is my hope that the lessons and insights contained within these pages will not only prepare you to meet today's challenges but also inspire you to lead in shaping the future of legal practice.

Let us embark on this journey together, exploring the possibilities and confronting the challenges that legal technology presents. In doing so, I hope this book serves as both a guide and a catalyst for your continued growth and success in this ever-evolving field. Whether you are a student just beginning your legal career, a practitioner seeking to modernize your practice, or an academic exploring the theoretical implications of technology in law, this book is for you. Together, we will uncover the ways technology can enhance our profession while remaining vigilant about its potential pitfalls. The journey may be complex, but it is one worth undertaking. After all, at the heart of the legal profession is a commitment to justice, and embracing technology is an essential part of fulfilling that commitment in the twenty-first century.

Learning Legal Technology

CHAPTER 1

Computer Parts and Processes: Introduction and Basics

The legal technology field may seem daunting initially, but it becomes more approachable when broken down into its component parts. The most simplified description of technology I have ever seen was a meme that circulated a few years ago where IT professionals reminded one another that when they felt overwhelmed with their job, they should remember that a CPU is just a rock that we have tricked into thinking. Legal tech is, simply put, the contemporary areas in the world of technology that are currently impacting the professional legal field. It is a fluid mix that changes frequently and often without warning.

A prime example is the recent introduction and subsequent flood of generative AI tools and issues. In November 2022, OpenAI introduced the public to Chat-GPT, a generative AI model trained on a massive dataset to be a conversational model or Chatbot. Without spoiling too much of Chapter 5, generative AI is a form of artificial intelligence intended to create new content based on patterns learned from training on large datasets. As of the writing of this book, nearly two years later, an astounding number of generative AI tools based on the GPT framework have been released, including legal-oriented tools like Casetext's Co-Counsel and Lexis+ AI. Additionally, a new type of copyright infringement case has evolved based on the methods of training AI models using copyrighted materials. In two years, a single platform changed the face of multiple industries and threw many others into upheaval.

My goal is to provide you with basic competency in a broad range of topics to remove some of the stigma associated with technology. This familiarity will enable you to approach new fields of legal technology with a sound fundamental base, not ossify you into a doctrine of what is and isn't legal tech. In the spirit of keeping things simple, we will begin with why it is essential for law students and, ultimately, attorneys to have a basic but holistic understanding of technology. From that understanding, we will discuss the computer's vital components, the cornerstone of all legal tech, and proceed outward in subsequent chapters, discussing the technological trends currently impacting the professional legal world.

Attorney Duty of Technology Competence

The American Bar Association (ABA) publishes a set of Model Rules of Professional Conduct (MRPC) that guide the ethical behavior of attorneys. Many states adopt the ABA's MRPC as a requirement for the practice of law in that state. Of interest in this chapter specifically is MRPC 1.1, which states:

> A lawyer shall provide competent representation to a client. Competent representation requires the legal knowledge, skill, thoroughness, and preparation reasonably necessary for the representation.[1]

In 2012, the ABA added Comment 8 to Rule 1.1, which brought to light an implicit requirement of Rule 1.1:

> To maintain the requisite knowledge and skill, a lawyer should keep abreast of changes in the law and its practice, including the benefits and risks associated with relevant technology, engage in continuing study and education, and comply with all continuing legal education requirements to which the lawyer is subject.[2]

Admittedly, the standard in Comment 8 is unclear as to what degree of technological competence a lawyer should maintain. Rule 1.1's lan-

1. Model Rules of Pro. Conduct r. 1.1 (Am. Bar Ass'n 1983).
2. Model Rules of Pro. Conduct r. 1.1 cmt. 8 (Am. Bar Ass'n 1983).

guage requiring lawyers to maintain the level of competency "necessary for the representation" sheds little, if any, additional light on the issue. It reminds me of many conversations I've had with my children:

> Child, upon seeing a large cake: "I want that!"
> Me: "Well, I don't think it would be good for you to eat all that."
> Child, gravely: "Oh, I don't want to eat it all."
> Me: "Well, how much do you want to eat?"
> Child, after serious thought: "Enough."

Many great thinkers in the legal community have asked the same question of Comment 8 as I laughingly asked my four-year-old: "What is enough?" This topic has been the subject of discussion panels, and many talented attorneys have weighed in on the contours of technological competency in modern practice.[3]

The tentative consensus seems to be that "enough" is something beyond being able to Google but shy of being able to code. As maddening as that statement may be, it is essential to note that a lawyer's duty of technological competence is a sliding scale. By the very language of Rule 1.1, that duty doesn't look the same to a general practitioner in rural Tennessee as it does to a firm counseling a large corporate client on eDiscovery or information governance. The shape of technology competence is discerned more from the industry in which an attorney practices and not as a uniform standard applied across the field.

That being said, a general understanding of the tools currently in use in the legal field helps to contribute to the foundation of knowledge available to lawyers and law students when confronted with the ABA's technological competency standard. In the following pages, we will cover the basic anatomy of a computer and the fundamentals of how the Internet operates. This knowledge will help inform subsequent chapters, as computers and networked communication are the foundation of the current technological landscape.

---

3. *See* Katy (Yin Yee) Ho, *Defining the Contours of an Ethical Duty of Technological Competence*, 30 Geo. J. Legal Ethics 853 (2017); *see also* Lori D. Johnson, *Navigating Technological Competence in Transactional Practice*, 65 Vill. L. Rev. 159 (2020).

Basic Anatomy of a Computer

My experience is that when you begin talking about the inner workings of a computer, most people immediately limit themselves with phrases like "I'm not techy" or "I'm not an IT person." Fortunately, you don't have to be. If I can promise you anything from this book, it is that you will not finish reading it and be ready to build your own personal computer (PC). Still, hopefully, you will understand the functions and pieces well enough to have more meaningful conversations with IT staff than "It's not working."

At its most general level, a computer consists of three major types of parts: a processor, input and output devices, and a memory unit. As illustrated in Figure 1-1, multiple types of input and output devices can be employed, but at their most basic level, these are simply the senses that transmit data to the central processing unit (CPU). It's very simple, nothing frightening. The PC tower still has its case on, and it's not flaunting its motherboard.

Figure 1-1: Basic computer setup.

Taking things a step further, let's talk about the computer process. As you can see from Figure 1-2, it operates in a loop. The user starts by inputting data either by typing, clicking with a mouse, using a webcam, or even speaking. Using an input device is a technical way of saying that you are communicating to the computer what you want it to do; that's all there is to it. The computer, of course, doesn't speak the same language, but it has built-in translators that take your input and convert it into machine language. So, once you have completed your input and the translators have converted it to machine language, it continues to the CPU, which receives your communication and carries out your instructions. After processing your instructions, the CPU returns a message to you through the output devices, again acting through translators to convert machine language to human language. The output devices can be a monitor, speaker, printer, or projector. You review the output and decide if the computer has completed the task or if you need to communicate further until you are satisfied.

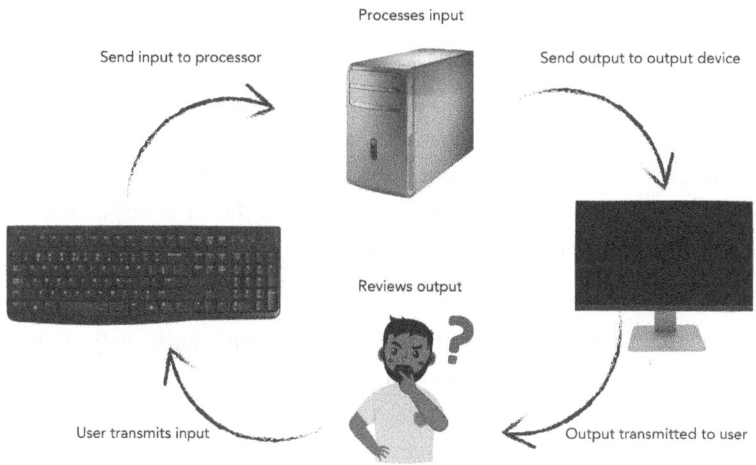

Figure 1-2: Superficial computing process.

Let's take things a bit deeper by comparing the parts of the computer we've discussed to a typical office environment. This time, we'll add the motherboard to demystify it. We'll start by putting the office workers in the role of the CPU, processing instructions and making the computer operate.

Central Processing Unit: The Office Workers

The central processing unit (CPU) is often described as the brain of a computer. The analogy of the CPU as the attorneys and staff of the office is apt because the CPU is responsible for processing information and executing instructions that drive all computer operations, similar to how a senior attorney oversees all the processes within the office, ensuring everything runs smoothly. The CPU is comprised of several key components, each with a particular function.

The control unit can be likened to the managing partner of a law office. It directs the flow of data and instructions between the various parts of the CPU and other components of the computer. The control unit fetches instructions from the computer's memory, decodes them to understand what actions are needed, and then sends signals to other components to execute these instructions. Just as a managing partner allocates tasks and ensures that the legal team follows procedures correctly, the control unit coordinates the CPU's operations to maintain order and efficiency.

The arithmetic logic unit (ALU) is the part of the CPU responsible for performing arithmetic and logical operations. Some examples of functions performed by the ALU include the following:

- Arithmetic Operations: The ALU performs basic arithmetic operations such as addition, subtraction, multiplication, and division.
- Logic Operations: It executes logical operations like AND, OR, and NOT. These operations are fundamental in decision-making processes and manipulating data.
- Bitwise Operations: Directly manipulating individual bits of information. We will not go in depth and explain binary, just know that part of what the ALU does is to manipulate these bits.
- Comparisons: It compares numbers to determine equality, greater than or less than conditions. These operations are essential for decision-making in programs.
- Increment/Decrement Operations: A technical way of saying that the ALU can increment (add 1) or decrement (subtract 1) values.

The ALU is akin to the associate attorney in our example handing the essential work of the firm, like arguing cases, preparing discovery, and making logical decisions based on the law. The efficiency and speed of the ALU directly impact the CPU's performance, just as an attorney's skills and efficiency affect the success of legal proceedings.

Next, much like paralegals who manage case files, keep track of essential documents, and ensure that necessary information is readily accessible to the attorney, the registers store immediate data that the CPU needs to execute instructions efficiently. They are small, fast storage locations within the CPU that hold data temporarily while it is being processed. You will notice through the walkthrough that there are three major levels of storage, each with varying degrees of size and speed. The hard drive has the most significant capacity but is the slowest of the three, RAM is faster than the hard drive but slower than registers and similarly situated in the middle for size, and the registers are the quickest of the three with the smallest storage capacity. RAM refers to Random Access Memory and, for our purposes, can be thought of as handling the information that a computer may need at any given time, though not necessarily being directly manipulated at the time. Think of the operating system functioning in the background or open applications that may be minimized but still open. Registers, on the other hand, represent data storage within the CPU and are typically only concerned with the data being manipulated at the time.

Finally, we have the cache, which is a small, high-speed memory storage location close to the CPU. Where the registers store the data currently being manipulated by the CPU, the cache stores frequently used instructions and data. Imagine a law librarian who provides access to frequently referenced treatises, cases, and statutes that are maintained for quick consults. By reducing the time it takes to access data from the main memory, the cache improves the CPU's efficiency, just as having a well-organized law library can significantly enhance a legal team's productivity. While this may seem confusing since we just discussed there being three levels of storage in this process, it can be helpful to think of the cache as simply a bit of RAM that has been added to the CPU to speed things up. The CPU always processes faster than the RAM can supply data. To increase computing speed, a bit of RAM is attached to the CPU to hold commands or data that will be used frequently in a program. This is a simplification but helpful in visualizing how the process works.

Now that we have our components identified let's take a look at the operation process. The CPU operates through a cycle known as the fetch-decode-execute cycle. As you can see in Figure 1-3, the cycle engages all of the components we just discussed.

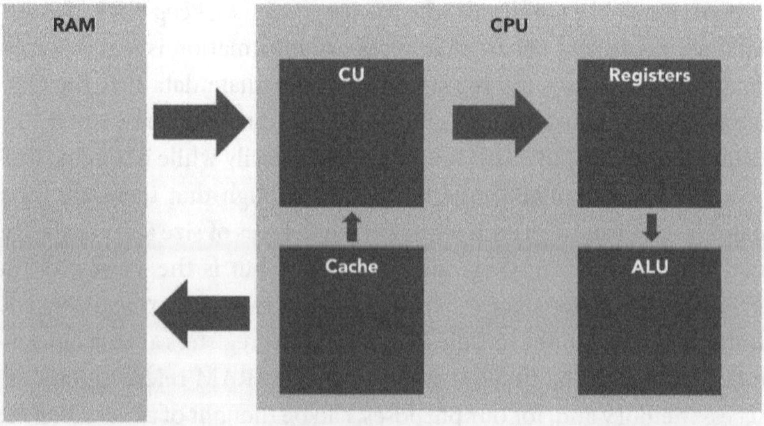

Figure 1-3: A deeper look at computing process.

During the fetch step, the CPU retrieves an instruction from the computer's memory. The CU fetches the instruction by sending the appropriate address to the memory, and the instruction is then transferred to the CPU for processing. Once the instruction is fetched, the CPU decodes it to understand what action is required. The CU translates the instruction into signals that other components of the CPU can understand and act upon. In the execute phase, the decoded instruction is carried out. If the instruction involves arithmetic or logic operations, the ALU performs the necessary calculations. If data needs to be moved to or from memory, the CU coordinates this action.

This can also be analogized to our law office scenario. The managing attorney receives a case from a client and sends it to an attorney within the firm, cc'ing their paralegal and the firm's law library. The paralegal assists the attorney as they read and interpret the task while the law librarian sends along tools and resources typically used in this type of action. The attorney performs the required task with the assistance of their paralegal and requests access to special resources through the managing partner if necessary.

Understanding how the CPU works will help users appreciate the intricacies of legal software as well as AI systems. For example, consider using an in-house database to store client matters and details. When the lawyer inputs a query, the CPU processes this request by fetching data from memory, performing necessary calculations, and delivering the results swiftly. The control unit oversees the entire process; the ALU handles logical comparisons within the query, registers hold temporary data, and cache memory speeds up access to frequently used database repositories and query processes. Moreover, AI and machine learning, as you will see in later chapters, rely on powerful CPUs to process vast amounts of data and perform complex computations. Understanding the CPU's role equips future attorneys with the knowledge to better leverage these technologies, making their use of them more efficient and effective.

Motherboard: Office Floorplan

The motherboard serves as the anchor point which ties everything else together. Continuing our previous analogy of the computer as a traditional office space, it is helpful to think of the motherboard as the office floorplan. Each part of the computer may have different forms and functions, but they are all ultimately tied back to the motherboard in some fashion, and the motherboard ensures smooth interaction between the parts.

Imagine walking into a modern office building. The floor plan will have been meticulously designed to ensure efficient workflow, communication, and power distribution. Similarly, a motherboard is a large, flat circuit board that connects all the components of a computer, allowing them to communicate and work together seamlessly.

We will discuss three key characteristics that define a modern motherboard: form factor, chipsets, and components. For our purposes, form factor can be thought of as the square footage and placement of doors and windows of our metaphorical office. Those who are computer building enthusiasts will probably cry out in anguish over this simplification, but since I want this book to remain approachable, computer construction and case selection will remain outside its scope.[4]

The chipset determines what type of CPU and other devices (type of RAM, number and type of USB ports, network connections, and so on) the motherboard will support. There are two major producers of CPUs in the PC world: Intel and AMD. Their competitive relationship through the birth of the PC age has significantly influenced the evolution of form factors and chipsets. Their intense rivalry and how they rose to their competitive market shares is a fascinating story.[5] For our purposes, consider the chipsets to be the office manager who oversees the coordination and communication between different departments. The chipset is responsible for managing data flow between the CPU, memory, storage devices, and peripherals.

Finally, the components on a motherboard are the physical interfaces that the circuity of the chipsets support. So, it is possible to have a motherboard that has a chipset that supports up to eight USB devices, but only have four physical USB component ports. A port is simply the location on a computer for physically connecting a device. In our office analogy we can compare the components on a motherboard to physical spaces on the office floorplan.

Every motherboard provides a connection for the CPU, which is specifically called a socket. If the CPU is made up of the attorneys and their staff, then the CPU socket would be their physical office space, where the majority of their work is done and where they interact with the other components. Equally ubiquitous are the RAM slots; there are different connection types, but for our purposes, it is sufficient to understand that the RAM slots on the motherboard hold the memory modules, or sticks, that temporarily store data for quick access, just like the physical desks in the offices.

This is also where the input and output devices of your computer physically connect to the system. So, no matter if it is a USB or older connection, this is where your keyboard, mouse, speakers, monitor, and any other peripheral device connects to the system and where it receives

4. For a more detailed discussion, I highly recommend Mike Meyers, CompTIA A+ Certification Exam Guide (10th ed. 2019).

5. *See* Greg Tang, *Intel and the x86 Architecture: A Legal Perspective*, Harv. J.L. & Tech. (Jan. 4, 2011), https://jolt.law.harvard.edu/digest/intel-and-the-x86-architecture-a-legal-perspective.

its instructions on how to interact with the rest of the system. If you have ever heard your IT technician say that you need updated BIOS files, a chip on the motherboard is where they are stored. It is the central location where all parts of the computer speak to one another and are instructed on how to interact.

As the floor plan of our office, the motherboard determines the physical space and connections available to connect.

Storage:
Filing Cabinet

As law students, you are no doubt familiar with the concept of a filing cabinet in a traditional law office. Imagine a typical filing cabinet used by lawyers to store essential documents—case files, client records, contracts, and legal memoranda. Each drawer is meticulously organized, with folders neatly labeled, ensuring quick retrieval of information when needed. Now, let us apply this familiar analogy to understand computer storage.

In our analogy, the entire filing cabinet represents a computer's storage system. Just like the cabinet stores physical documents, a computer's storage stores digital files—documents, e-mails, software programs, and multimedia; these digital files are essential to a lawyer's practice today, just as paper files were in the past.

Each drawer of the filing cabinet is akin to a storage drive on a computer. In modern computers, there are various types of storage drives: hard disk drives, solid state drives, or external drives connected via USB. These drives serve as the drawers where digital information is stored.

Hard disk drives (HDDs) and solid state drives (SSDs) are two types of storage devices used in computer data storage, but they differ significantly. HDDs use magnetic disks, or platters, to store data, with read/write heads moving mechanically to access the information. The moving mechanical parts of the HDD mean it is typically slower, more prone to damage, and consumes more energy than an SSD. HDDs' remaining benefit is the cost-to-storage ratio, which offers much larger storage capacities at lower cost. Many computers still in operation utilize HDDs, but the tide is shifting towards SSDs. HDDs are suitable in applications where budget and high storage capacity are more critical than speed, such as for archiving or storing large media files.

SSDs, on the other hand, use flash memory technology with no moving parts, resulting in faster data access speeds, greater durability, and lower power consumption compared to HDDs. SSDs provide quicker boot times, faster file transfers, and more responsive performance in applications, making them ideal for operating systems, applications, and frequently accessed data. The drawbacks of SSDs come from their cost and data retention capabilities over longer periods. As time progresses, SSDs will come to dominate the PC world, barring any paradigm-shifting developments in data storage architecture. Many HDDs, however, will still be relevant in the legal world for their use as archival data tools. HDDs tend to be better equipped for long-term data storage, as SSDs need a power supply to ensure data integrity. Depending on the physical conditions of storage, earlier generations of SSDs may begin to lose data in as little as a few months without power. Like other aspects of developing technology, this is changing, and newer versions tout data security for 10–15 years, but with an eye towards preserving data for eDiscovery, it is important to be aware of this possible flaw with early version SSDs.

Within each drawer, we have folders. Folders in a filing cabinet help us categorize and organize documents, making them easy to find. Similarly, on a computer, folders (or directories) organize files. These folders can be nested within one another, creating virtually limitless (depending on comparative file and hard drive sizes) layers of files as opposed to the limited space within a filing cabinet.

A NOTE ON FILE SIZES AND CONTEXT

File sizes are typically measured in bytes, with larger units used to represent increasingly large quantities of data.

Byte

- The smallest unit of digital data.
- A single byte consists of 8 bits (think Binary 0s and 1s).
- Represents a single character, such as a letter or number.

Kilobyte

- 1 Kilobyte = 1,024 Bytes
- Often used to measure the size of small files, such as text documents or small images.

Megabyte

- 1 Megabyte = 1,024 Kilobytes = 1,048,576 Bytes
- Commonly used to measure the size of medium-sized files, such as MP3 audio files, high-resolution images, and documents.

Gigabyte

- 1 Gigabyte = 1,024 Megabytes = 1,073,741,824 Bytes
- Used to measure larger files or storage capacities, such as high-definition videos, software applications, and most smartphone and computer hard drives.

Terabyte

- 1 Terabyte = 1,024 Gigabytes = 1,099,511,627,776 Bytes
- Typically used to measure the storage capacities of large hard drives, servers, and cloud storage services.

Petabyte

- 1 Petabyte = 1,024 Terabytes = 1,125,899,906,842,624 Bytes
- Used in large-scale data storage systems, such as data centers or large-scale cloud storage providers.

You'll notice a pattern in the increasing capacity measures. The next higher measure on the scale is 1,024 times the size of the measure before it. This is because computer data storage is built around a binary system where data is converted into binary code 0s and 1s. A complete overview of binary is beyond the scope of this book, but as a brief example. The phrase "Hello, World!", is a very common introductory coding phrase. To convert it down to a form the computer understands it is converted to ASCII (the standard code for information interchange), and in preparation for its transmission to other parts of the computer or a networked device, it is paired down even further to a series of 0s and 1s, representing "off" and "on states respectively. So basically, when a computer is using binary it is simply applying different degrees of electricity to represent 0 or 1 since it doesn't have an actual voice with which to communicate or understand plain text per se. So, where we see "Hello, World!" the computer would read:

```makefile
H: 01001000
e: 01100101
l: 01101100
l: 01101100
o: 01101111
,: 00101100
(space): 00100000
W: 01010111
o: 01101111
r: 01110010
l: 01101100
d: 01100100
!: 00100001
```

Figure 1-4

All of this is to say that the different size measures for data storage are organized around powers of 2 instead of base 10, with 1,024 being the closest power to 1,000. If you are keen to drop some insider terms when chatting with IT professionals refer to the different measures of data as Kibibytes, Mebibytes, or Gibibytes instead of Kilobytes, Megabytes, and Gigabytes. The alternate terms may sound silly, but they're more accurate and the only reason the more inaccurate terms persist is largely marketing.

Random Access Memory: Desk or Workspace

Now that we have our legal team assembled and our office laid out, let's talk about the actual information being processed. As discussed in the previous section, there are various filing cabinets throughout the office filled with files, books, and documents representing your computer's permanent storage. However, when you're working on a case, you don't stand at an open filing cabinet to do your work; instead, you use your desk.

Unlike the permanent storage devices discussed earlier, RAM (random access memory) is considered volatile memory. This means it requires power to retain data and loses its contents when the system is powered off. Similar to tidying up your desk and putting away files at the end of the day, the data you are working with through RAM is either stored or discarded when you shut down the computer.

Your desk represents the RAM in your computer. Just like your desk provides space to spread out all the documents, case files, and memoranda you need for the case you're currently working on, RAM provides space for your computer to temporarily store data it needs to access quickly.

If your desk is large, you can have many documents and tools spread out and readily accessible, allowing you to work more efficiently. Similarly, if your computer has a large amount of RAM, it can handle more tasks simultaneously without slowing down. As you begin to run more programs, they consume varying amounts of your available space. For instance, you might have a word processor open to draft your first-year memo, an internet radio application running in the background, an internet browser with multiple tabs open to different cases on your preferred legal research database, and an e-reader application open to a forgotten page in your downtime book.

You might begin to notice occasional lag as you switch between programs, realizing that you have slowly filled your desktop, and your RAM is being heavily used by the programs you have running.

The documents on your desk are there temporarily. Once you're done with them or need to make space for new projects, they are either returned to the filing cabinets or thrown away. Similarly, data stored in RAM is temporary. When your computer is turned off, everything in RAM is cleared. This is why your IT technician often asks if you have tried shutting your machine down and turning it back on as the first step in troubleshooting. It forces the computer to clear its memory and return to its initial operating state.

Finally, having essential documents within arm's reach on your desk means you can access information quickly without wasting time searching through filing cabinets. RAM is much faster than your hard drive and can be rapidly accessed by the computer's processor. To simplify, the closer the memory is to the CPU, the quicker it is processed. In our analogy, if the permanent storage device is the filing cabinet, and the

RAM is the desk, then memory stored on the CPU's cache is like having the document in hand.

Peripherals: Office Tools

The final components that we will cover are known as computer peripherals. These are the devices that allow you to meaningfully interact with your computer and to give it instructions. The peripherals communicate with your operating system through drivers. This is an important concept, as many times when a device malfunctions or fails to function at all, it is because the driver is either missing or out of date. If you remember, in our broad overview of the anatomy of a computer, we discussed input and output devices; these are peripherals.

Input devices used to provide data to the computer include keyboards, mice, scanners, microphones, and webcams. Output devices that receive data from the computer and present it to the user include monitors, printers, and speakers. Additional storage devices beyond the computer's hard drive (e.g., external hard drives and USB flash drives) are also considered peripherals.

Peripherals are important because they enhance the capabilities of a computer. Input devices allow users to interact with the computer and input data. Output devices enable users to see, hear, or physically receive information processed by the computer. Storage devices provide additional space for storing files and backups, expanding the computer's capacity beyond its internal storage. Most computers are mass-produced and, therefore, share very similar construction; peripherals allow for the customization of computers for specific purposes and tasks.

These devices connect to your computer through various interfaces that tend to change as technology improves. Currently, the most common peripheral interfaces include USB (universal serial bus) ports, Bluetooth, HDMI/VGA/Display Port, audio jacks, and network interfaces (see Figure 1-4).

Concluding the office analogy, peripherals are similar to the multitude of office supplies that allow you to complete your work.

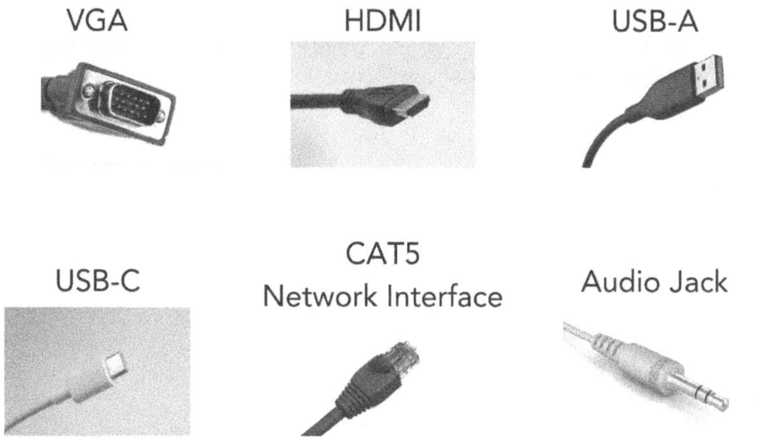

Figure 1-5: Peripheral connection types.

How the Internet Works

Introduction

Now that we've covered the essential components and processes of the computer, we'll touch on network communications and how the Internet works. There is very little in the computer world today that doesn't rely upon internet connectivity in some way. Stand-alone software packages are becoming a thing of the past in favor of subscription cloud-based apps; e-mail and other communications are stored on third-party servers, and even the stand-alone programs that still exist rely upon internet connectivity for security updates and bug patches. Whether you're navigating eDiscovery, safeguarding client data, or employing digital legal research tools, your ability to comprehend how information is transferred across networks is crucial.

The Basics of Network Communications

The Internet is probably the most widely recognized form of network communication, but to truly understand its complexity, it is important to understand basic networking principles. At its most basic level, network communications are two or more devices transferring information through a shared pathway, whether it is through physical cables or wireless transmissions. There are several classifications of networks depending on that network's purpose and scope:

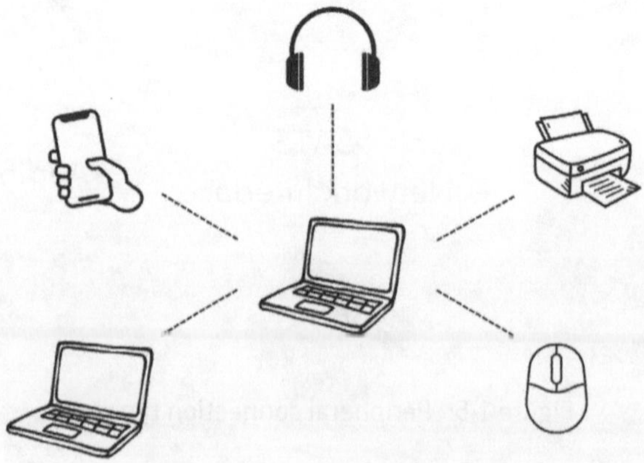

Figure 1-6: Personal area network.

A personal area network (PAN), as seen in Figure 1-5, is a network organized around an individual within a single building. Think about studying at home with your laptop connected to your home printer, headphones, and mouse. They may be connected by different means, but together, they can all communicate with one another, forming a personal network.

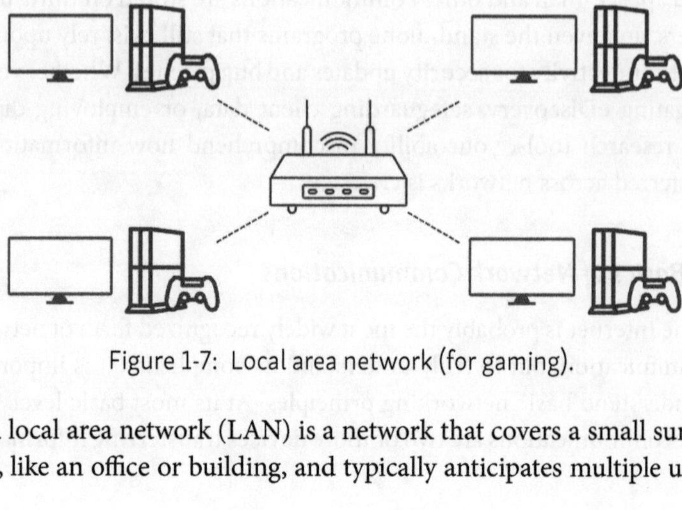

Figure 1-7: Local area network (for gaming).

A local area network (LAN) is a network that covers a small surface area, like an office or building, and typically anticipates multiple users.

It is generally used to connect personal computers, printers, and servers in an office to create an "intranet." A more entertaining use for LANs that was popular in the past is pictured in Figure 1-6. Before the surge in online gaming, many players would connect their individual consoles to an ethernet router and create their own networks to game with friends.

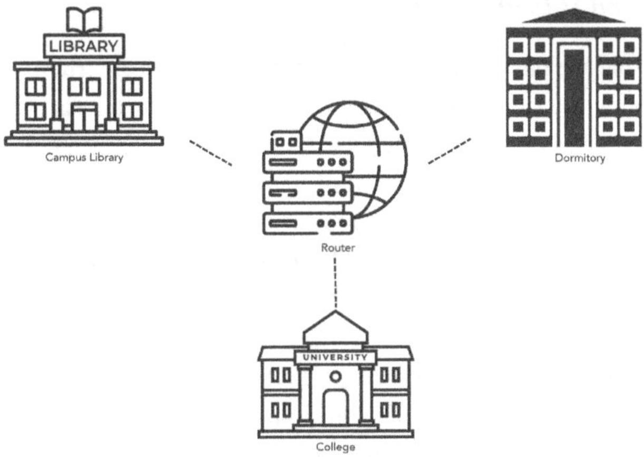

Figure 1-8: Metropolitan area network.

A metropolitan area network (MAN) covers a larger area than a LAN, encompassing multiple buildings and many more users. The MANs that people are probably the most familiar with would be cable television or university campus networks (as pictured in Figure 1-7). Frequently, MANs will involve networking multiple LANs together.

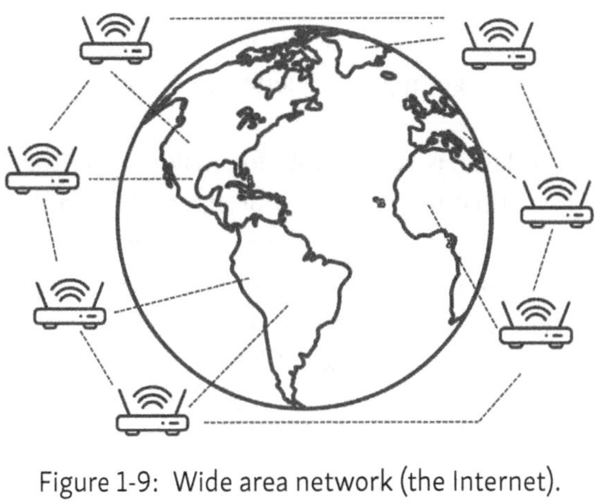

Figure 1-9: Wide area network (the Internet).

A wide area network (WAN) is the largest area network. It is intended to span large geographic areas, often encompassing multiple cities or countries. The largest and most well-known WAN, spanning the globe, is the Internet itself.

The OSI and TCP/IP Models

Now that we have established the different physical structures of the various networks, it is time to address how the information is transmitted between devices on those networks. A network is merely a collection of interconnected devices that communicate with each other. Understanding how data travels across a network requires a grasp of something called the Open Systems Interconnection (OSI) or the Transmission Control Protocol/Internet Protocol (TCP/IP) model, which are conceptual frameworks used to understand how networks interact and transfer data. The OSI model is more idealistic, while the TCP/IP model is more functional.

The OSI model is more theoretical and is often used to explain how communication should work in a perfect system. It has seven distinct layers, each with a specific role. These layers include the physical, data link, network, transport, session, presentation, and application layers. Think of these layers as a funnel with the application layer being at the top and the physical layer at the bottom connected to the physical wires or wireless signal of your device.

The physical layer is the "hardware" layer. It's all about the physical connection between devices—like the cables, switches, and signals that physically connect computers. For this layer, imagine sending a letter. The physical layer is the mailbox, the mail trucks, and the roads they drive on. It's about getting your letter from one place to another physically.

The data link layer is responsible for making sure data can travel across the physical connection without errors. It organizes data into frames and handles error detection and correction. Think of this as the envelope that you put your letter in. It protects the letter and ensures that it doesn't get damaged in routine transit.

The network layer determines the best path for the data to take to reach its destination. This is where IP addresses come into play. This layer is like the post office, which decides the best route for your letter to take to reach its destination. If your letter needs to go from New York to

California, the post office figures out the most efficient way for it to get there.

The transport layer works to ensure that when data is sent from one point to another, it arrives as intended. This includes ensuring that the data arrives complete and uncorrupted, in spite of any network issues, and reassembled correctly if the data must be broken down into smaller packets. Many data transfers are too large to be sent in one piece, so the transport layer breaks them down into smaller packets, which are then sequenced so the recipient device has instructions on how to reassemble the information. In addition, this layer acts to ensure that all packets arrive intact by adjusting transmission speed to avoid data loss, checking for packet corruption, and also ensuring that all packets are sent to the correct location, even if you are sending multiple signals simultaneously.

The session layer manages the communication session between two devices. It keeps the connection open while they are talking and closes it when they're done. This is like a conversation between pen pals, keeping track of whose turn it is to send a letter and ensuring that the conversation continues smoothly.

The presentation layer translates data into a format that the application layer can understand. It is responsible for encryption, compression, and formatting. In the letter analogy, it serves as a translator between people writing in a language that isn't their native one. It ensures that the recipient can read the letter.

Finally, the application layer directly interacts with the user. It's where the actual communication happens, using applications like web browsers, email programs, or instant message platforms. When you open an e-mail or browse the Internet, the application layer is the interface you use with the data. It's like reading the letter that you received.

To summarize the process, when you send an e-mail, your computer goes through all seven layers of the OSI model. Your e-mail client (the application layer) is where you compose and send your e-mail. The e-mail is then translated into data, packaged, routed, and finally transmitted through physical wires or wireless signals. At the other end, the receiving device goes through the exact same funneling process but in reverse, translating data signals up the funnel until the recipient's e-mail client can display the e-mail in plain text (see Figure 1-9).

Tying everything back to our office example, if OSI is the aspirational office policy manual detailing the approved channels through which in-

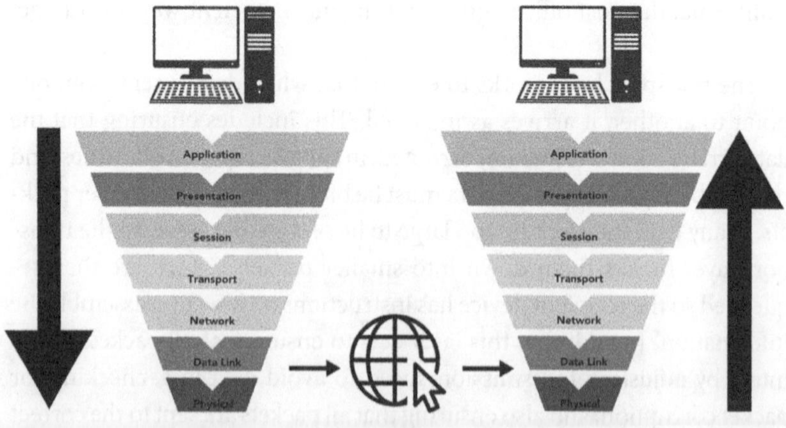

Figure 1-10: Data traveling through the OSI model.

terdepartmental communication and interaction should occur, TCP/IP is the imperfect but actual way in which departments work together. It only has four layers, combining some of the OSI layers. The network interface layer combines the OSI's physical and data link layers, ensuring that data moves physically between devices. The internet layer is similar to OSI's network layer and handles routing data across different networks. The transport layer is like its OSI counterpart, ensuring data integrity and reliability and making sure everything arrives as intended. Finally, the application layer merges the OSI's top three layers (application, presentation, and session), focusing on what most users interact with on the screen—the user interface of your email client, web browser, or file-sharing system (see Figure 1-10).

The main difference between OSI and TCP/IP is that OSI is mainly an academic construct used to explain how information is transferred over a network. TCP/IP, however, is what has been implemented on the Internet and, therefore, more widely used.

The Internet: The World's Largest WAN

The Internet is the most expansive network ever created, connecting billions of devices worldwide. With the sheer number of devices and geographic surface area covered, there are, understandably, a few more layers involved than your typical Friday night LAN party. Every device

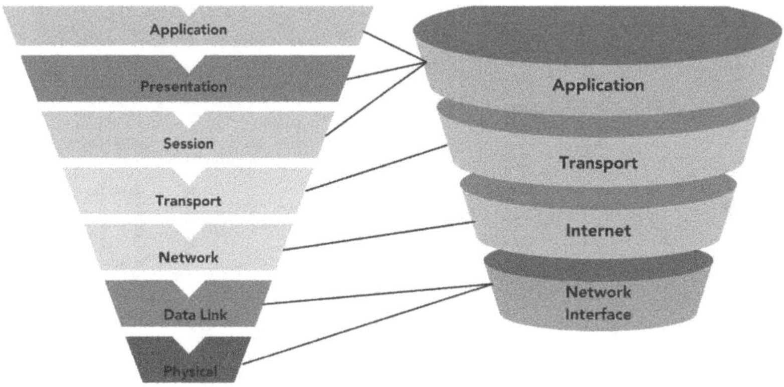

Figure 1-11: Comparing OSI to TCP/IP models.

connected to the Internet has a unique identifier known as an Internet Protocol (IP) address. There are two primary versions:

- IPv4: The older standard, utilizing a 32-bit address, which supports about 4.3 billion unique addresses.
- IPv6: The newer standard, utilizing 128-bit address, supporting 34 undecillion (that's a 34 with 37 zeros after it!) unique addresses.

Domain names are human-readable addresses that map to IP addresses through something called the Domain Name System (DNS). DNS servers are basically the phone book of the Internet; they translate domain names into IP addresses to direct traffic to the correct destination. Think of it this way: how easily would you remember 2607:f8b0:4005:812::200e as opposed to www.google.com? Additionally, that IP address is going to be associated with only Google, whereas Google may purchase multiple domain names to ensure that any time someone makes a typo, they will still be directed to Google's servers. Any time they enter the correct address or any typo or variation of the domain name that Google has purchased, it is checked against the DNS phonebook, which maps it directly to Google's unique IPv6 address.

Once your device has acquired the address of the website, it attempts to establish a connection with the web servers of that site. Your device then initiates a request for specific content from that server—typically an HTML file displayed as a website by your internet browser. The re-

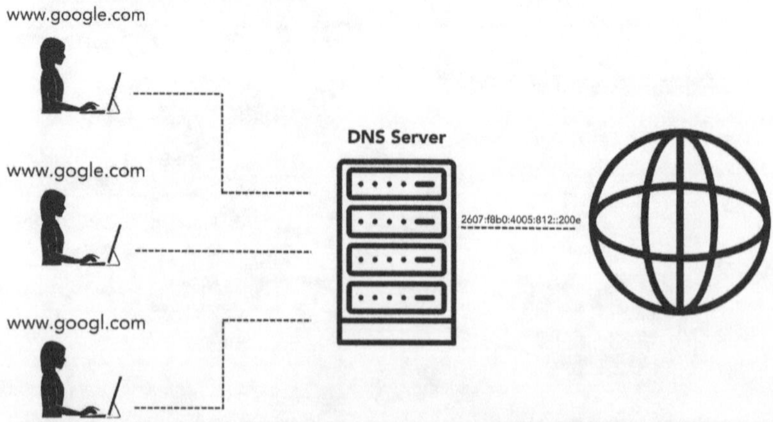

Figure 1-12: Visualization of DNS concept.

quested data is broken up into a series of packets that are then sent to your device. These packets all include a header and footer that instructs your device on how to reassemble the file. Sort of like a jigsaw puzzle. Remember back to the OSI and TCP/IP models: once the packets arrive, they are sent back up the funnel—reassembling according to the rules of different protocols and the instructions from the data packets' headers and footers—until the data file is reconstructed and displayed on your internet browser. A similar process occurs for e-mails, instant messages, or video files. What devices allow the transmission and receipt of these packets, though?

Internet Service Providers

If we imagine the vast WAN, which is the internet as a highway, Internet Service Providers (ISPs) are the ones that maintain the highways and direct traffic. ISPs like Comcast or Verizon are the gatekeepers that provide access to the internet. They connect your devices, assign them unique addresses, and manage the infrastructure that makes the whole system work.

Now, depending on where you live and the technology available, there are different types of vehicles that ISPs might use to connect you to the internet. Let's explore a few:

1. Dial-Up: This was the "Model T" on a country road of internet connections operating through telephone lines. It was slow and noisy (literally, your parents aren't making it up when they say the internet used to scream at them). It crawled along at speeds so sluggish you could brew coffee while a single webpage loaded. Thankfully, it's mostly a relic of the past.
2. Broadband: Welcome the highways of the modern internet. Broadband connections, like DSL, cable, or fiber optics, provide faster, more reliable access. DSL uses telephone lines but doesn't tie up your phone, while cable connections share the same lines as your TV. Fiber-optic cables are the luxury express lanes, transmitting data as light signals at blazing speeds—perfect for streaming, online research, and attending virtual classes.
3. 5G Wireless: Picture this as a network of high-speed drones delivering data to your devices. It's the latest generation of wireless technology, offering speeds that rival fiber optics without the need for cables. It's great for mobile devices and cutting-edge applications like virtual reality, but coverage can be spotty outside major cities. As the extension of our metaphor exists, it is still dependent on direction from ISPs, but it doesn't rely as much on physical cabling to connect point A to point B
4. Quantum Teleportation: Now, here's where things get futuristic. This technology, still in its experimental stage, aims to use the principles of quantum physics to transmit information instantly. Instead of physically sending data, quantum teleportation relies on "entangled particles" that share information no matter how far apart they are. It's like sending a message that appears instantly at its destination—no roads, no delays, and no interception by malicious actors.

There are three key tools that ISPs use to keep internet data moving smoothly: routers, bandwidth allocation, and peering agreements.

At the heart of the ISPs' operations are routers, the traffic lights and signposts of the internet. These devices guide data packets from one location to another. When you type in a web address, your request is broken into packets and sent to a router. This router determines the best path for those packets to take, avoiding congestion and ensuring they arrive at the correct destination. If you're accessing a legal database from your law school's library, the packets might hop through multiple routers—managed by your ISP and others—before reaching the database server and returning the results to your screen.

But managing traffic isn't just about finding the best path; it's also about balancing demand. This is where bandwidth allocation comes in. Bandwidth is the digital equivalent of lane space on a highway. During peak hours, when everyone is streaming videos, attending online classes, or downloading files, ISPs allocate bandwidth to prevent the network from grinding to a halt. For example, a busy evening might mean slower speeds for non-essential activities, ensuring that critical tasks still get through. ISPs sometimes enforce limits, such as throttling speeds after reaching a data cap, to ensure fair use among customers.

Another vital part of this ecosystem is peering agreements, which are like treaties between neighboring countries that agree to share their roads. ISPs don't operate in isolation; they interconnect with other ISPs to form the global web. Through peering agreements, ISPs allow data to flow seamlessly between their networks without charging each other, much like exchanging courtesies for mutual benefit. For example, when you access a website hosted on another ISP's network, the peering agreement ensures that your data can pass through without additional tolls. These agreements are carefully negotiated to maintain the balance of traffic and costs, allowing the Internet to function as a unified whole.

Why Is This Important?

As a future attorney, it is crucial to recognize the legal implications of network communication. The intersection of law and technology presents unique challenges and opportunities. The global nature of the Internet complicates traditional questions of jurisdiction. Understanding how the internet functions can help you develop a more holistic view of how data is stored and transferred, allowing you greater insight when unraveling a court's authority to hear a case involving online activities, particularly when the parties are located in different countries. Understanding that many websites and communications are stored on networked third-party servers can also grant you insight into the collection and production of electronically stored information (ESI) during eDiscovery. As an adviser to your client, you must be adept at working with IT professionals to preserve relevant data, identify potential sources of ESI, and ensure that data is collected in a legally defensible manner. Additionally, as a responsible custodian of your client's information, a healthy understanding of how data is stored and transferred will prompt questions when your firm employs cloud-based third-party storage solutions.

The rapidly evolving landscape of legal technology demands a proactive approach to understanding and integrating new tools and systems. As we've explored in this chapter, the foundational elements of technology—ranging from the basic anatomy of computers to the intricate workings of the Internet—are not just abstract concepts but practical knowledge that equips attorneys with the competence necessary to navigate the modern legal environment.

The duty of technological competence, as highlighted by the ABA's Model Rules of Professional Conduct, underscores that staying informed about technological advances is no longer optional but a professional obligation. This competence is a fluid concept tailored to the specific needs of one's practice and the ever-changing nature of technology itself.

By breaking down the complexities of technology into more relatable analogies, such as comparing computer components to office environments, we aim to demystify the intimidating aspects of legal tech. This approach not only makes the subject more approachable but also emphasizes that mastering these basics can empower legal professionals to have more meaningful interactions with IT experts, make informed decisions, and ultimately better serve their clients.

As we move forward into the following chapters, which will delve deeper into specific technologies and their direct impact on legal practice, keep in mind the foundational knowledge laid out here. Whether you are managing data, safeguarding client information, or engaging in eDiscovery, your understanding of these basics will serve as the cornerstone of your technological fluency in the legal field. The journey through legal technology may be intricate, but with each step, you will gain the skills and confidence to navigate the future of law with a tech-savvy edge.

Review

1. Why is it important for legal professionals to have a fundamental understanding of technology?
2. What is the significance of the ABA's Model Rule 1.1 and Comment 8 in relation to technology competence for attorneys?
3. What are the three major types of components in a computer and what are their broad functions?
4. How do the Control Unit and Arithmetic Logic Unit contribute to a computer's processing power?
5. Explain the difference between HDDs and SSDs.
6. Differentiate between PAN, LAN, MAN, and WAN.
7. What is the purpose of the OSI model, and how does it differ from the TCP/IP model?
8. Describe how the DNS works and its importance in internet navigation.

CHAPTER 2

Document Manipulation

Introduction

There is no other product that has kept me busier than Microsoft Office. It is the workhorse software suite for the legal industry. There are alternatives to the specific programs included. However, it is impossible to deny that Office occupies the lion's share of firm and law school devices. There are a multitude of different ways to perform tasks within this suite of software, and everyone has their own way of doing things. There are some methods, however, that are just a bit more efficient than others. In this chapter, we will explore several programs from the Microsoft family of software and address some of the most common questions that come up when using them in both law school and practice.

The diversity of approaches to using Office is so prevalent that there are entire companies built around training law students in effective practices when using these programs. For those who learn better from hands-on practice with software, I highly recommend the programs offered by Procertas and the National Society of Legal Technology (NSLT). Procertas sticks primarily to everyday tasks performed in the law on Microsoft Office and Adobe Acrobat. As you can see in Figure 2-1, it provides training and an assessment of each module for which the user is seeking certification. The company recommends an assessment → trainer → assessment sequence for these modules. The thought is that the initial assessment will highlight the areas where the user will benefit from additional training, the subsequent trainer will address those areas, and the repeat assessment will allow for an improved score. With Procertas, the user is allowed to complete the modules as many times as they want, allowing for improved scores on the assessment modules and eventual mastery. The assessment is auto-graded, and users are evaluated based on accuracy and time of completion to arrive at a score of beginner, intermediate, qualified, or expert.

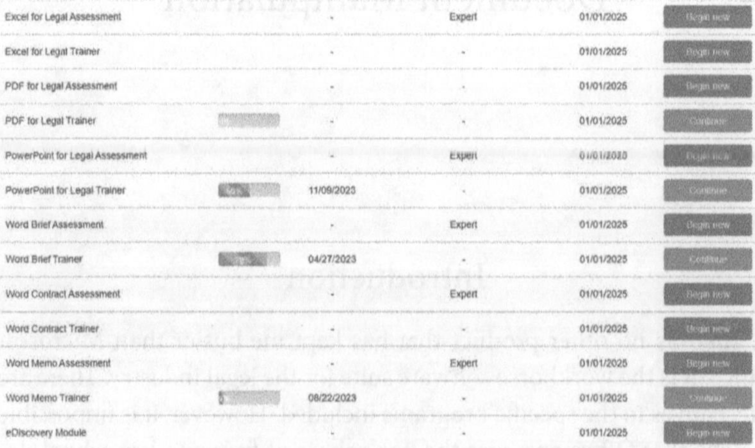

Figure 2-1: Modules offered by Procerta's Legal Technology Assessment.

NSLT provides a broader range of topics but also includes modules on Microsoft Office and Adobe (see Figure 2-2). The major difference between the trainers is that Procertas requires you to work in the actual programs being evaluated and NSLT provides a simulation with images of the software and interactive markers mapped on the images to evaluate performance, a boon considering most law students don't have TrialDirector or Clio pre-installed on their devices.

Word

In the following section on Word we will be covering the use of styles to apply formatting across a document, methods of inserting various finding aids, inserting and formatting helpful organizational tools

LEGAL TECHNOLOGY CERTIFICATE MEMBER PAGE

NSLT is proud to offer a Legal Technology Certificate of learning that provides training and verifies members' knowledge of legal software. The certificate cost is included as part of the $160 NSLT 1-year Membership Fee. The certificate process requires members to complete training modules on 12 different software programs chosen from the list of 28 available courses. Each software title is broken into several 5 - 10 minute modules. This allows members to complete the certificate at their own pace and as their own time schedule allows.

Some of the courses students may learn and test on are:

- Adobe Acrobat Pro 2023
- Best Authority 5
- CaseMap 13
- Clio Manage
- CloudNine Concordance
- DocuSign eSignature
- Excel 365 Basic & Intermediate
- Excel 365 Advanced
- Google Workspaces
- iManage Work 10 Desktop
- Kofax Power PDF Advanced 3
- Litera DocX Tools
- Litera Workshare Compare
- Microsoft SharePoint
- Microsoft Teams
- NetDocuments & NDOffice
- OneNote 365
- Outlook 365
- Payne Numbering Assistant 11
- PowerPoint 365
- Slack
- TimeMap 6
- TrialDirector
- Windows 11 Pro
- Word 365 Basic & Intermediate
- Word 365 Advanced
- WordRake
- Zoom 5.5

This certificate is a great way for members to demonstrate their skill and knowledge of legal technology to their current and potential employers!

Figure 2-2: NSLT topics.

(breaks, page numbers, and so on), keeping track of your edits, and finally a touch of security as we remove your document's metadata.

Applying and Modifying Styles

Styles help maintain consistency and a uniform appearance for documents. By applying a particular style to text elements across a document, users ensure that headings, subheadings, and body text have consistent fonts, sizes, and colors. This uniformity is crucial for professional and clear communication. Using styles enables users to apply multiple formatting attributes with a single action. Instead of formatting each block of text individually, a style allows for simultaneous adjustments to many parts of a document, saving time and effort.

Additionally, when you need to make changes to the format, instead of updating each instance individually, you can modify the styles, and all elements using that style in the document will update automatically. This makes the editing process much faster and less prone to errors. So, if you wish to edit all of the text that is not associated with a specific style, instead of having to go through and highlight large chunks of text to edit individually, you can simply edit the "Normal" style and have it update all the text associated with that style.

Finally, headings, are integral in many advanced features in Word and for accessibility. A style is simply a set of formatting instructions that are labeled within Word and can be found on the "Home" tab, as pictured in Figure 2-3. Headings, not to be confused with headers, improve the navigation of your document by organizing it into sections, thus allowing readers and editors the ability to locate the information they are seeking quickly and efficiently. Headings are included in the broader category of styles in Microsoft Word that allow you to apply formatting broadly across any document and are essential in building an automated table of contents. Additionally, using heading styles, particularly in Word, enhances the accessibility of documents. Screen readers use these styles to navigate through the document effectively, which is vital for users with visual impairments.

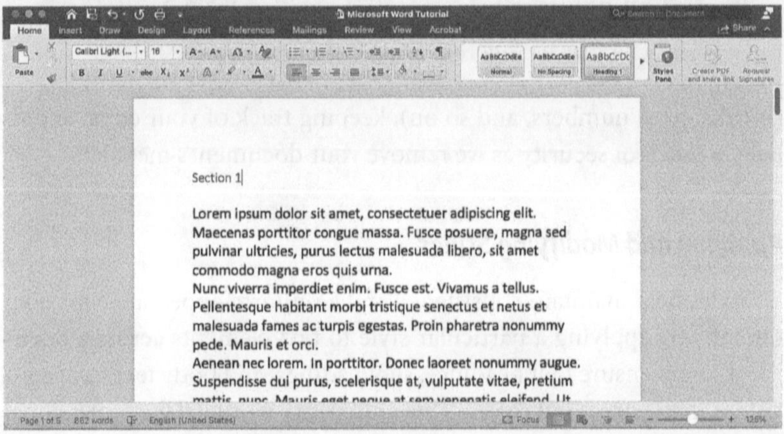

Figure 2-3: "Styles" window in Microsoft Word.

There can be up to nine different heading styles in a document on Word. Correspondingly, as you will see later, there are nine levels to a table of contents generated by Word. Do not be intimidated by the number of levels; most users stick to 3–4 heading levels.

In Figure 2-3, we have applied a Heading 1 style to the text "Section 1." As you can see, it has altered the font, color, size, and other aspects of the text. Word has default formatting associated with each heading style. You can change the formatting options of each heading by either right-clicking the desired heading level and clicking "modify" from the dropdown menu or by opening the "Styles" pane to the right of the "Styles" window and selecting "modify style" from the dropdown menu option that appears when the cursor hovers over the desired style (see Figure 2-4).

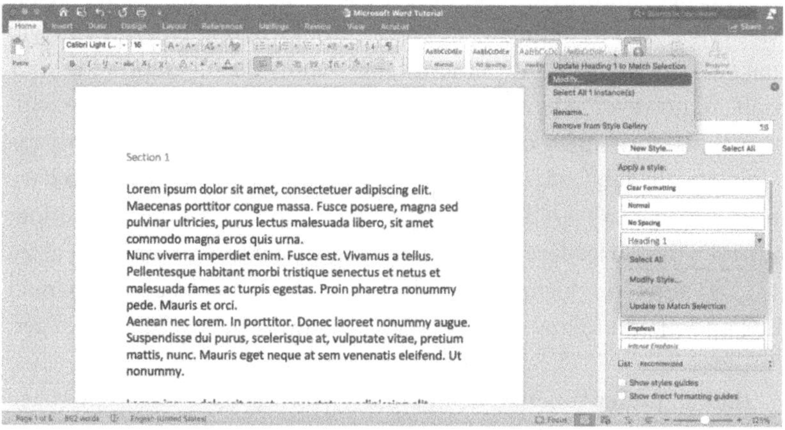

Figure 2-4: Styles format editing.

From the modify screen, users are presented with all the formatting options that are generally applied ad hoc throughout their documents. The key difference is that any edits made to the formatting in this window will apply throughout the document to any section of text where the selected style has been applied. So, your section and subsection headings will be easily formatted simply by highlighting the text and applying the desired style. A notable feature of the "Styles" pane is that it will tell you what style your selected text is associated with. So, if you are unsure what level of heading you need to format, open the "Styles" pane and click on the heading in question to see whether it is Heading 2, 3, 4, and so on; if it has yet to be associated with a style, the "Styles" pane will display "Normal."

Table of Contents Tool, Manual and Automated

The table of contents (ToC) is the bane of many a first-year law student's legal writing career. You have put weeks into finely honing your arguments, countless hours refining your prose, and days you'll never see again have gone into updating cases and statutes. Now, why won't these demonic page numbers align on your ToC? There is an easier way; as a matter of fact, there are two easier ways: the automated ToC tool in Microsoft Word and the tab leader function. The usefulness of each is dependent mainly on the situation in which you find yourself. If you are near the beginning of the drafting process or facing a document that has relatively little formatting, going back through and applying styles will make the automated ToC a more robust and valuable option for your draft. If, however, you are dealing with a group-created template with convoluted formatting or facing a tight deadline and all your drafting is complete, the tab leader function can be a useful quick-fix tool to have in your arsenal. Overall, the automated ToC tool is the better solution; however, the tab leader function can be a good band-aid solution if there just isn't time to reformat. We will start with the tab leader or manual ToC option and follow up with a broader discussion of the automated ToC tool.

The tab leader function in Microsoft Word is used to fill the space between tab stops with a repeated character, typically dots, dashes, or underscores. It is oriented around a specified point on the document ruler, the tab stop, so in a ToC the page number and dot leaders are uniformly placed across the line, meaning that they line up perfectly without the vertigo-inducing wavy lines resulting from simply holding down the period key between your chapter name and the corresponding page number.

To create a ToC using the tab leader function, place your chapter titles left aligned on the page with the page number immediately following the chapter titles. In order to better predict where your page numbers will align, it is helpful to have the ruler enabled from the view tab of the ribbon at the top of the window. After you have your chapter title and page number in place, right-click with the cursor between the chapter title and page number and select "Paragraph" from the dropdown menu that appears. You will need to choose "Tabs" from the bottom left of the "Paragraph" window; the window you are looking for is pictured in Figure 2-5.

From the menu in Figure 2-5, you will want to select "Right" alignment, the type of leader/filler you want between your title and page numbers (dashes, dots, or a solid line), and put the inch mark where you want your page numbers to appear in the box under "Tab stops," then

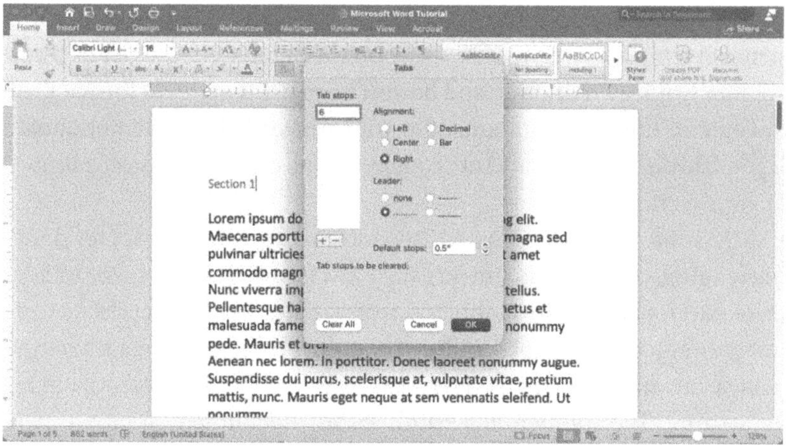

Figure 2-5: "Tabs" window in Microsoft Word.

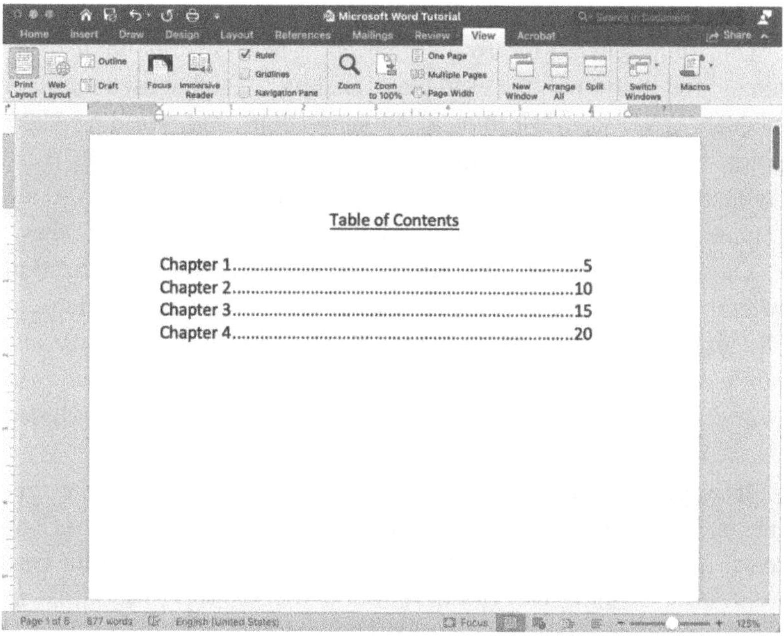

Figure 2-6: Sample tab leader table of contents.

click the add symbol and "OK." After completing all of this information, you will be able to click the "Tab" key, and Word will automatically align your page numbers at the desired location (see Figure 2-6).

The tab leader route for creating a ToC can suffice with preconstructed templates whose formatting doesn't lend itself to styles or if you are totally finished drafting and haven't been using styles to format your document. It is entirely manual, so your page numbers will not update if you add content or if any subsequent editing changes the page number of your sections.

Microsoft Word's automated ToC tool is a significant asset for drafting lengthy, complex documents such as case briefs, legal memoranda, or research papers. The ability to create, customize, and update a ToC not only enhances the readability of documents but also streamlines the navigation and referencing of critical sections, which is essential in legal writing. The ability to hyperlink within a document or cross-reference sections definitely weighs in favor of the automated ToC tool over tab leaders.

As discussed earlier, the first step in using the ToC tool is to format the headings in your document correctly. Word uses these headings to organize and generate the ToC. Each heading level corresponds to a different level in the ToC; for example, "Heading 1" is often used for main chapters or sections, "Heading 2" for subsections, and "Heading 3" for points made within those subsections. As a brief review, to apply these styles, highlight the text you want to designate as a heading, go to the "Home" tab, and select the appropriate style from the "Styles" window.

Once your headings have been set, place the cursor in the location where you want the ToC to appear. Navigate to the "References" tab and click on "Table of Contents." For a quick, pre-formatted ToC choose one of the automatic styles provided by Word. The program will then scan your document for headings and automatically generate the ToC based on the hierarchy of the applied styles.

If the pre-formatted ToC styles do not meet your formatting requirements, you can customize the ToC by selecting "Custom Table of Contents" from the "Table of Contents" menu (see Figure 2-7). In the customization window, you can decide how many levels of headings to include, customize the tab leaders that Word will incorporate, and modify the formatting of the individual levels of your ToC. Adjusting these settings can make the ToC more functional and better suited to the specific needs of your document.

To access the "Style" menu, click on "Modify" from the "Table of Contents" window. From the "Style" menu, you can see that each level of the

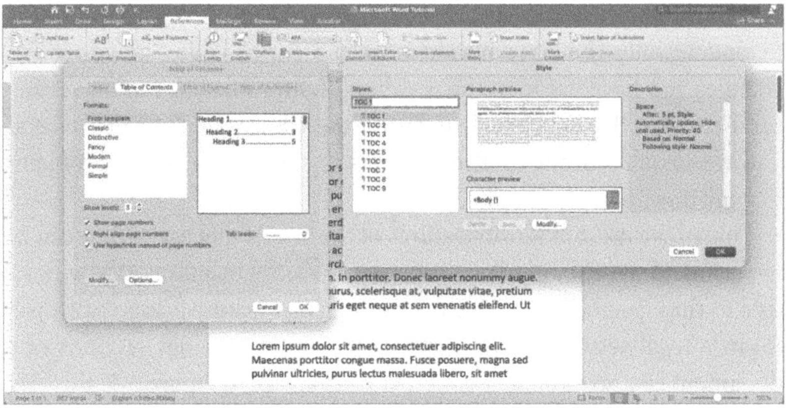

Figure 2-7: ToC formatting menu.

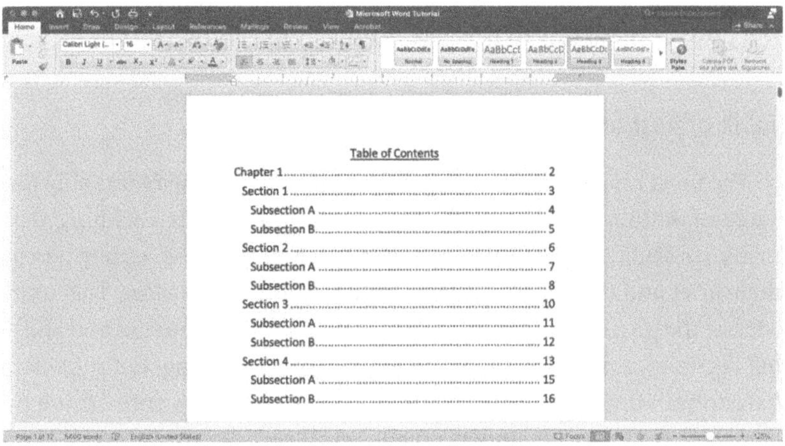

Figure 2-8: Sample generated ToC.

ToC can be formatted individually. The greyed-out window to the rightmost of the menu screen provides details about the current formatting of each level as you highlight it. As with styles, if you want to edit the formatting and change font size, spacing, or text treatment (bold, underline, italics), you simply click on "Modify," and the formatting window will appear. Once you are satisfied with the formatting of your ToC, simply click "OK" on the two menus, and Word will scan your headings and create a custom ToC (see Figure 2-8).

As you modify your document, adding or deleting sections and pages, your ToC will need to be updated to reflect those changes. To update the

ToC, right-click the ToC and choose "Update Field." You have the option to update only the page numbers or the entire table, including any changes you have made to the wording of your headings or any structural changes. I recommend updating the whole table at least once as you are closing out the drafting process to spot any potential problems in your headings.

One of the most practical features of the ToC is that each entry can be hyperlinked. By clicking on a ToC item, Word will automatically navigate to that specific part of the document. This feature is especially useful in a legal setting where quickly accessing particular sections of a document can save valuable time. As you can see in Figure 2-7, the "Table of Contents" menu offers an option to use hyperlinks instead of page numbers. This will not affect a printed document since the page numbers will still appear, but for a digital document circulated in-house, it will provide the ability to navigate between sections quickly.

Table of Authorities Tool

The most underutilized tool in Word for brief writing is arguably the Table of Authorities (ToA). The process seems so overwhelming that many students simply opt to keep a running tab of the authorities in their brief and cobble it together at the last minute. Leaving ToA until later in the process is not necessarily a bad idea since rewrites and shifting sections can cause issues with your page numbering, but it doesn't have to wait until the end, and you don't have to do the entire thing by hand. For the first-year students reading this section, a ToA is a list of all the legal citations in a document—cases, statutes, regulations, and more—along with the page numbers where they appear. Very similar to a table of contents, the ToA helps readers quickly locate essential references. Each citation can be categorized (e.g., "Cases," "Statutes," "Regulations," and so on), which allows you to break down the ToA into sections for easy navigation.

To encapsulate the process, you are effectively just going through your document and marking each citation with a set of tags that tells Word: "This citation is to a legal source that should be included in the table of authorities, and this is how it should be categorized. Keep track of the page number where it and any additional short cites appear." Before beginning this process, you will want to ensure that the majority of your primary writing is completed and that you have a backup copy of the document before you begin. Shifting significant sections of text can cause problems with this process. You must start the process by labeling the first full cite of any given resource in your document so that any subsequent cites are nested under its heading. If you identify the first occurrence of a citation and subsequently delete that entry, it can cause problems with your page numbering when you insert your ToA.

To begin, click the "¶" (Show/Hide) button on the "Home" group. This will help you see the hidden codes that Word inserts for citations and makes troubleshooting easier. Next, carefully review your document to identify the references you want to include in the ToA. Navigate to your first citation and highlight the entire text of the citation. With the citation still highlighted, switch to the "References" tab at the top of the application window. In the "Table of Authorities" group, you should see a button labeled "Mark Citation." Click it, and a small pop-up window titled "Mark Citations" should appear. Let's say you have marked a case, *Smith v. Jones*, 123 F.3d 456. The selected text from the citation will automatically display in the dialog box. This is Word recognizing precisely what you have highlighted (see Figure 2-9). It can be a little confusing, but remember to make sure the text that appears in the "Short Citation" box on your first occurrence of an authority is the full citation as you want it to appear in the Table of Authorities.

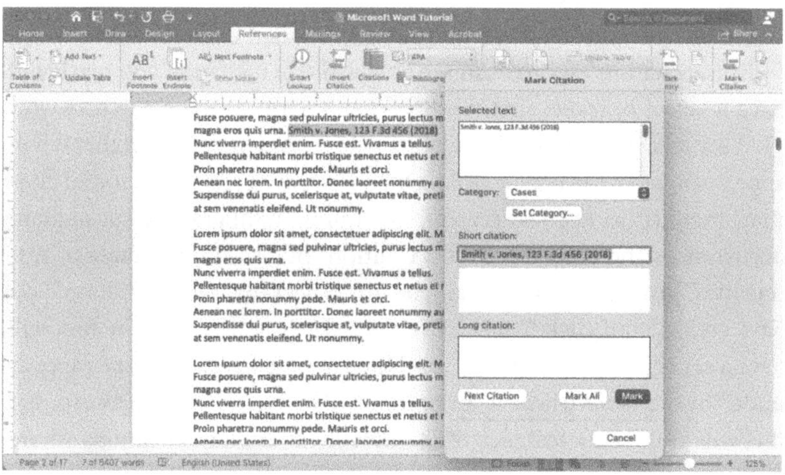

Figure 2-9: Marking a citation.

Next, you select "Category." Obviously, *Smith v. Jones* would be a case; however, there are other options for how to classify a given citation, including as a statute, regulation, or even a customized category (see Figure 2-10). Be aware of what category you are selecting; I have heard many a chagrined exclamation in the library after students have had to start over from their backup draft because they accidentally marked every citation as a case.

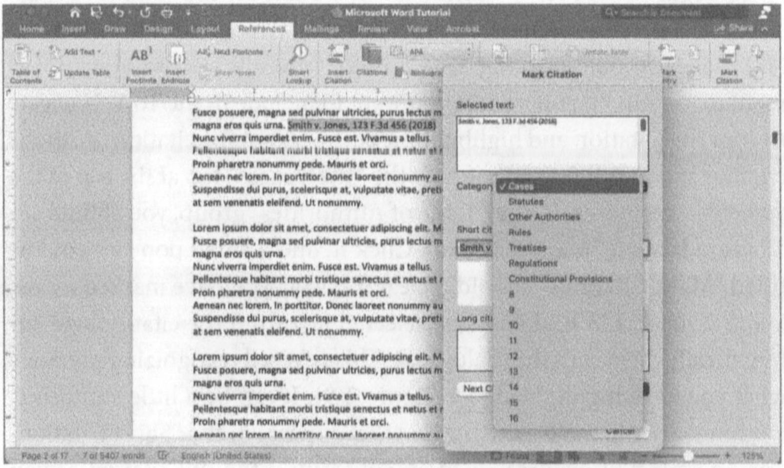

Figure 2-10: Selecting a category after marking a citation.

Finally, you click "Mark" to insert the hidden code that tells Word: "This is a citation." As you can see below, the first citation you mark will have a set of brackets surrounding the citation, tagging the text with "TA" for table of authorities and a "/s" identifying the citation that it will appear under in the actual table. Once you have created the initial citation, there is no need to recreate it; simply highlight any subsequent occurrences and click the "Mark Citation" button in the "Table of Authorities" group, and in the dialogue box, select the "Short Citation" you have created and click "Mark." Every marked citation after the first will have a set of brackets with "TA" and the citation as you want it to appear under in the table. There is an option to "Mark All," but be aware that this will grab every instance of *Smith v. Jones*, even in situations where you are quoting another court that is only discussing the *Smith* case, which doesn't constitute a citation in your brief.

After diligently marking every case, statute, and regulation, you will reach the point where you're ready to generate the ToA. It will most likely be placed after your table of contents but before your substantive writing. From the "References" tab, you will click on the "Insert Table of Authorities" button, which will open a dialogue box for you to format your table just like with your table of contents (see Figure 2-11). A significant distinction is the option to use "passim." If a particular authority is cited frequently throughout your brief, Word can replace the long list of pages with the single word "passim," indicating it appears often throughout the document. This is a situation where you should consult with your professor for style guidance or the style guidelines of your local court. Similar to the table of contents, if you later need to add citations, you can simply mark them, right-click the table, and click on "Update Field" to have the table automatically update with the new citations included.

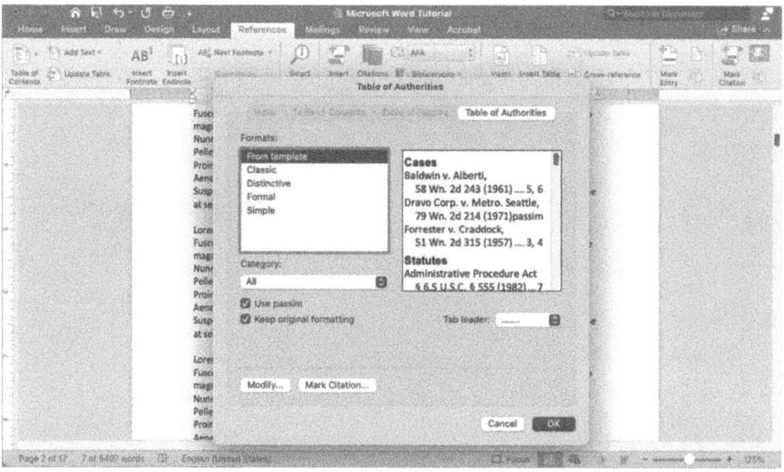

Figure 2-11: Generating the Table of Authorities.

Page Numbering

Page numbering doesn't seem like it would be incredibly difficult and in most academic papers it is as simple as navigating to the "Insert" tab and following the prompts from the "Page Number" drop down. Many legal documents have page numbering requirements that specify unique page numbering for different portions of the document, which is where the problems begin to arise.

I have overheard many a one-sided pleading between students and their laptops, and if I can pierce the haze of trauma from my first brief, I remember having similar conversations. "Why do you hate me? Just change the 2 to a 1!" "Ignore the cover sheet; I don't need it numbered!" "Please just put Roman numerals and regular numbers in this section!" It can seem a bit daunting at first, but the process becomes simple once you understand the steps. Whether you're creating a basic page number sequence or customizing numbers for different sections, Word offers tools to make it all possible.

We'll start easy; from your document navigate to the "Insert" tab. From there, select "Page Number" in the "Header & Footer" group. A dropdown menu will offer various placement options: at the top or bottom of the page, in the page margins, or at the current cursor position. Once you select a location, you'll be presented with styles to choose from. With a single click, your chosen page numbers will appear in the document.

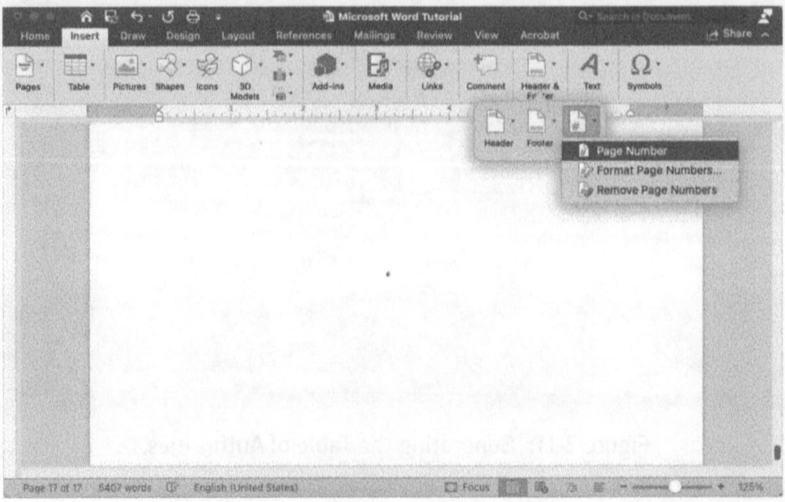

Figure 2-12: Inserting page numbers.

Formatting the numbers can refine their appearance. Double-click the header or footer to access the Header/Footer Design toolbar, then select "Page Number" > "Format Page Numbers." In the dialog box, you can select a numbering style, such as Arabic numerals or Roman numerals. You can also specify whether the numbering should start at a specific number. Clicking "OK" applies these settings instantly.

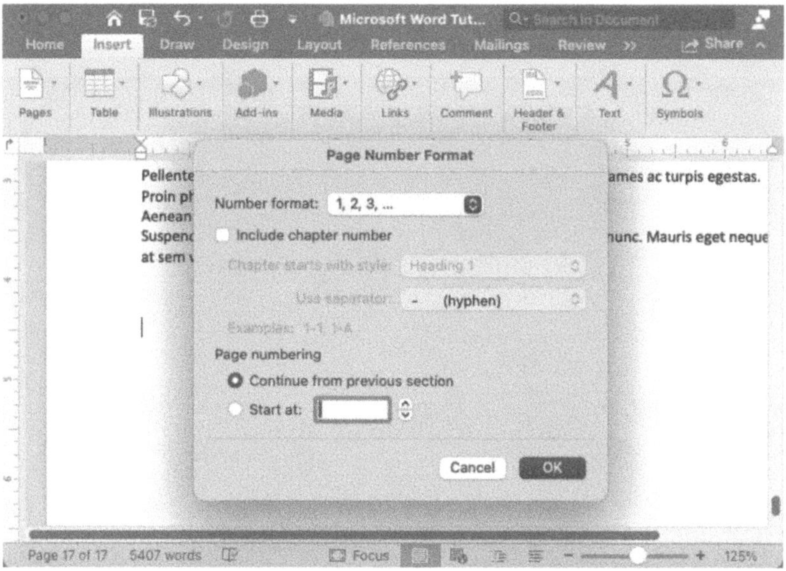

Figure 2-13: Page number formatting.

If your document requires different numbering styles or a restart of numbering in specific sections, you'll need to divide the document. Place your cursor at the point where a new numbering style should begin and go to the "Layout" tab. Select "Breaks" > "Next Page" to insert a section break. Then, double-click the header or footer in the new section. Looking at the toolbar at the top, you will see an option that says "Link to Previous." This option is selected by default to preserve consistency in your document. In order to break this section away from the styles of the previous section, you will need to click this option to deselect it. You can now insert and format page numbers for this section independently. For example, you might choose to restart numbering at "1" and change to Arabic numbering after your Table of Contents and Table of Authorities, which would be in Roman numerals.

At times, you might want to exclude the page number from the first page. Activate the header or footer and check "Different First Page" in the "Header/Footer" design toolbar. This option hides the page number on the first page while retaining it on subsequent pages. It's especially useful for cover pages depending on the style requirements of your first-year writing class or the jurisdiction for which you are drafting.

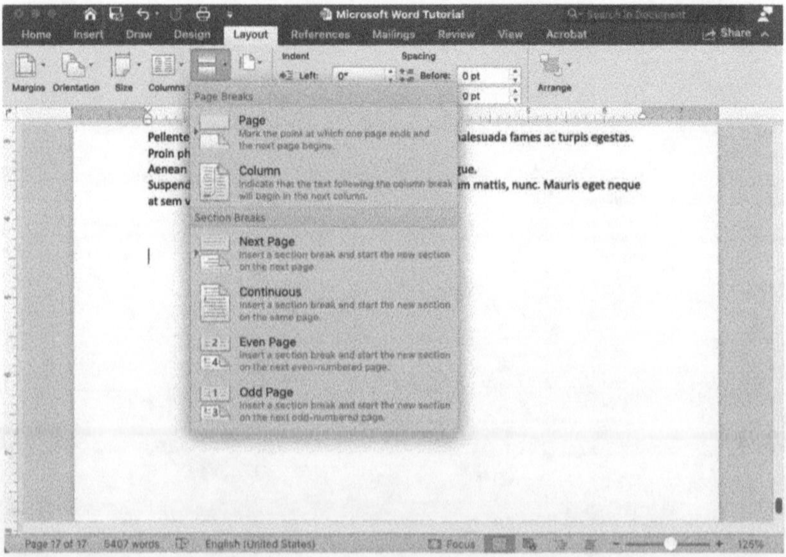

Figure 2-14: Making a new section in document in order to number it separtately.

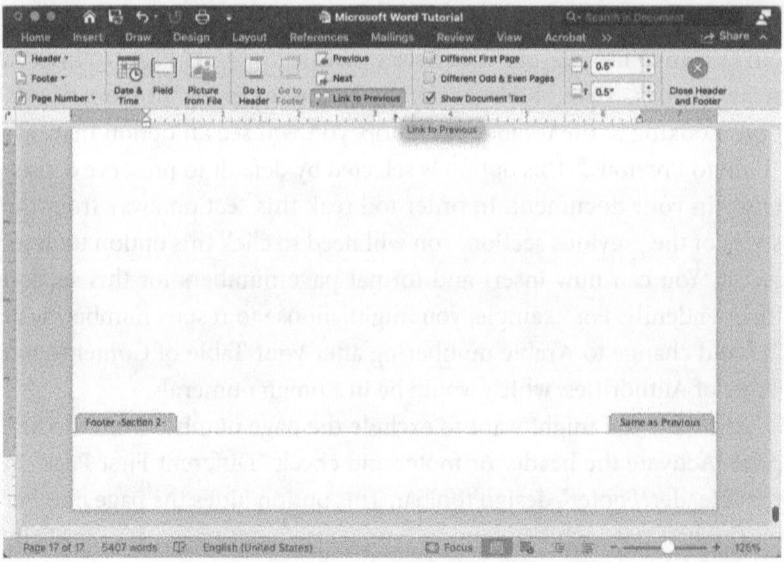

Figure 2-15: Deselect "Link to Previous."

It's a good idea to preview your changes using "Print Preview" to ensure the page numbers appear as expected and that your section breaks haven't inserted any superfluous pages. If unnecessary page breaks have been created by inserting a section break, activating the "Show/Hide" button (¶) on the "Home" bar is invaluable for tracking down the formatting changes that resulted in the errant page.

Track Changes and Comments

In law school you will encounter many situations where a professor wishes to provide feedback on your assignments through the use of comments or will want to see edits made to a document through track changes. In practice it will not be uncommon to be working on a large document like a multi-district litigation brief with other attorneys. Comments and track changes are invaluable tools for collaborations and editing in these situations. They allow users to suggest, review, and discuss changes in a document without altering the original text.

When using track changes, every edit—such as additions, deletions, or formatting adjustments—appears visibly marked. Inserted text is highlighted, often in a different color, while deletions appear struck through. This feature ensures that the original document remains intact, making it easy to compare changes or revert to earlier versions if needed. It's particularly beneficial for teams, as it allows contributors to track who made each edit.

Comments, on the other hand, provide a space for discussion. Instead of modifying the text directly, users can add notes in the margins of the document. This is ideal for asking questions, suggesting alternative phrasing, or pointing out areas that need clarification. Comments appear as speech bubbles alongside the text, keeping the main content clean and focused.

To enable the track changes feature, you'll need to navigate to the "Review" tab on the Word ribbon. Clicking on the "Track Changes" button activates the feature, and from that moment, any edits you make are tracked. You can also customize how changes appear—for example, whether they are shown inline or in balloons in the margin.

Adding comments is equally straightforward. Highlight the section of text you'd like to comment on, then click the "New Comment" button in the "Review" tab. A speech bubble will appear in the margin, where you can type your note. These comments can later be resolved or deleted, ensuring the document stays organized as feedback is addressed.

When reviewing a document with tracked changes and comments, use the "Accept" and "Reject" buttons in the "Review" tab to approve or dismiss suggested edits. For a comprehensive view of all changes, you can toggle between different views, such as "Simple Markup" or "All Markup," which adjust the level of detail shown. Finally, to share a clean version of the document, turn off track changes by clicking the button again and either accepting or rejecting all changes in the document. Comments can be deleted by right-clicking on them and selecting "Delete Comment."

Removing Metadata

While metadata will be discussed in more detail in the eDiscovery chapter, we are going to quickly cover the process of removing metadata from Word documents here and from PDFs a little later in the chapter. For lawyers, removing metadata from a Word document is a crucial step in maintaining client confidentiality, protecting professional integrity, and minimizing risk. Metadata, often called the "data about data," includes hidden information embedded in the document, such as the author's name, tracked changes, comments, and even the document's editing history. While this information might seem harmless, it can inadvertently reveal sensitive details about the drafting process, such as legal strategies, internal discussions, or confidential client information.

Imagine a scenario where a lawyer drafts a settlement agreement. The metadata in the document could disclose earlier versions of the agreement, show concessions initially considered but later withdrawn, or include litigation strategies or sensitive client concerns in comments that informed the offer. If this document is shared with opposing counsel without removing metadata, it could weaken the client's negotiating position or even lead to potential ethics violations. Similarly, metadata could inadvertently reveal co-authors or contributors, breaching confidentiality agreements or privileged communications.

The process of removing metadata from a Word document is simple and should be part of every lawyer's standard workflow when sharing documents externally. Begin by opening the document and navigating to the "File" tab in Microsoft Word. From there, select "Info," which will

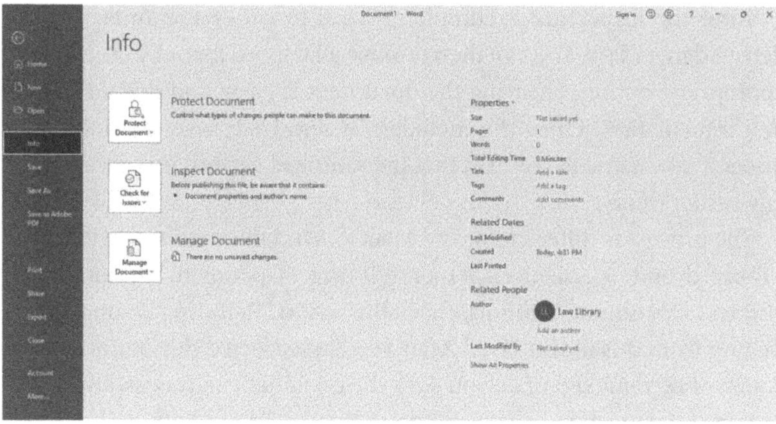

Figure 2-16: The "Info" panel.

display details about the document, including its properties and potential metadata.

Within the "Info" panel, locate and click on the "Check for Issues" dropdown menu. Choose "Inspect Document," which activates Word's inspection tool. This tool allows you to check for various types of metadata, such as comments, tracked changes, document properties, headers, footers, and hidden text. Select the categories you wish to inspect, and Word will scan the document for any embedded information.

Figure 2-17: Inspecting the document for metadata.

After the inspection is complete, Word provides a summary of the detected metadata. You can then remove all flagged items by clicking the appropriate option, ensuring the document is clean and devoid of hidden information. Once the metadata is removed, save the document under a new name to confirm that the sanitized version is separate from any earlier drafts.

The process is different for the MacOS. On Office for Mac within the "Tools" dropdown menu click on the "Protect Document" option. In the "Protect Document" window, check the box to "Remove personal information from this file on save." After you have selected this option, metadata will be removed once you save the document so stay aware of this option if you wish to save versions of the document with and without metadata attached.

Compare Documents

The compare documents feature in Microsoft Word is invaluable in situations where accuracy and attention to detail are paramount. This feature streamlines the review process for contracts, pleadings, agreements, or any other critical documents that undergo multiple rounds of revisions. For instance, when negotiating a contract with opposing counsel, a lawyer may receive a revised draft without a clear record of changes. Instead of manually scouring the document for edits, the compare documents feature highlights every alteration, such as additions, deletions, or formatting changes, in an organized and visually intuitive way. This ensures that no modification goes unnoticed and allows the lawyer to focus on assessing the implications of the changes rather than expending valuable time finding them.

To use this feature, simply navigate to the "Review" tab on the ribbons. Within this tab, you'll find the "Compare" button. Clicking on it opens a menu with two options: "Compare" and "Combine." For a simple comparison, select the "Compare" option. Word will prompt you to choose the two documents you wish to compare: the "Original document" and the "Revised document." Once chosen, you can adjust settings to specify which elements—such as comments, formatting, or text changes—should be included in the comparison. After confirming your selections, Word generates a new document displaying a side-by-side comparison of the original and revised versions, along with a detailed summary of all changes.

The resulting comparison document uses markup to show differences clearly. Additions appear underlined, deletions are struck through, and a "Review" pane provides an itemized list of changes for easy navigation. This visual clarity allows lawyers to quickly evaluate revisions, decide whether to accept or reject them, and prepare an updated draft if needed.

Orphan Control

Finally, an aesthetic tool to preserve consistency across the document without the need to constantly review and insert lines is Orphan Control. In Word formatting an "orphan" refers to the first line of a paragraph that appears alone at the bottom of a page, separated from the rest of the paragraph. This can disrupt the flow of reading and make a document look unpolished or disjointed.

Orphan Control ensures that at least two lines of a paragraph are kept together on the same page. By doing so, it maintains the visual integrity of the text, making it easier for readers to follow the content without unnecessary breaks or distractions. This is particularly useful in professional documents such as legal briefs, contracts, or academic papers where presentation and clarity are critical.

Orphan control can be applied on an as-needed basis to individual paragraphs, or it can be applied globally to the entire document. To simply select the text you wish to apply the feature to, either select the particular section or hit Ctrl-A to select all text in the document. Right-click on the highlighted text and choose "Paragraph" from the drop-down menu that appears, or select it from the options in the "Format" dropdown menu at the top of the document. In the "Paragraph" dialog box, switch to the "Line and Page Breaks" tab. Here, you'll find several options for controlling how text flows across pages. Check the box labeled "Widow/Orphan Control" ("widows" are similar to "orphans," referring to the last line of a paragraph appearing alone at the top of a page). Once selected, Word automatically adjusts the pagination to prevent orphans.

Adobe Acrobat

Portable Document Format (PDF) is a widely used file format that preserves the layout, fonts, images, and other elements of a document regardless of the software, hardware, or operating system used to view it. PDFs are designed to be a universal format that ensures documents appear the same on all devices. This consistency makes the format particularly useful for professionals like lawyers who need reliable, unalterable documents for communication and record-keeping.

For lawyers, PDFs have become an indispensable tool for several reasons. First, they ensure document fidelity. Whether it's a contract, court filing, or memorandum, the content and formatting remain intact, avoiding potential distortions that can occur when sharing Word files or other editable formats. PDFs are particularly useful in eDiscovery because of their universality, since many documents from different devices are exchanged between parties and the attributes of those documents are preserved in the exchange, thus preventing confusion and delay.

Security is another significant advantage. PDFs can be encrypted and password-protected, ensuring sensitive client information or confidential documents remain secure. Digital signatures can also be applied to PDFs, making them a convenient tool for executing contracts or verifying authenticity without requiring physical paperwork. Moreover, PDFs are optimized for legal processes. Many courts now require filings in PDF format because they are easy to archive, search, and annotate. Features like optical character recognition (OCR) allow scanned documents to be converted into searchable text, which is invaluable for quickly locating key terms in lengthy documents such as case files or discovery materials.

Finally, PDFs are platform-agnostic, making them an excellent choice for collaboration. Whether working with opposing counsel, clients, or colleagues, lawyers can share PDFs with confidence that the recipient will see precisely what was intended. Tools for commenting and highlighting further enhance their utility for collaborative review. This book will provide tutorials on a key handful of features available through Adobe Acrobat for working with PDFs. For a more in-depth exposition on working with PDFs in the legal field, I recommend consulting Daniel

Siegel and Pamela Myers's book *The Ultimate Guide to Adobe Acrobat DC* from the American Bar Association.[1]

OCR

The OCR feature in Adobe Acrobat DC is a powerful tool for lawyers, allowing them to convert scanned documents and image-based files into searchable and editable texts. Documents created through Microsoft Office and other text editing software and exported as PDFs are searchable by default. The PDF version of the document preserves the attributes of the underlying document, including the formation of words and font. With scanned documents, however, what effectively happens is the scanner takes a picture of the document and converts it into PDF format. With a picture, there is no text for the program to identify, so something has to fill the gap in order for PDF readers to conduct text searching within the scanned document; this is where OCR comes into play.

A single scanned document without OCR may not create a problem depending on its length, but imagine working on a case that involves hundreds of pages of scanned documents. Without OCR, finding specific clauses, names, or dates would require time-consuming manual reading. With OCR, lawyers can quickly search for keywords, annotate the document, or even copy and paste relevant sections into briefs or memos. This not only saves time but also reduces the risk of missing critical details hidden within the text.

Technically speaking, OCR exists under the broad umbrella of AI as a form of machine learning based on pattern recognition as it analyzes the shapes and patterns of pixels in an image and converts them into a digital text format that can be edited, searched, or processed by software. Here's a more detailed breakdown of how OCR works:

1. Image Acquisition: The OCR process begins with an image of the text. This could be a scanned document or a photograph. The software first analyzes the image and prepares it for character recognition.

---

1. DANIEL SIEGEL & PAMELA MYERS, THE ULTIMATE GUIDE TO ADOBE ACROBAT DC (2d ed. 2022).

2. Preprocessing: Before recognizing text, OCR software may clean up the image to improve accuracy. This includes tasks such as:
   a. Deskewing: Correcting any tilt in the scanned image.
   b. Denoising: Removing spots, specks, or other visual white noise.
   c. Binarization: Converting the image to black-and-white to focus on contrasts between text and background.
3. Text Segmentation: The software divides the image into zones, isolating text from non-text elements like images or graphics. It then further breaks the text into individual lines, words, and, eventually, characters.
4. Pattern Recognition:
   a. Template Matching: The software compares each character in the image against a stored library of fonts and shapes to find a match. This is effective for clean, consistent text but less so for handwriting or unusual fonts.
   b. Feature Extraction: The software identifies unique features of each character, such as lines, curves, and intersections, and matches those to known patterns. This approach is more robust for varying text styles.
5. Postprocessing: Once the characters are recognized, the OCR software may use contextual analysis to improve accuracy. For example, it checks recognized words against a dictionary or applies grammar rules to suggest corrections for unclear text.
6. Output Generation: The final step is converting the recognized text into a usable format, such as searchable text overlaid on the original image in a PDF.

To use the OCR feature in Acrobat DC, open a scanned PDF. A very simple way to see if the PDF already has OCR included is to find a term on the first page of the document and do a Ctrl+F search for that term. If the search returns no results, you can safely assume that OCR is not enabled in the document. If OCR is not available, navigate to the "Scan & OCR" tool, which is available on the right-hand pane. Select the option to "Recognize Text," and Acrobat will prompt you to choose the specific pages or the entire document for OCR processing. Acrobat then scans the document, identifies the text, and overlays it onto the original PDF.

After running OCR, you may need to correct errors, especially in documents with complex layouts, poor-quality scans (smudges, blurred images, and so on), or unusual fonts. Acrobat makes this process intuitive. Once the text recognition is complete, open the "Correct Recognized Text" tool from the same "Scan & OCR" panel. This feature highlights suspected errors in the text, allowing you to review and edit them directly. For example, if there are signature lines at the bottom of the document, OCR might not be able to recognize the signatures; you can click on the highlighted words and replace them with the correct version. This is also handy when dealing with legalese, as OCR might not pick up on more obscure legal terminology and may need to be corrected.

Indexing

While OCR allows for text searching of a single or group of documents, Acrobat provides an option to create a more robust set of entry points for large groups of documents. The index feature in Adobe Acrobat DC is handy when managing large, complex sets of documents. It allows you to create a searchable index for a collection of PDFs, enabling rapid access to specific information. For lawyers working on cases involving large discovery sets, multi-document contracts, or extensive research files, the ability to quickly locate relevant keywords and phrases is invaluable.

Imagine handling litigation with thousands of pages of evidence spread across a vast multitude of produced PDFs. Without an index, searching for a specific clause, term, or name would require scanning each document individually, wasting precious time. By creating an index, Acrobat allows you to search all the documents in a fraction of the time, ensuring you can locate critical information efficiently and accurately. This is particularly useful during depositions or court proceedings when time is of the essence.

Using the index feature begins with opening Acrobat DC and navigating to the "Tools" section. Look for "Catalog," the tools used to create and manage indexes. If you don't see it, you can add it from the available tools list. Once inside "Catalog," you'll create a new index by specifying the PDFs you want included. These documents can be a single file, multiple files, or an entire folder of PDFs. For organizational purposes, it is handy to locate the files you wish to index in a single folder.

Next, you'll configure the index settings. Acrobat allows you to customize how the index is generated, such as specifying metadata, indexing bookmarks, or including document properties. Once your preferences are set, start the indexing process. Acrobat will analyze the files and generate the index, which is saved as a separate file. This indexed file allows Acrobat to search the included documents instantly. To use the index for searching, open the "Advanced Search" tool in Acrobat and select the option to use an index. This ensures that the search draws directly from the pre-built index, delivering results far more quickly than a standard text search. The indexed search supports advanced queries, including Boolean operators, making it even easier to pinpoint relevant results.

Comments

Similar to Word's comment feature, Acrobat's comment feature allows users to add annotations, notes, and feedback directly onto a PDF without altering the underlying document. This feature also helps in preparing for litigation or trial. Lawyers reviewing evidence, affidavits, or court filings that are typically submitted in PDF form can annotate key points, flag issues, or jot down strategies for quick reference. Using comments in Acrobat is essentially as simple and straightforward as in Word.

To begin, open the PDF and navigate to the "Comment" tool, which can be found in the right-hand pane or by selecting "Tools" from the top menu and then choosing "Comment." Once activated, the toolbar provides various annotation options, such as adding sticky notes, highlighting text, underlining, strikethroughs, or drawing shapes. The sticky note feature is a bit different than the comment feature in Word as it allows you to attach a virtual sticky note to the document, similar to adding one to a physical document. To add a sticky note, simply click the "Note" icon and then click anywhere on the document where you want to place the comment. A text box appears, allowing you to type your thoughts. This is ideal for general feedback or pointing out sections that need attention. For more targeted feedback, you can highlight a specific portion of text and right-click to choose "Add Comment," linking your note directly to the highlighted area.

Comments can be managed and organized using the "Comments List," which provides an overview of all annotations in the document. Each comment appears with the author's name, timestamp, and content, making it easy to track input from multiple reviewers. You can reply to comments, mark them as resolved, or delete them when no longer needed, ensuring the document remains tidy as revisions are implemented.

Redacting Text

Unlike superficial redaction practices, such as drawing black boxes over text in word processors or image editing software, Acrobat's redaction tool removes the targeted content entirely from the file's metadata, making it unrecoverable. This distinction is crucial in situations where improperly redacted documents can lead to accidental disclosures, ethical breaches, or legal liabilities.

For lawyers, redaction is often required when sharing documents during litigation, regulatory reviews, or client communications. For example, during discovery, a lawyer may need to provide opposing counsel with a document while concealing privileged information, personal identifiers, or sensitive client details. Acrobat's redaction feature ensures this process is secure, precise, and compliant with confidentiality obligations.

To use the redaction tool, start by opening the PDF in Adobe Acrobat DC. Navigate to the "Redact" tool, which can be found in the "Tools" pane. Once selected, Acrobat offers various options to redact content. You can choose to redact text, images, or specific areas of the document. For text, simply highlight the words or phrases you want to redact. If the image is a scan, you may need to run the OCR feature to allow for text selection. Acrobat will mark them for redaction, enabling you to review your selections before finalizing the process.

If the document contains recurring sensitive terms, such as names or identification numbers, Acrobat provides a "Search and Redact" option. This feature scans the document for specific terms and allows you to redact them all at once, saving time and ensuring consistency. Additionally, you can customize the appearance of redacted areas by adding placeholder text, such as "Redacted" or a reason for the redaction.

Once you've marked all the content for redaction, finalize the process by selecting "Apply Redactions." Acrobat will permanently remove the selected text or images and overwrite the file to prevent recovery. At this stage, it is advisable to save the redacted document under a new file name to preserve the original version for your records. The security and thoroughness of Acrobat's redaction tool make it superior to other methods that merely obscure the text visually but leave the underlying data accessible.

Bates Numbering

The process of Bates numbering assigns a unique, sequential identifier to each page in a set of documents, ensuring that every page is easily traceable and distinguishable. This practice is particularly useful in litigation, where legal teams must organize, reference, and share extensive document collections such as discovery materials, case files, or trial exhibits. It streamlines document organization by creating a systematic reference system, reducing confusion when working with lengthy filing or shared evidence. Additionally, it facilitates communication between legal teams, clients, and opposing counsel by providing a universal method for referencing specific pages. Bates numbering provides a systematic process for referencing specific documents in pleadings, memoranda, and briefs. For example, during depositions or court proceedings, a lawyer can quickly direct attention to "Bates Number 12345" instead of describing a document's location or contents. As you will see in Chapter 7, this dramatically reduces confusion and increases efficacy when presenting evidence with a trial technician. Courts often require Bates numbering for submissions to ensure clarity and consistency.

Start by opening the PDF or batch of PDFs you wish to number. Navigate to the "Tools" section and select "Edit PDF," where you'll find the "Bates Numbering" option. Choose "Add Bates Numbering," which opens a dialog box for customizing the numbering process. In this dialog, you can specify the files to include. Acrobat allows you to add multiple PDFs, combining them into a single sequence or numbering them individually. After selecting your files, you can adjust the numbering's format and placement. Options include font styles, size, and color, as well as the numbering's position on the page, such as the header, footer, or margin. You can also append prefixes or suffixes to the numbers to include case-specific identifiers or timestamps.

Once configured, Acrobat previews the numbering to ensure accuracy. After confirming the settings, apply the Bates numbering to your document set. The software processes the files and embeds the numbering directly onto each page, creating a consistent and professional reference system. For added security, save the numbered set under a new file name to preserve the original files. With the Bates numbers in place, you can share the documents with your co-counsel or opposing counsel at your discretion, confident that every page is accounted for and easy to reference.

Securing Documents

Chapters 3 and 4 discuss the need for and the concept of data encryption in more detail, but Acrobat provides tools to ensure document security that are well worth familiarizing yourself with. One of the most straightforward tools for ensuring document security is password protection. This feature restricts access to a document, ensuring only authorized recipients can open or modify it. For example, when sending a contract draft or confidential client memo via email, lawyers can apply a password so only those with the correct credentials can view or edit the file. This protects sensitive information from unidentified exposure, even if the email or file is intercepted.

To apply password protection, open the PDF in Acrobat and navigate to the "Protect" tool in the right-hand pane. Select "Encrypt with Password," and Acrobat will prompt you to choose between two options: requiring a password to open the document or another to restrict specific actions like editing or printing. After setting your password, save the document, and it will be securely locked.

Another form of document security is the process of creating a certified document. Certification ensures the authenticity of a document and confirms it has not been altered since it was signed or sent. For lawyers, this is particularly useful when sharing contracts, affidavits, or court filings where the integrity of the document is paramount. A certified document includes a visible signature or certificate that assures the recipient of its legitimacy.

To certify a document in Acrobat, use the "Certificates" tool, which can be accessed from the "Tools" section. Once there, select "Certify (Visible Signature)" and choose the area of the document where you want the certification to appear. You can then add a digital signature, which acts as a tamper-evident seal. Save the document, and any future changes will invalidate the certification, alerting the recipients to potential alterations.

The secure envelope feature adds an additional layer of protection when sending multiple files or sharing sensitive documents via email. A secure envelope allows you to package one or more files into a single PDF that is encrypted and password-protected, functioning like a digital lockbox. To create a secure envelope, go to the "Tools" section and select "Send for Review" or use the "Adobe Sign Integration" to create a secure package. You can add files to the envelope, apply encryption settings, and set permissions.

Once the envelope is ready, you can share it with recipients through secure email or other file transfer methods. Recipients will need the designated password or certificate to access the envelope and its contents. This ensures that even if the envelope is intercepted during transit, the contents remain secure and unread.

Digital Signatures

Finally, the digital signature feature in Acrobat offers a secure and efficient way to sign, share, and authenticate documents. Unlike a traditional handwritten signature, a digital signature provides an added layer of security by embedding cryptographic information that verifies the signer's identity and ensures the document hasn't been tampered with after signing. For lawyers who frequently deal with contracts, affidavits, and court filings, digital signatures streamline workflows and enhance the integrity of legal processes.

Digital signatures are particularly useful in scenarios requiring fast and secure document execution. For instance, when finalizing a settlement agreement, multiple parties can digitally sign the document without needing to meet in person, saving time and reducing logistical challenges. Additionally, a digital signature provides a clear audit trail, confirming the date and time of signing and ensuring compliance with standards for electronic transactions. To use the digital signature feature, open the document you want to sign and navigate to the "Certificates" tool in the "Tools" pane. Once in the "Certificates" interface, select "Digitally Sign," and Acrobat will prompt you to draw a signature box in the desired location on the document.

After placing the box, Acrobat asks you to choose a digital ID. If you already have one, select it and proceed. If not, you can create a new digital ID directly within Acrobat, either as a file-based certificate or linked to a trusted certificate authority. Once you've selected or created your digital ID, Acrobat allows you to customize the appearance of your signature, including options for a typed name, an image of your handwritten signature, or a simple digital seal. When you're satisfied with the settings, apply the signature. Acrobat embeds the signature into the document, along with cryptographic data that ensures its authenticity. The signed document can then be saved and shared, with recipients able to verify the signature's validity through Acrobat's built-in verification tools.

Conclusion

Mastering document manipulation tools is an essential skill for anyone working in the legal field. The comprehensive functionalities offered by Microsoft Office and Adobe Acrobat empower legal professionals to create, format, and share documents efficiently while maintaining accuracy and professionalism. From applying styles and generating automated tables of contents to leveraging tools like Track Changes and metadata removal, these techniques ensure streamlined workflows and polished outputs. Similarly, Adobe Acrobat's features for securing, annotating, and organizing PDFs provide unparalleled control over document management, making them invaluable for collaboration and compliance.

Incorporating these tools into your daily practice will save time, reduce errors, and enhance your ability to produce clear, organized, and professional documents. Whether you are a law student learning the fundamentals or a seasoned attorney handling complex cases, proficiency in these applications will support your success in an increasingly technology-driven legal landscape. By continually refining your skills and exploring the full potential of these tools, you will not only improve your efficiency but also elevate the quality of your legal work.

CHAPTER 3

Cybersecurity: Protecting Your Firm and Your Client

Cybersecurity is an increasingly critical area of focus within legal technology, as law firms, courts, and other legal institutions face unprecedented challenges in safeguarding sensitive data. A question I frequently pose to my students, and on which I would ask you to ruminate, is why law firms are preferred targets for threats in the digital world. Can you think of anything the world's most wealthy people or organizations have in common? Answer: They tend to seek out legal advice on their activities to protect or enhance their monetary gains. Clients need guidance on patenting their innovations, navigating government contracts, and conducting due diligence on corporate mergers, all of which require reviewing highly sensitive information. The shift toward digitization within the legal sector has undoubtedly amplified productivity, enabling attorneys to access, store, and transmit vast amounts of information with relative ease. However, with this advance in productivity comes a concomitant increase in risk. In addition to the traditional risks associated with hard copy files stored and transmitted by a firm, legal professionals now grapple with the complexities of data protection. A task that, handled improperly, can expose sensitive client information, erode public trust, and even jeopardize the integrity of the judicial process.

According to the *2023 ABA Legal Technology Survey Report*, between 15% and 36% of firms surveyed reported a security breach of their firm in 2023.[1] Looking at Figure 3-1 below, there tends to be a trend wherein most breaches occurred in mid-size firms, and there was a bit of a fall-off

1. Am. Bar Ass'n, 2023 Legal Technology Survey Report Combined 150 (2023).

with solo practitioners and larger firms of 100 attorneys or more. This is not to say that solo practitioners and larger firms are safe, as seen from the numbers. Mid-size firms present a sweet spot where there is enough staff to present a target-rich environment for attacks while possibly not having as robust a cybersecurity presence as the largest firms. Hopefully, this figure illustrates that cyber threats are a very real concern for legal professionals entrusted with sensitive client data.

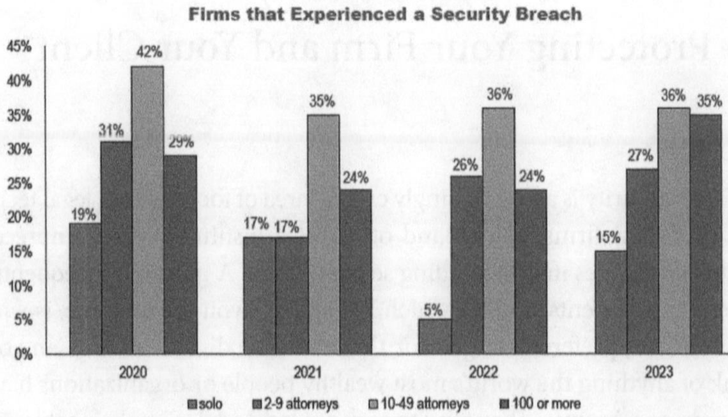

Table 3-1: Percentages of surveyed firms that experienced a security breach, by number of attorneys, 2020–2023.

So, what does cybersecurity entail, you may ask? According to the Cybersecurity & Infrastructure Security Agency, it is the art of protecting networks, devices, and data from unauthorized access or criminal use and the practice of ensuring confidentiality, integrity, and availability of information.[2] The term *confidentiality* should probably make your attorney senses start tingling. When we're dealing with client information, confidentiality is paramount. Specifically, Rule 1.6 of the ABA *Model Rules of Professional Conduct* obliges lawyers to keep client data confiden-

2. Cybersecurity & Infrastructure Security Agency, *What is Cybersecurity?*, CISA Blog (Feb. 01, 2021), https://www.cisa.gov/news-events/news/what-cybersecurity.

tial and avoid intentional or inadvertent disclosure absent permission to the contrary.[3] Additionally, ABA Opinion 483 states that:

> [A]n obligation exists for a lawyer to communicate with current clients about a data breach ... [a data breach is a cyber episode in which] material client confidential information is misappropriated, destroyed, or otherwise compromised, or where a lawyer's ability to perform the legal services for which the lawyer is hired is significantly impaired by the episode.[4]

So not only do cyberattacks put you in hot water ethically, but if they occur, you have to report to your client that an obvious threat has accessed either the sensitive information they entrusted to you or that a malicious actor is hobbling your efforts to represent them, neither of which paints a flattering picture of you professionally. Some might be tempted at this point to think, "Well, if I have an IT guy, I've done my part to protect my client's data." Unfortunately, Rule 5.3(c) suggests that lawyers may be responsible for any negligence on the part of their non-lawyer IT employees.[5] Luckily, this chapter reveals the only surefire way to ensure absolute immunity for your devices from cyber threats; for details, consult Figure 3-2.

Figure 3-1: A little humor.

3. *See* Model Rules of Professional Conduct r. 1.6 (Am. Bar Ass'n 1983).

4. ABA Comm. on Ethics & Pro. Resp., Formal Op. 483 (2018) (discussing a lawyer's obligations after an electronic data breach or cyberattack).

5. *See* Model Rules of Pro. Conduct r. 5.3 (Am. Bar Ass'n 1983).

Unfortunately, the only way that your devices and data can be utterly impervious to cyber threats is if they are entirely disconnected from any network and wholly encased in cement. To be fair, if the data on those devices was valuable enough, those absurdly extreme measures still might not be sufficient protection. So, let's review what we've covered so far. Recent practices digitizing client data have made it vulnerable to new forms of threats; those threats are pervasive and insidious; everyone is susceptible; you might be responsible for mistakes you didn't personally make; and there is no practical way to be 100% secure. Ready to go back to Microsoft tutorials?

A peer in the field articulated a concept that resonated with me when I began studying cybersecurity. It is impossible to build an utterly foolproof system; cyber attackers can find a way in if they want in badly enough, but frequently, they are like carjackers wandering through a parking lot. If your doors are locked, the alarm is armed, and there are no valuables clearly visible, they will move one. As odd as it may sound, the goal is not always to form an impregnable wall of defense. It is to make sure that you are not the most appealing target in view. The ABA model rules recognize the necessity for scaling protections based on the preceding concept. Paragraph 18 of the Comment to Model Rule 1.6 identifies criteria for when security should be scaled upward. Specifically, it states that additional protection may be required based on:

1. The sensitivity of the information,
2. The likelihood of disclosure if additional safeguards are not employed,
3. The cost of employing additional safeguards,
4. The difficulty of implementing the safeguards, and
5. The extent to which the safeguards adversely affect the lawyer's ability to represent clients (e.g., by making a device or important piece of software excessively difficult to use.).[6]

Beyond confidentiality, cybersecurity in legal technology intersects with two other vital principles that make up what is called the CIA Triad: data confidentiality, integrity, and availability. Data must remain unaltered and accessible to preserve their validity in legal proceedings. A cybersecurity breach that corrupts or deletes essential data could jeop-

6. MODEL RULES OF PRO. CONDUCT r. 1.6, cmt. 18 (AM. BAR ASS'N 1983).

ardize the chain of custody for vital evidence. Ensuring data integrity and availability requires robust measures, including regular data backups, secure access protocols, and disaster recovery plans. These measures are essential not only for ongoing cases but also to retain data availability for productivity and workflow within the firm.

In addition to the ethical considerations imposed by the ABA Rules of Professional Conduct, regulatory compliance further complicates the cybersecurity landscape. Legislation such as the General Data Protection Regulation (GDPR) in Europe,[7] the California Consumer Privacy Act (CCPA),[8] and industry-specific privacy laws impose strict requirements on how data should be handled, stored, and protected. These regulations carry substantial financial penalties for non-compliance and necessitate proactive security measures.

Finally, in the face of mounting cyber threats, legal practitioners need to consider the implications of a breach on their relationships with clients and the public at large. Data breaches can damage a firm's reputation, eroding client trust and confidence. For clients, entrusting their most sensitive information to a law firm is a profound act of faith; a data breach, therefore, feels like a betrayal, with potential impacts on future business. In this way, cybersecurity has become an essential component of client service, as the measures a law firm takes to protect data directly influence its credibility and reliability.

This chapter delves into the aspects of cybersecurity within legal technology, exploring best practices for protecting client information, maintaining data integrity, ensuring regulatory compliance, and educating legal professionals about potential threats. Through practical examples and insights, law students and professionals can better understand and protect themselves, their clients, and the integrity of the justice system, adapting to the challenges of a digital age that shows no signs of slowing down.

---

7. EU General Data Protection Regulation (GDPR): Regulation 2016/679 of the European Parliament and of the Council of 27 April 2016 on the Protection of Natural Persons with Regard to the Processing of Personal Data and on the Free Movement of Such Data, and Repealing Directive 95/46/EC, 2016 O.J. (L 119/1).

8. Cal. Civ. Code §§ 1798.100-199 (West 2018) (effective Jan. 1, 2020) (codifying CCPA).

Threats and Vulnerabilities

In cybersecurity, a threat and a vulnerability are two distinct but closely related concepts, each playing a different role in the overall risk landscape. A threat is any circumstance or event with the potential to adversely impact organizational operations, organizational assets, or individuals through an information system via unauthorized access; destruction, disclosure, or modification of information; and/or denial of service.[9] A vulnerability is a weakness in an information system, system security procedures, internal controls, or implementation that could be exploited or triggered by a threat.[10] Essentially, a threat is something that has the potential to cause harm and a vulnerability is a weakness in a system that could be exploited by a threat to cause that harm.

Threats can include such things as a cyber attacker attempting to access data, malware exploiting weak points in a system, or a phishing attack designed to trick users into revealing sensitive information. Vulnerabilities can include unpatched software with known security flaws, weak passwords, lack of two-factor authentication, or misconfigured network settings that expose sensitive data. We're going to walk through some of the more prevalent threats and vulnerabilities that occur in an organization, followed by some tools and strategies that you should at least be aware of in order to effectively collaborate with your security team to protect firm and client data.

Social Engineering

Let's start with a hypothetical situation in which you are a potential malicious actor analyzing a mid-size firm with loads of juicy information about some very wealthy clients. After some research and reconnaissance, you have decided that there are really only two viable ways to gain access to the information you are seeking. They are:

---

9. Joint Task Force Transformation Initiative, National Institute of Standards and Technology, NIST SP 800-30, Rev. 1, Guide for Conducting Risk Assessments (2012), https://nvlpubs.nist.gov/nistpubs/Legacy/SP/nistspecialpublication800-30r1.pdf.

10. National Institute of Standards and Technology, FIPS Pub. 200, Minimum Security Requirements for Federal Information and Information Systems (2006), https://nvlpubs.nist.gov/nistpubs/FIPS/NIST.FIPS.200.pdf.

Figure 3-2: Meet Joe Law

Meet Joe! Joe works as a law clerk at the firm you are surveilling while attending law school at night. Joe has a new family, and he has a lot of things going on in his life. He enjoys his work and needs the experience, but Joe isn't interested in the corporate work this firm typically handles. He hopes to go into the non-profit sector someday and maybe create his own NPO to support overburdened social workers. Joe is a friendly person who holds doors for stragglers and is always willing to carry boxes or books if someone looks overwhelmed. Joe doesn't judge people for forgetting their keycards because he knows he's made mistakes, too. Joe is good people.

Figure 3-3: Hacker-Smasher EX9000

Meet the Hacker-Smasher EX9000! It is an unholy abomination created by the collaborative will of 150 cyber security experts fueled by the tears of 9000 interns. It integrates the best practices of every known framework ever created and refined by the latest AI technology available. It monitors data across every available network connected to the firm and integrates biometric identification from a closed database of known employees housed in a secure room guarded by sharks with lasers attached to their heads.

Given the two options, which of the two targets do you think would provide the more accessible entry point to the firm's information? Obviously, this example is a bit bombastic, but it highlights the differences between technical-oriented attack strategies and a concept known as social engineering. Social engineering is a psychological manipulation tactic used to deceive individuals into either revealing confidential information or bypassing security protocols to gain physical access to a target's systems.

At its core, social engineering is employed because, while systems can be fortified with robust security protocols, people and interpersonal relationships are built on behaviors that are often encouraged in the workplace. In the above example, although Joe's willingness to give access to the building with his keycard to individuals who have forgotten theirs isn't necessarily a good trait, the willingness of a team to help one another is a trait that is cultivated for efficiency.

In addition to preying on people's propensity to be helpful, social engineering also looks to exploit pervasive biases. For example, there are certain things that generally make people uncomfortable, such as crying babies, loud arguments, and public displays of affection. In the movie *9 to 5* with Jane Fonda, Dolly Parton, and Lily Tomlin, Tomlin manages to steal the body of her presumed dead boss from a hospital morgue and make a getaway only to discover it is the wrong body, which she subsequently returns. The entire scene is based around the known discomfort people generally feel for being around dead bodies. Social engineering is effective because it taps into human psychology and exploits natural tendencies, making people more susceptible to manipulation.

Some of the more common tendencies it plays upon are:

1. Exploitation of Trust: Pretending to be trusted individuals or authority figures, relying on people's inclination to help or obey. This trust can prompt individuals to share information or grant access without questioning motives.

2. Emotional Manipulation: By playing on emotions like fear, urgency, sympathy, or curiosity, social engineers bypass rational decision-making, e.g., "Your account will be locked" or "You have missed a payment."
3. Lack of Awareness: Many people are unaware of social engineering techniques, making them easy targets. Social engineers use common scenarios or plausible stories, which seem ordinary, to avoid raising suspicion.
4. Over-Reliance on Technology: People often trust technology and assume digital systems are secure.
5. Authority and Conformity Pressure: People tend to comply with authority figures and imitate group behavior. Social engineers exploit this by creating scenarios where victims feel pressured to conform, like posing as an executive or tech support agent.
6. Routine Interruption: Another tactic is to approach individuals during busy times or through unexpected calls and emails, catching them off guard when they are less likely to assess a situation critically.
7. Scarcity: An effective sales tactic that creates the illusion of a product's scarcity can apply pressure to override a person's good judgment and cause them to click on a link when they might not normally do so.

Social engineering is successful because it preys on behavior so universal that it is hard to develop training against since, most of the time, people don't know they're being manipulated. Many of the tools employed by social engineers aren't based on a sophisticated knowledge of technology. They don't manipulate systems. They manipulate people, as you will see from the description of some of the more common tools below.

1. Phishing
   Phishing is one of the most common social engineering tactics, where attackers send fraudulent emails or messages that appear legitimate, aiming to trick recipients into revealing sensitive information. Phishing messages often contain a sense of urgency, such as fake security alerts or claims of account issues, directing users to a fraudulent website to "confirm" credentials or personal information.

2. Spear Phishing
   Unlike broad phishing attacks, spear phishing is highly targeted and personalized. Attackers research their target and tailor messages with specific details (like their name, job title, or recent purchases) to increase credibility. These attacks often target individuals within an organization aiming to gain access to critical systems or data.
3. Pretexting
   In pretexting, attackers create a fabricated scenario or "pretext" to gain the target's trust and obtain sensitive information. This might involve pretending to be a co-worker, IT support, or another trusted figure, using details gleaned from social media or other sources to make the story more convincing. For example, an attacker might claim they need personal information to verify an account or reset a password.
4. Baiting
   Baiting involves offering something enticing to lure targets into a trap, such as fake freebies, gift cards, or even job offers. The bait might direct the user to click a link that installs malware, or it could take the form of a physical device, like a USB drive left in a public place. When the user inserts the drive into a computer, malware is installed, granting attackers access to the system.
5. Quid Pro Quo
   In quid pro quo attacks, the attacker offers a service or benefit in exchange for information. For example, they might pose as tech support, offering to fix a problem but asking the user to disable security settings or reveal login details. Once the target complies, the attacker has the access they need.
6. Tailgating (or "Piggybacking")
   Tailgating occurs when an unauthorized person gains access to a restricted area by following an authorized individual. Attackers might ask someone to hold the door open as they juggle items or wear a uniform to appear legitimate. Once inside, they can access restricted systems or areas to steal information.

7. Vishing (Voice Phishing)
   Vishing uses phone calls instead of emails to gain sensitive information. Attackers might impersonate an IT professional or bank representative, claiming they need account verification or security details. This technique takes advantage of the sense of urgency and legitimacy that people often associate with voice communications.
8. Scareware
   Scareware involves frightening victims into believe their system has been compromised or infected with malware, prompting them to click on a link or download software that will "fix" the problem. In reality, clicking the link often leads to malware installation, giving the attacker control over the system.

See WM. ARTHUR CONKLIN ET AL., ALL IN ONE COMPTIA SECURITY+ EXAM: SY0-601 EXAM GUIDE, Ch. 1 (6th ed. 2021).

Guarding against Social Engineering and the Three Types of Control

Discussed in the abstract, many of these strategies probably prompt an eye-roll, but they are effective nonetheless. They prey on the principle that employees are not going to be perfectly vigilant 100% of the time, and they look for that one mistake. Training and compartmentalization can help remedy the vulnerabilities that are exploited by social engineering attacks and the negative consequences of mistakes made by any one employee. Awareness and training will assist employees in identifying potential errors and reduce the amount of time between suspicion and reporting, thus allowing a security team member more time to minimize the impact.

As a personal example, I purchased an ASUS ROG Ally and went through the process of downloading files and software to customize it for all the wild ideas I had concocted. In the process of downloading a public-domain book in PDF format, a notification box popped up asking me to give the file permission to make changes to my system. I can only plead button fatigue, as I had been customizing and installing software for hours, but I gave permission. Luckily the training and education I had received kicked in immediately thereafter as I sheepishly realized there was no reason for a PDF file to ask for permission to do anything when opened, and I realized that I had downloaded malware instead of Moby Dick. I was quickly able to reset to factory settings and begin the laborious task of customization from the beginning as penance for my blunder. At least I was left with an incredibly ironic anecdote about literally being baited while searching for a book on whale hunting.

The difficulty with awareness training is not that employees are incapable of learning about the practices of social engineering; it's maintaining the sense of urgency needed to keep the knowledge at the forefront of their minds. Everyone laughs at the trope of the guard, who looks like a fool as the hero quietly creeps past on the rooftops overhead, but how long has that guard been standing at his post with nothing happening? How long since he was reminded to look overhead even though 98% of threats have approached from ground level? Frequent training and awareness campaigns help offset the complacency that sets in from guarding a post no one seems to attack. Additionally, tactful organization-wide notification of social engineering attacks helps remind employees that the threats against the organization are real and that they are still occurring, even if not to every individual.

Finally, compartmentalization helps to offset the risk that a successful social engineering attack will compromise the keys to the kingdom. Compartmentalization is a strategy used to limit the impact of a security breach by dividing networks, systems, or data into distinct segments or compartments. Each compartment is designated to operate independently, with its own access controls and permissions, so that if one area is compromised, the breach is contained within that segment and does not spread to the entire system. Keeping access limited to that which is necessary for an employee to complete their job can prevent a successful attack from accessing all of an organization's systems. As an example, consider Figure 3-5 below; if Employee A has access only to financial details and they are compromised by a phishing attack, it is still bad, but in this example, the other compartments are still secure. The contact details are still protected, meaning that the client is not at risk of additional social engineering attacks when using the contact details provided to the firm. Likewise, the proprietary files and matter details are still protected, thus preserving the confidentiality of the matters being handled by the firm.

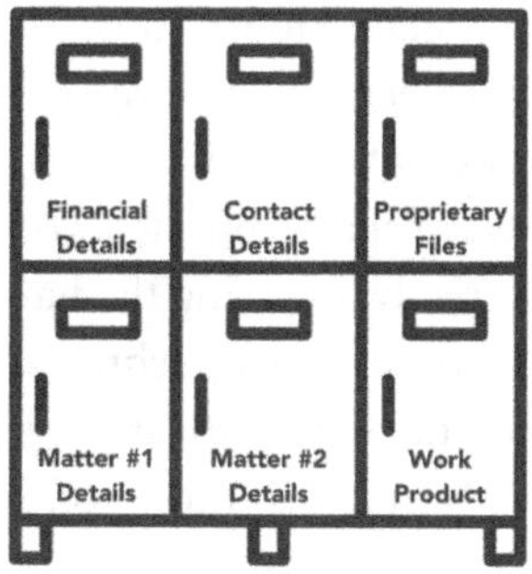

Figure 3-4: Compartmentalization.

The practice of compartmentalization is a good example of a practice that can employ all three types of control. In the field of cybersecurity, defense measures used to minimize threats to an organization are typically categorized as either physical, logical, or administrative controls. Each type plays a specific role in building a comprehensive defense strategy, and many security guidelines recommend creating layered defenses that employ all three. Let's break down each type in terms of what they are and use our example of the principle of compartmentalization to illustrate the distinction between them.

Physical controls are the security measures that protect the physical spaces where data is stored and processed. These measures include locks, security cameras, access badges, and even guards who control entry to secure areas like data centers or server rooms. In a legal setting, physical controls are essential because client files may still be stored in hard copy, and even digital data resides on servers that must be physically secure. With compartmentalization, data storage centers may have separate physical areas for servers that house different types of sensitive data, with physical access restricted to authorized personnel. Physical access controls are often overlooked when discussing cybersecurity because the name itself suggests strictly digital-oriented security measures, but it is essential to understand that an unauthorized person physically downloading data to a thumb drive is just as much a breach as if someone initiated a complex network attack. The data is just as compromised.

As mentioned before, a layered approach is often the best defense. Logical, administrative, and physical controls complement each other to create a well-rounded security strategy. For example, a firm might implement logical controls like multi-factor authentication (MFA) to restrict digital access to a system. However, without administrative controls like mandatory cybersecurity training, employees might still fall victim to phishing attempts, inadvertently compromising their MFA-protected accounts. Similarly, physical controls prevent unauthorized individuals from directly accessing the hardware that stores data.

Logical controls (sometimes called technical or digital controls) are security measures applied through software or hardware to manage access and protect digital information. These controls include encryption, firewalls, anti-malware programs, and access control mechanisms like passwords, two-factor authentication, and biometric scans. Compartmentalization is often implemented through logical controls such as firewalls, access control lists, and encryption. These tools are used to create virtual barriers within networks or between applications, limiting access and interactions based on defined policies. Logical controls also allow monitoring of system activity, so if there is unauthorized access, it can be detected and traced back to its source.

Administrative controls are the policies, procedures, and training that govern how people in an organization interact with its systems and data. These controls are essential because technology alone cannot secure information; human actions and decisions play a significant role. Administrative controls generally include data handling policies, background checks for new hires, incident response plans, and cybersecurity training for employees. Policies, procedures, and guidelines are part of the administrative controls that enforce compartmentalization. For example, an organization might define specific roles, permissions, and access levels based on job functions, ensuring that employees only access the compartments necessary for their tasks. The administrative controls are typically informed by strict regulations (like HIPAA or GDPR) and ethical standards for data protection. These controls also address how an organization must respond to breaches, including the process for reporting incidents to clients or regulatory bodies.

Malware: Keyloggers, Trojans, and Worms, Oh My!

Now that we've talked a bit about social engineering, let's take a look at some of the flashier tools that threat actors may deploy. Consider this section a primer on the different types of attacks. It should give you broad exposure to many of the various types of threats being deployed, but don't consider it exhaustive in either scope or detail. To clarify, you will walk away knowing roughly what a Ransomware attack is, but the details on how to initiate or guard against one are a bit beyond the scope of this text.

Malware is an amalgamation of the term "malicious software," and as the name implies, it refers to any software that is designed with malicious intent. Malware is commonly created with the intention of either stealing sensitive information, disrupting operations, gaining unauthorized access to a system or device, and/or spreading to other systems. Social engineering attacks are typically deployed with the aim of either obtaining sensitive information or distributing malware. Additionally, malware is commonly distributed through either malicious downloads or by exploiting software or system vulnerabilities.

Before we get into the specifics of the types of malware out there, it is essential to note the importance of installing security patches and updating software. When Apple, Microsoft, or any other publisher releases a security update what has happened is that hackers (either ethical or malicious) have discovered a flaw in the previous system that can be exploited and create security concerns. The patch is the publisher's response to correct or eliminate that vulnerability for its users before they are exposed to any threats. The longer that a user waits to install the patch, the more opportunity they give to potential attackers to access their devices or systems. The interesting thing is that a user's vulnerability to a particular threat will actually increase after a patch has been released because the patches provide information on what is being patched and why. So effectively, the security patch broadcasts to a broader pool of potential threat actors the vulnerabilities of a given device or system, both increasing the number of people who know of the flaw and decreasing the work needed to identify a vulnerability.

BRUTE-FORCE ATTACKS

As the name implies, these attacks typically lack any type of finesse and rely on sheer overwhelming force. The idea is to run a script that inputs a massive number of password combinations, usually from a list of commonly used credentials. The hope is that by attempting thousands or millions of combinations, the malicious actor will gain access through the sheer number of attempts. These types of attacks are the reason many well-known sites employ a limit on the number of login attempts permitted.

RANSOMWARE

Ransomware is malicious software that encrypts a victim's files, rendering them inaccessible. Attackers then demand a ransom in exchange for the decryption key, often paid in cryptocurrency for anonymity. Many are automated with a short window to pay the ransom, or the data is either destroyed or disclosed. Ransomware attacks are especially devastating because they can halt business operations until the ransom is paid or the data is restored from backups. Probably the most well-known recent examples of ransomware attacks are the Colonial Pipeline attack of 2021[11] or the WannaCry attack of 2017.[12]

TROJANS

Trojans disguise themselves as legitimate software or files to deceive users into installing them. Once installed, trojans provide unauthorized access to attackers, who can steal data, install additional malware, or disrupt systems. The name signifies how Trojans differ from traditional viruses; it refers to the story of the Trojan horse and the fact that as long as the horse stood outside the gates of the city, it appeared to be harmless. It was only after the citizenry took the horse into the city, or in this scenario, installed the program, that the attack occurred. The more advanced Trojans are programs that perform the functionalities expected of them, thus not alerting the target, but concealing additional functionality that the attacker wishes to employ. The ILOVEYOU trojan cause roughly $10 billion in damage in 2000.[13]

---

11. Sean Michael Kerner, *Colonial Pipeline hack explained: Everything you need to know* (TechTarget, Apr. 26, 2022), https://www.techtarget.com/whatis/feature/Colonial-Pipeline-hack-explained-Everything-you-need-to-know.

12. Cloudflare, What was the WannaCry ransomware attack? (n.d.), https://www.cloudflare.com/learning/security/ransomware/wannacry-ransomware/.

13. James Griffiths, 'I Love You': How a badly-coded computer virus caused billions in damage and exposed vulnerabilities which remain 20 years on (CNN, May 3, 2020), https://www.cnn.com/2020/05/01/tech/iloveyou-virus-computer-security-intl-hnk/index.html.

WORMS

Unlike trojans, worms are self-replicating programs that spread through networks without user interaction. Once they infiltrate a system, worms can consume resources, slow down networks, and cause systems to crash. Worms are designed to exploit network vulnerabilities, making them especially destructive in interconnected environments. The significant distinction between a worm and a virus is whether the malicious program can survive on its own (worm) or if it has to be attached to something else in the system to survive (virus). Although there is some dispute over its classification as a worm or virus, the program MyDoom caused an estimated $38 billion in damage before it was dealt with in 2004.[14]

BOTS

Bots are pieces of software that are controlled remotely by another program, often without the owner's knowledge. Typically, they result in devices being controlled remotely through a Command and Control (C&C) attack to control systems, exfiltrate data, or launch additional attacks with distributed computing power. When an attacker controls a network of these devices, it is referred to as a botnet. Botnets are generally used in large-scale attacks and can be used to deploy other malware on a large scale.

LOGIC BOMBS

Logic bombs are interesting in that they demonstrate the necessity of compartmentalization and overlapping controls for defense. Typically, logic bombs are malicious code installed by authorized users and trigger upon a specific event or time. For example, if an organization's payroll is uploaded and the installing authorized user no longer appears on that payroll the logic bomb may trigger, engaging in whatever malicious activity it has been set to accomplish (deleting files, crashing systems, and so on).

---

14. Karolis Bareckas, THE MYDOOM WORM: HISTORY, TECHNICAL DETAILS AND DEFENSE (NordVPN, Mar. 19, 2022), https://nordvpn.com/blog/mydoom-virus/.

SPYWARE

Spyware is designed to secretly monitor user activity. It can collect data such as browsing habits, login credentials, and credit card information. Because spyware often operates in the background, it can be challenging to detect. The information collected is sent to the attacker, who may use it for financial gain, identity theft, or other malicious purposes.

KEYLOGGERS

A keylogger is a type of spyware that records every keystroke made by a user. This data, including usernames, passwords, and other sensitive information, is then sent to the attacker. Keyloggers can be hardware devices plugged into a keyboard or software programs hidden on a device. They are frequently used in identity theft and credential stealing attacks.

ROOTKITS AND BACKDOORS

Rootkits are especially dangerous in that they can mimic any action the infected operating system can do. They modify an operating system to allow the attacker to control the device while hiding their presence from user security tools. This malware is so invasive and well-camouflaged that many organizations practice installing a clean system image instead of attempting to remove it. Similarly, backdoors are unauthorized access points. Developers create some backdoors for maintenance purposes, but they can leave systems vulnerable. Typically, they are made by attackers after a successful phishing attempt. Once a backdoor or rootkit is in place, attackers can re-enter the system at will.

Network and Application Attacks

Hopefully, you can see that social engineering and malware are not necessarily distinct from one another. Many times, social engineering techniques are used to gain access to a system in order to deploy malware onto that system or device. Additionally, network vulnerabilities or applications can be used to deploy malware. There is quite a bit of overlap between the topics, and it is important to understand that even though they are being discussed as distinct topics here, they are often deployed as part of a layered attack by threat actors. In addition to social engineering strategies, there are more technical methods for gaining access to a system. Application attacks exploit vulnerabilities in software applications, including web applications, to gain unauthorized access, steal data, disrupt organizations, or compromise user trust. These attacks target flaws in the code, configuration, or design of an application. Network attacks target the infrastructure that connects systems, including hardware (routers and switches), protocols, and data transmission processes. The goal is to disrupt communication, intercept data, or gain unauthorized access to resources. These types of attacks tend to require a significantly higher degree of technical acumen than social engineering attacks, thereby necessitating a more sophisticated degree of protection than the typical lawyer is prepared to deploy alone. Most likely, these types of attacks will require the attention of dedicated IT staff or will be protected against by security patches from software vendors or through the deployment of standard cybersecurity tools like firewalls, endpoint protection, or virtual private networks (VPNs).

Attacks that focus on exploiting software installed directly on your device are best defended against by installing software and security updates as they become available to limit the scope of your vulnerabilities and to employ runtime security, which we will discuss shortly. Some of the more common web application attacks include cross-site scripting, injection attacks, and buffer overflow. The best protection against these attacks is to not engage in casual web browsing on a device that stores or has access to sensitive client data and to vet any web application services you use in conjunction with your practice to ensure they adhere to some sort of recognized cybersecurity framework. That being said, understanding how these attacks function may help you spot them and communicate with your IT staff or security programs.

CROSS-SITE SCRIPTING (XSS)

This type of attack relies on a combination of websites that allow users to input and share content, like comments in a news article or a message board, and scripting languages. A form of scripting that most people are probably familiar with is the process of scrolling on a social media site or app. As the user scrolls, the script lets the site know that the user has reached the end of the page, and additional posts are populated for the user to look through. With XSS, a potential attacker posts a comment or message that includes some sort of scripting code that gives instructions to other users' devices. So, when a user's device comes across the comment, it performs the action included in the code. An example might be:

```
Hello everyone! Check out this link: <script>alert('You got hacked!')</script>
```

If the website doesn't "sanitize" user input, making sure only safe text is allowed and no harmful code gets through, then every user who views the code will see a pop-up with the message "You got hacked!" This is a fairly innocuous example, but this type of attack can also be used to steal credentials or sensitive information and can even hijack a user's session, allowing the attacker to impersonate the user.

INJECTION ATTACKS

This type of attack attempts to manipulate the databases in which user credentials generally reside. Typically, websites with login requirements rely on databases to store those credentials, and specific languages are used to verify a user's login credentials against that database. Structured Query Language (SQL), Extensible Markup Language (XML), and Lightweight Directory Access Protocol (LDAP) are the languages typically used to store data. When a user inputs their username and password, a command is generated by the website that queries the database and compares the credentials input with those stored in the database. If the credentials match, the user is given access to the account associated with those credentials. With an injection attack, the attacker attempts to trick the system by inputting commands in the Username and Password field to force the system to generate a command that the designer did not intend. I will avoid any in-depth discussion of SQL, XML, and LDAP and provide a simple example.

Imagine you are having a conversation with an exchange student whose native language is Spanish but who can also speak English. The conversation proceeds in English as the exchange student has grown accustomed to people in the host country speaking only English. Partly through the conversation, you change your tone and command, "Dame las llaves de tu auto" (Give me your car keys). Chances are the change in tone and language may disorient the other person enough that they may move to comply without thinking even if they ultimately stop. The difference between a human interaction and an injection attack is that, with Spanish being representative of one of the command languages, unless the application has been programmed to treat user input as plain text only, it won't have any of the restraints a human would have that would prevent it from carrying out the command. Thus, the keys to the application are unwittingly turned over to the malicious actor.

BUFFER OVERFLOW

Buffer overflow accounts for a staggering number of application exploits historically. A program is generally designed to store a fixed amount of data (e.g., 100 characters in a text box). In this scenario, the attacker has identified a vulnerability where they can input a number of characters that forces the program to accept a number of characters that exceeds its limit (e.g., 1,000 characters). The extra data has to go somewhere. In this scenario, it spills over into other areas of memory, potentially overwriting important system information or allowing the attacker to insert malicious instructions.

This attack is most easily depicted by the figures below. Let us say that you owe John Smith $10,000, and it is written thus in your ledger:

Name	Amount Owed
John Smith	10,000

After paying him off, you incur a $1,000 loan from another individual who gives her name as "Jane Doexxxxxxxxxxxxxxxxxxxxxxxxxxxxxxxx xxx999999"

Name	Amount Owed
Jane Doexxxxxxxxxxxxxxxxxxxxxxxxxxxxxxxxxxxx	9999990

In this example, the additional characters fill the textbox, and the overflow overrides the amount owed, changing it from $1,000 to $9,999,990. Similar to the last example, lacking human powers of cognition, the program executes the command, and you are suddenly $9.9 million poorer.

DOMAIN NAME SYSTEM ATTACK

Recall from Chapter 1 the explanation of how the internet works, specifically dealing with Domain Name System (DNS). For the point of explaining this type of attack, it is sufficient to visualize DNS as a directory of the internet, providing addresses and directions to the websites you want to visit based on the URL you type in. Let's say that you are trying to visit your favorite bakery, Pleasant Pastries. Typically, you'd look up its address in your neighborhood's directory (DNS), drive to the address listed, and buy your goodies. But what if someone sneaks in and changes the bakery's address to a fake bakery, trying to trade on Pleasant Pastries' good reputation? When you arrive, it looks similar to your favorite bakery, but it's not the same. The pastries are bad, and they steal your credit card information when you pay for your purchase. This is known as DNS Spoofing, wherein a malicious actor alters the DNS records of a legitimate website so that when users attempt to visit the legitimate site, they are directed to a malicious site controlled by the attacker instead. This malicious site retains the same look and feel as the legitimate website to aid in tricking the user into inputting their login credentials or payment information, which are then made available to the malicious actor.

DISTRIBUTED DENIAL OF SERVICE ATTACKS

Let's stick with Pleasant Pastries to explain Distributed Denial of Service (DDoS) attacks. Imagine that you are the new owner of Pleasant Pastries. It has become very well-loved in the community. Every morning, loyal customers line up to grab their coffee and pastries before heading to work. Your shop runs smoothly, handling a steady flow of customers without issue.

One day, a massive group of pranksters shows up. They aren't here to buy coffee—they just fill the shop, block the door, crowd the line, and clog the parking lot. Real customers can't get in to place orders, and your deliveries don't arrive. Eventually, your shop's resources are so stretched that you have to shut down temporarily. This scenario mirrors what happens during a DDoS attack.

A DDoS attack is a type of attack where malicious actors flood a website, server, or online service with so much fake traffic that it becomes overwhelmed and unable to serve legitimate users. The goal is simple: to take the target offline and disrupt its normal operations. Picture when a new movie trailer releases and receives so much traffic that the website hosting the video collapses. Only in this case, the traffic is artificially inflated to achieve the same result by the malicious actors.

A DDoS attack is "distributed," meaning it uses multiple sources (often thousands or even millions of infected devices worldwide) to attack the target. Recall the explanation of bots from earlier; in this scenario, malicious actors create a network of bots from internet-connected devices. The bots send a massive number of requests to the target website or server at the same time. The target's resources are exhausted trying to handle the flood of requests, leaving no capacity to serve real users. The result is legitimate users experiencing slow loading times or inability to access the website at all.

MAN IN THE MIDDLE ATTACKS

Imagine you're working on a sensitive case and have a trusted courier to deliver confidential documents and exhibits to your client. You box up an exhibit, seal it, and give it to the courier to deliver to your client. The courier sets off, but unbeknownst to you, someone intercepts the package halfway through the journey. This person opens the box, switches the contents of the box, and reseals it before allowing your courier to deliver it. When your client receives the exhibit, they have no idea it has been tampered with—or that someone else is aware of the contents.

This scenario is referred to as a Man in the Middle (MITM) attack in the cybersecurity world; here's how it works. Let's say you want to catch up on your client communications by connecting to the airport's free public Wi-Fi. To set up a MITM attack, a malicious actor sets up a fake network called "Airport-FreeWiFi" or something similar that looks like the airport's wireless network. When you connect to it, you're unknowingly connecting to the attacker's system. As you log in to your email, your username and password travel through the attacker's network, where they capture it in real time. If the attacker is particularly surreptitious, your communications will not stop on their network but will be forwarded to the intended recipient. With your credentials, the attacker can access your account, steal sensitive information, or change the data being sent (like modifying a document you're uploading, downloading, or sending). What makes this attack particularly insidious is that the user tends to remain unaware since the communications are still going through, albeit not as securely as the user expects, and possibly altered depending on the goals of the attacker.

The types of attacks included in this chapter are not exhaustive, as malicious actors are constantly refining their processes and looking for new access points and vulnerabilities. Hopefully, this gives you a feel for the field and the commonly deployed strategies and avenues (personnel, applications, and networks) used by cyber-attackers. Having established that you will be the custodian of valuable client information and responsible for its safekeeping and that cyber-attacks occur frequently and pervasively, how can you defend yourself?

Defending against Cyber-Threats: Frameworks, Tools, and Tips

While it seems that malicious actors have the upper hand with the frequency of attacks and the numerous news stories of successful data breaches and ransomware attacks, a great deal of time, money, and human effort has gone into developing defenses against cyber threats. Tools exist that are dedicated to preventing, compartmentalizing, and tracking intrusions. Frameworks have been designed to highlight and train organizations on best practices to minimize exposure to cyber threats and to minimize their impact. Additionally, laws have been implemented to force new technology into compliance with reporting standards and increase data security. Hopefully, you have noticed that many threats rely on malicious actors seeking out vulnerabilities like chinks in armor instead of attacking well-protected organizations head-on. This is not to say that a clever attacker couldn't get around an organization's security directly, but an organization that adheres to well-maintained security policies is a more difficult nut to crack than one with less refined security practices.

Cloud Services and Security

Let's not forget that not every organization has the same financial resources available to deploy security tools and policies. This is where the conversation of in-house vs. cloud-based tools can come into play. Picture beloved actor Rowan Atkinson, best known for his role as Mr. Bean. Now, do a quick Google search for "Mr. Bean Terminator." One of the first images you are likely to encounter is a meme combining Mr. Atkinson in an armchair with Arnold Schwarzenegger's Terminator character, Cyberdyne Systems Model 101, carrying him, as well as a fairly nasty arsenal. In a scenario where you face both options as a malicious actor of the two potential targets, would you rather encounter Mr. Bean or Mr. Bean with his own Terminator?

To put it another way, would an attacker be more likely to target a small to mid-size firm with a handful of IT staff or Amazon/Google's dedicated cybersecurity team that just happens to handle file storage for a small firm? Cloud services and virtualization are becoming standard tools to manage cost and risk while still fielding a robust security presence.

Cloud services come in a variety of forms, each serving a unique purpose. Here's a breakdown to make sense of the different types:

- Infrastructure as a Service (IaaS): Imagine renting the hardware and network infrastructure you need instead of buying and maintaining it yourself. This is essentially the barest layer of service; you are provided the hardware, but you are responsible for customizing it with your own virtual machine.
- Platform as a Service (PaaS): Imagine renting a fully equipped workshop for application development, where the tools, workspace, and utilities are provided. Think of this type of service as being primarily for developers.
- Software as a Service (SaaS): Imagine accessing software over the internet without the need to install or maintain it on your own devices. Arguably the most prevalent example would be Microsoft Office 365, where you are able to access the programs without downloading or updating them.

These services provide firms with the ability to scale their needs to a certain degree without purchasing expensive new hardware or altering their security protocols. The leading providers also invest heavily in state-of-the-art security measures, such as encryption, firewalls, and intrusion detection, without firms having to configure these tools independently or employ a security team to maintain them. Additionally, many of the leading cloud platforms are designed to meet stringent legal and regulatory requirements, making it easier for firms to stay compliant and ensure that client data is backed up so that it can be restored quickly in case of ransomware or physical disasters.

While there are many benefits to cloud-based services because they are marketed to large groups of people, there is necessarily some loss of control in the process. Essentially, your organization's flexibility with these tools is going to be governed by the user agreement. This could result in needing to negotiate customization options, indemnity provisions for data breaches, notification responsibilities for cyber-attacks, and data retention and storage provisions for sensitive client data. The last is particularly important as you are effectively communicating confidential information to a third party, which means you need to be aware of the companies' data transfer and storage policies as well as the policy for data destruction if the contractual relationship ends. While we will discuss cryptography in more detail in the next chapter, two concepts to be aware of when evaluating vendors for data storage or cloud platform access are encryption-in-transit and encryption-at-rest. In simplified terms, encryption-in-transit means that your data is scrambled while it is being transmitted, and no one can unscramble it but you; encryption-at-rest means that while the cloud-based vendor is storing it, your data remains scrambled and can only be unscrambled by you. Both concepts are essential for confidential data; encryption-in-transit means that your data will be much more difficult to intercept in a useful format, and encryption-at-rest means that your duty of confidentiality is not breached by having a third-party company store client data since they cannot access it any meaningful way.

Cybersecurity Frameworks

A cybersecurity framework is a structured set of guidelines and best practices designed to help organizations identify, manage, and reduce risks related to cybersecurity. Think of it as an extremely detailed checklist that ensures everyone in an organization is on the same page about protecting sensitive information—similar to the way a Restatement brings together convoluted or sometimes conflicting doctrine into clear, black letter pronouncements of the law.

Perhaps the best-known framework in the U.S. is the National Institute of Standards and Technology (NIST) Cyber Security Framework. The NIST Framework was established in response to Presidential Executive Order No. 13636, "Improving Critical Infrastructure Cybersecurity." The order was intended to increase competency in managing cyber risk to critical infrastructure. NIST released the Cybersecurity Framework version 2.0 in February of 2024 with resources tailored to small and medium businesses with little or no cybersecurity plans currently in place. It is a great place to start when familiarizing yourself with these types of resources.

The NIST framework is organized around five stages of the lifecycle of cyber threats:

1. Identify: Understand what needs protection (e.g., client data) and recognize potential threats.
2. Protect: Set up safeguards like passwords, encryption, and access controls.
3. Detect: Monitor for unusual activity that could indicate a breach.
4. Respond: Have a plan for mitigating damage if a breach occurs.
5. Recover: Restore operations quickly and learn from the incident.[15]

Additional frameworks include:

- The Center for Internet Security Critical Security Controls (CIS)
- The International Standards Organization (ISO) frameworks ISO/IEC 27001 and 27002
- The Health Insurance Portability and Accountability Act (HIPPA)
- Service Organization Control (SOC2)

15. National Institute of Standards and Technology, NIST SP 300, NIST Cybersecurity Framework 2.0: Small Business Quick-Start Guide (Feb. 2024), https://nvlpubs.nist.gov/nistpubs/SpecialPublications/NIST.SP.1300.pdf.

- North American Electric Reliability Corporation Critical Infrastructure Protection (NERC-CIP)
- General Data Protection Regulation (GDPR)
- Payment Card Industry Data Security Standard (PCI-DSS)
- Control Objectives for Information and related Technology (COBIT)
- The Healthcare Information Trust Alliance Common Security Framework (HITRUST-CSF)
- Cloud Security Alliance's Cloud Control Matrix (CCM)

Physical Protection Controls

Physical controls are largely self-explanatory but are essential to bear in mind. What good is a six-figure cybersecurity budget dedicated to all the latest tech toys if someone can walk in and out of your front door with one of your devices? You should also bear in mind that even though a great deal of this chapter is dedicated to malicious actors, cyber-security also entails protecting your digital systems from natural disasters and environmental hazards. Think fire suppression systems and moisture detection. While we won't go as overkill as covering how to install Faraday cages in your firm, hopefully some of the following controls will provide insight into the layered utility of some physical controls.

As simple as printed paper in a badge holder or as complicated as radio-frequency identification (RFID), badges help employees recognize individuals in the building who are authorized to be there. Even visitor badges can serve this purpose by demonstrating that a person has met whatever requirements management has put in place permitting a person to visit the premises and that their presence is known. As organizations grow, interpersonal recognition can grow more attenuated, making badge systems very valuable in validating an individual's presence.

Signage can provide information about whether an area is restricted or what precautions should be taken. They can serve to remind employees of existing administrative policies to increase adherence and reduce forgetfulness. Commonly used in conjunction with badges, signage can delineate restricted versus open-access areas where badges signify an individual's level of access, thus making unauthorized entrants stand out. Additionally, employing security cameras can allow for recording the activities of visitors as they are on the premises. Some of the more advanced cameras even allow for motion recognition to engage, eliminating hours of useless recording and object detection, drawing a reviewer's eye to relevant portions of the recording.

Reception areas can serve as buffer zones between different areas within an organization's offices, segmenting the building into separate areas for distinct purposes. Employing a visitor check-in desk and lobby allows the control of visitors, logging their presence, tracking deliveries, and providing authorized personnel as escorts to ensure unauthorized personnel do not access restricted areas. In addition, employing biometric sensors can significantly increase the difficulty of gaining access to unauthorized areas. Fingerprint scanners are perhaps the most prevalent biometric scanning devices; however, devices exist for scanning retinas/corneas, hand geometry, and facial shapes. While useful in increasing security, biometric scanners are not foolproof, and ways exist to bypass them, which reinforces the need for deploying a layered approach to defense.

Preventing unauthorized physical presence within an organization is not the only purpose behind physical controls. They can also prevent unauthorized access to restricted information even if a visitor gains access to an unauthorized area. USB connectors on devices provide a perfect access point for malicious actors. Even without login credentials, someone with physical access to a device can use a USB device to deploy code into that system. There are ways to disable USB ports, but this isn't always practical as many peripheral devices connect through USB ports and draw power from them now. An interesting physical control in this situation is a USB data blocker. USB connectors have four connections: two for power and two for data access. USB data blockers, as the name implies, can block data access while still allowing devices like a keyboard or mouse to draw power from the port, thus allowing authorized users to continue making use of USB peripherals while preventing unauthorized users from accessing data from the ports.

Finally, in addition to protecting an organization's physical locations from unauthorized access, physical controls also serve to protect information about an organization's physical resources by providing avenues for the secure disposal of physical resources. This can cover everything from the need to have a secure method of shredding documents to the need to safely destroy data storage containers as they become obsolete and new devices are deployed. Physical files can be destroyed in a variety of ways, including burning, shredding, or even recycling the paper into a new form through pulping. These options seem pretty obvious for print files, but what do you do with a computer once it is obsolete and needs to be disposed of? You could recreate the scene from Office Space where the error-prone printer is taken to a field and cathartically destroyed. Some companies simply remove the hard drives from existing equipment and destroy them instead. There are other options that will ensure that sensitive data is removed. With some existing equipment, if it contains an HDD instead of a SSD, there is the option of degaussing. Degaussing is the process of using a strong magnetic field to realign the magnetic particles on the hard drive, which effectively destroys all of the data present. Many organizations engage third-party companies that specialize in data destruction, but there is a window between handing over the data and its destruction where you again have a third party that has access to sensitive client information. That isn't necessarily a deal breaker, but you need to pay attention to the details of your agreement with the data destruction company to ensure that your client data is protected from third-party access. This is another situation where data encryption concepts are important to bear in mind. If your data is encrypted while in the possession of the data destruction company, it will be protected from prying eyes.

Logical Security Controls

Now that we've covered the physical barriers to your firm's data, let's move on to logical controls. If physical controls represent, and in a very real sense can be, physical locks preventing unauthorized access to your organization's data, then logical controls are the digital locks that serve a similar purpose. Logical controls are security measures implemented in software, hardware, or digital systems to regulate access, protect data, and ensure proper use of technology resources. Unlike physical controls, logical controls focus on the digital realm. They enforce rules that determine who can access information, what they can do with it, and how they are monitored.

We'll be looking at authentication and access controls, firewalls, intrusion detection systems, endpoint and run-time protection, network segmentation, and virtual private networks. Data encryption is a crucial logical control, but we will discuss it in more detail in the next chapter.

It is important to remember that with logical controls, you aren't looking solely at prevention; to have a fully rounded protection plan in place, you have to anticipate that some unauthorized users will find ways to bypass your security controls. With that in mind, some aspects of logical control include minimizing the effects of a breach and tracking what systems were breached for reporting and remediation.

AUTHENTICATION AND ACCESS CONTROLS

Authentication and access controls are closely aligned, but it is helpful to understand the difference between them. Imagine the Westlaw or Lexis account at a law firm; when you attempt to log in, you are met with a request for a username and password. Once you provide these details, you have proven to the system that you are an authorized user of the system. This doesn't mean, however, that you will be given unfettered access to all the resources on every database. Your credentials serve to *authenticate* you as a user, but your firm's subscription terms determine access. You may be relegated to all primary sources for a jurisdiction and a handful of subject-specific secondary resources, or you may have access to a broader range of resources.

Probably the most widely recognized authentication control is the username and password combination to log in to a system. This is an example of a knowledge-based control which, as the name implies, relies on information possessed by the user for authentication. Other examples of this type of authentication are personal identification numbers (PINs) or security questions. These controls are easy to implement but, as you can imagine, are prone to phishing attacks. Other types of authentication controls include possession-based authentication, inherence-based authentication, and what we'll call advanced authentication controls.

Possession-based authentication is reliant upon something the user has with them. This could be a physical device generating one-time codes, smart cards that identify the user by scanning or RFID, or mobile applications (e.g., Google Authenticator). It is harder for attackers to duplicate than passwords, but they are vulnerable to theft or being lost. Inherence-based authentication relies upon the physical or behavioral characteristics of the user. Biometrics, discussed earlier, would be a prime example of this type of authentication, but it can also include voice recognition or even patterns in the way a user walks (gait analysis). This type of authentication is more difficult to replicate or share, but it raises privacy concerns when an organization has records of users' fingerprints or retinas.

Advanced authentication methods include two-factor or multi-factor authentication, wherein multiple forms of the authentication methods discussed are used to verify a user's identity. For example, an attorney logging into their work email and being prompted for both a username and password as well as confirming their identity with a mobile app (i.e., knowledge-based + possession-based). Even more advanced methods of authentication exist wherein the level of authentication is adjusted based on the perceived risk of the login attempt. An example would be a student attempting to log in to library resources from off-campus being prompted for two-factor authentication while one accessing from on-campus only requires a username and password.

Access controls are interesting in that they have elements of logical controls and administrative controls in their makeup. Access controls refer to security mechanisms that determine who is allowed to access specific digital resources by verifying a user's identity and granting access based on some predefined schema. Their administrative control aspect includes determining the details surrounding what users and their characteristics are used in the schema. With access controls, an organization increases the difficulty of accessing a system and segments its system so that one user does not have access to all data. This limits the possibility that attackers might target a single employee to access everything. There are several types of access controls:

1. Attribute-Based Access Control (ABAC): uses attributes (properties or characteristics) of the user, resource, or environment to determine access permissions. These attributes are evaluated against policies to decide whether to grant or deny access. The attributes can include user attributes (job title, security clearance, or department), resource attributes (document type or sensitivity level), or environmental attributes (location, time, or device used). An example would be an associate working remotely from outside the U.S. not being able to access a firm's sensitive client files due to their location restrictions, even if their role is an adequate one.

2. Role-Based Access Control (RBAC): assigns permissions based on the user's role within an organization. Roles are predefined, and users inherit permissions based on their assigned roles. These types of controls are simple to implement and manage, and the roles are tied to job functions, not individuals. An example would be the role of a paralegal being able to view case files but not edit or delete them, while a senior partner is able to view, edit, and delete case files. This format has the advantage of being easily scalable as new users are added since they only need to be assigned a role.
3. Rule-Based Access Control (RuBAC): access is governed by rules defined by the organization. Rules are usually tied to specific conditions that must be met for access to be granted. Rules can be based on time, location, or particular actions. This type of control is often used alongside other access control methods. An example would be a legal research platform with rules specifying that (a) access is allowed only between 8:00 a.m. and 8:00 p.m. and (b) only users within the law school's network can access the platform. This type of control offers very granular levels of control based on specific conditions.
4. Mandatory Access Control (MAC): This is the strictest model, where access is dictated by a central authority based on security labels. Users cannot change permissions, and access decisions are made based on classifications. Security levels (confidential, secret, and top secret) are assigned to users and resources. Users can only access resources with classifications equal to or below their security level. An example would be a government attorney working with classified files. In this situation, only individuals with "Top Secret" clearance can access "Top Secret" documents. This model is highly secure and ideal for environments requiring strict confidentiality but has reduced flexibility.
5. Discretionary Access Control (DAC): In this model, the resource owner decides who has access and what permissions they have. The permissions are based on the resource owner's discretion, and users can share access to resources they own. An example would be a senior associate creating a case

file and deciding who can view or edit it. They grant editing permissions to one associate and view-only permissions to another. This is the most flexible and user-friendly model, but it entails a higher risk of unauthorized access because user discretion is so dispersed.

6. Conditional Access: This access applies access policies dynamically based on real-time conditions or circumstances, adding an extra layer of control. It is widely used in modern systems for enhanced security. It combines user context with environmental factors, and the policies adapt to current conditions. An example would be a university proxy server. It engages in an IF/THEN analysis when presented with access attempts. For example, IF located on campus, THEN grant access, or possibly IF off campus, THEN prompt for login credentials. This model balances security and flexibility by adapting access rules to specific scenarios.

FIREWALLS

Firewalls are probably the most recognized tool for preventing attacks from malicious actors. They serve as gatekeepers to your network or system, admitting some traffic and denying others based on a set of rules. Imagine your device or organization's network is a castle, and a firewall is a gatekeeper at the castle's entrance.

Figure 3-5: The firewall concept.

In this analogy, the gate is the only point of entry into your castle, just like a firewall, which is the primary filter for network traffic entering and leaving your system. The gatekeeper uses a set of rules, another example of an administrative control working in tandem with a logical one, to decide who can enter the castle or leave. For instance, users with permission from the castle lord (authenticated users) are allowed into the castle grounds, while those recognized as threats (see signature-based systems in the next section) are turned away. Additionally, before letting someone in or out, the gatekeeper may inspect their belongings to ensure they're not carrying harmful items (like a virus or malware) in or valuable property (financial or client data) out. Similarly, a firewall inspects data packets for suspicious content both as they enter and exit a system. As a point of inspection and filtering, firewalls also serve as natural data-gathering locations for intrusion detection and intrusion prevention systems.

INTRUSION DETECTION AND PREVENTION SYSTEMS

If a firewall is a gatekeeper, then an intrusion detection system (IDS) or intrusion prevention system (IPS) is its supervising officer, evaluating the observations of the firewall and issuing alarms or acting in defense of the castle as dictated by a pre-existing set of rules. An IDS is a tool designed to monitor a network or system for suspicious activities, security policy violations, or unauthorized access. Think of an IDS as a digital security guard who is watching all of the security camera footage at a museum. The museum would represent your organization's network, systems, or sensitive data that need protection. Authorized users, like employees or ticketed guests, represent regular visitors to the museum. The guard knows these people are allowed to be there. If someone starts behaving oddly—like lingering too long near a valuable painting or trying to force their way into restricted areas—the guard takes notice and will either alert the authorities or act to prevent the suspicious activity, depending on the type of system. Technically, an IDS only monitors and sends an alert to designated users, although a similar product known as an Intrusion Prevention System (IPS) can act to stop suspicious behavior based on a set of predetermined rules. An IPS can result in quicker response times to suspicious activity, but because it is designed to act immediately in response to specific criteria, there may be some frustration with initially calibrating it since it may prohibit certain behaviors because they meet the specified criteria even though they are technically permitted.

An IDS typically consists of a traffic sensor, detection engine, user interface, and alert system. The traffic sensor collects data for analysis. With a network-based sensor, this means that it monitors incoming traffic at firewalls or routers, whereas a host-based system would reside on the devices (e.g., servers or laptops), monitoring device activity like files accessed or processes executed. The detection engine analyzes the collected data, looking for suspicious patterns or behaviors. It compares the data against the signatures of known malicious activities (signature-based), looking for similarities or identifying behavior that deviates from normal user behavior (anomaly-based).

An example might be a user failing a set number of login attempts, which could indicate someone engaging in a brute-force attack on the system. Signature-based systems are very fast, with low instances of false positives; that being said, maintaining a library of signatures can become cumbersome as the markers of malicious behavior increase. Additionally, signature-based systems will be vulnerable to newly developed attacks as their patterns won't be present in the signature library. Anomaly-based systems, on the other hand, can have a very high rate of false positive alarms because any deviation from what the system has been trained to recognize as normal behavior can result in an alarm, but they may be more responsive to new attacks since they look at existing behavior patterns and would send alerts for new behaviors employed by a new attack. The user interface generally provides a centralized platform for administrators to monitor alerts, configure settings, and review logs.

Consider Figure 3-8 below, which is a simple representation of a network-based IDS. Traffic flows in from the internet through a router and is initially confronted by a firewall. The firewall inspects the data packets coming from the internet against its rules as the IDS monitors the traffic for suspicious activity. If the firewall detects something suspicious or if the traffic is from a domain that is blocked it will prevent the data from entering the organization's system. If the firewall allows the traffic through but the IDS detects suspicious activity, it will send an alert and log the interactions for further review. These logs might also be necessary later for reporting in compliance with frameworks or laws.

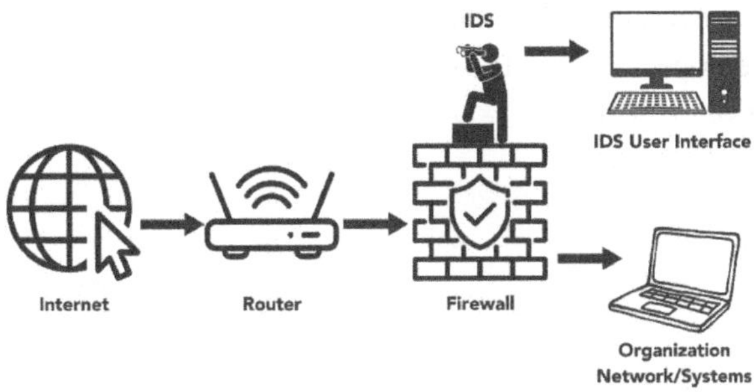

Figure 3-6: A network-based intrusion detection system.

ENDPOINTS AND RUNTIME PROTECTION

Another tool in an organization's repertoire for combatting cyber threats are endpoint protection and runtime protection. Endpoint protection focuses on securing individual devices, which are known as endpoints, while runtime protection focuses on securing applications while they are running. Endpoint protection acts to protect individual devices from threats like malware, ransomware, phishing, and unauthorized access. Runtime protection seeks to ensure that software behaves as intended and that malicious code cannot compromise the application during its execution.

The idea behind endpoint protection is to provide individual layers of security to individual devices (see Figure 3-9). The protections can take the form of antivirus/anti-malware, endpoint detection and response solutions, data loss prevention, and firewalls. We have already discussed firewalls and to some extent endpoint detection and response as it is conceptually similar to IDS and IDP solutions, only device oriented instead of network oriented. Antivirus and anti-malware solutions are very similar, and the terms are frequently used interchangeably though their focus is slightly different.

Antivirus software focuses on a specific subset of malicious programs (e.g., viruses, worms, Trojans). It monitors programs on a device, looking for indicators of behavior that are similar to traditional virus threats. These are similar to the IPS solutions we discussed earlier in that they compare program behavior against a database of signatures to identify and remove or quarantine specific threats. Anti-malware has a more expansive scope, targeting a broader range of malicious software beyond just viruses, including ransomware, spyware, and adware. It is frequently deployed alongside antivirus programs to form a more complete layer of protection.

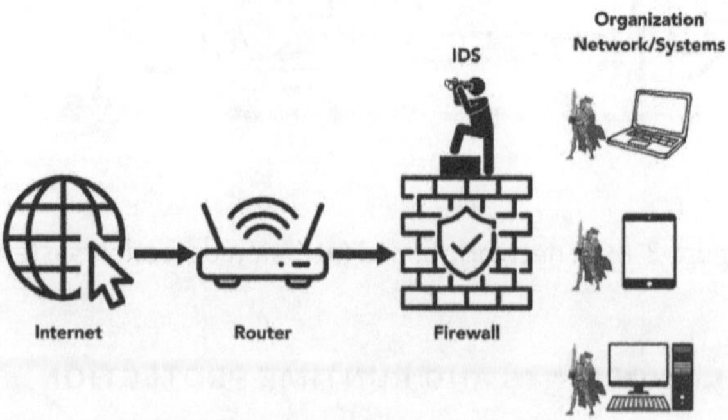

Figure 3-7: Endpoint protection.

Runtime protection includes features dedicated to ensuring that software applications, both local and web applications, run safely and as intended. These can include tools to monitor the program's behavior, intermittently check the code to ensure nothing has tampered with it, block attempts at exploiting vulnerabilities (again, install your security updates!), and monitor application memory to guard against buffer overflows or injection attacks.

Endpoint and runtime applications are complementary, with one ensuring that the device running an application is secure while the other ensures that the application itself remains secure during use. The conceptual similarity of many of these protections and their complementary nature help illustrate that when it comes to cybersecurity, a layered approach is best, with multiple overlapping tools in place to encourage attackers to seek other prey.

Administrative Security Controls

As you will remember, administrative controls are non-technical measures designed to guide, manage, and enforce an organization's cybersecurity posture. These controls focus on policies, procedures, and processes that reduce risks by influencing human behavior and ensuring that everyone within the organization understands their role in maintaining security.

Administrative controls help establish the framework for implementing logical controls like firewalls, encryption, and intrusion detection systems. Often, administrative controls are translated into configuration settings for logical controls. For example, an administrative policy requiring password complexity is translated into a logical control via password complexity settings in the tool that authenticates users.

Not all administrative controls can be enforced by logical controls; many must be implemented in a human-centric style. For instance, in a law firm setting, while the firm can make the tools available for encrypted emails, it is only through administrative controls that it can increase user adherence to the policy. In this situation, the policy might be that employees must use encrypted email when sending client information. The administrative controls employed to increase compliance might be a procedure providing a step-by-step guide on how to use the firm's encryption software or possibly frequent trainings or workshops on recognizing phishing emails and the need to safeguard client information.

Business guidance and leadership is beyond the scope of this book; however, some administrative controls that you are likely to encounter are:

- Acceptable Use Policy: Guidelines for proper and authorized use of an organization's IT resources. This policy is in place to prevent misuse of systems and protect data. It will typically include a policy prohibiting the use of company IT resources for non-work-related activities.
- Access Control Schemes: Policies determining who can access specific resources and what actions they can perform. The purpose is to segment users' permissions, thereby reducing the scope of access granted to any one user and reducing risk to the organization.
- Breach Notification Policy: Response plans for a data breach in order to bring the breach to the notice of company officers and accelerate its investigation outside of a normal cyber-incident response. Organizations face many requirements to report data breaches with stringent timelines. These policies ensure that company officers are aware of a breach in a timely

manner to help ensure timely communication to meet legal obligations and minimize damage.

- Business Continuity Plans: Strategies to ensure essential business functions continue during a disruption, such as a ransomware attack. These plans seek to minimize downtime and maintain critical operations. Frequently they will include plans for maintaining backup systems and alternate communication channels.
- Continuity of Operation Planning: A subset of business continuity plans that focus on essential functions continuing during attacks or natural disasters. While an organization most likely will not be able to maintain all functions, the presence of a remote command center, for example, may ensure that a core subset of critical activities continue.
- Data Classification Policy: Guidelines for categorizing data based on sensitivity and importance. This type of policy can help inform access controls by segregating data into different silos (e.g., public, internal, confidential) that are only accessible by specific user types.
- Data Retention Policy: Rules for how long data should be kept before it is deleted or archived. Exist primarily to balance the cost of data retention against legal requirements to preserve information and create a predictable data lifecycle within an organization. The data lifecycle manages information from creation, use, storage, and eventual disposal to optimize data use while ensuring compliance with security.
- Disaster Recover Plans: A detailed plan for restoring IT systems and operations after a disaster with a goal of minimizing downtime and recovering critical systems quickly. There can be a broader policy that includes a business continuity and continuity of operation plan.
- Incident Response Plans: A structured approach to identifying, managing, and mitigating security incidents with the goal of minimizing damage during an incident. It should be differentiated from a breach notification plan as the breach notification plan should have a separate avenue to notify company officers as quickly as possible.

- Least Privilege: A policy ensuring users have only the permissions necessary to perform their job duties, which reduces the risk of misuse or accidental data breaches.
- Separation of Duties: Similar to least privilege except the scope is oriented towards responsibilities instead of permissions. Splits critical tasks among multiple people to reduce the risk of error or fraud, ensuring checks and balances in processes.

Remember that physical, logical, and administrative controls do not tend to exist in a vacuum but act to inform and strengthen the resilience of one another. Physical and logical controls are informed and their rules crafted in adherence to company policy established by administrative controls. Likewise, the need for some administrative controls only exists after certain physical or logical controls have been implemented.

Conclusion

A final note on notification requirements: In addition to protecting its confidential and proprietary data, an organization may face notification requirements depending on its geographic location and industry. Each state has its own data breach notification requirements.[16] Additionally, different industries have separate notification laws that should be consulted as well in the event of a data breach. The industries that have the more robust reporting requirements are the chemical industry, communications, defense contracting, energy and utilities, financial sector, and health care and medical devices. The legal industry also has its own professional responsibilities when it comes to data breach notifications. These statutory and regulatory requirements create a complex interplay of responsibility that can be pretty confusing. I highly recommend consulting Practicing Law Institute's *Cybersecurity: A Practical Guide to the Law of Cyber Risk* for a detailed explanation of the landscape surrounding cybersecurity breach notifications.

---

16. Edward R. McNicholas and Frances E. Faircloth, Cybersecurity: A Practical Guide to the Law of Cyber Risk App. 2A-1 (2d ed. 2024).

Review Questions

1. What are the key components of the CIA Triad, and why are they critical in the context of cybersecurity for legal professionals?
2. According to the ABA Model Rule 1.6, what are an attorney's responsibilities concerning client data confidentiality?
3. List three examples of social engineering tactics and briefly describe how each exploits human behavior.
4. What is ransomware, and why is it particularly devastating for organizations?
5. Explain the concept of compartmentalization in cybersecurity and how it mitigates the impact of data breaches.
6. Describe the differences between physical, logical, and administrative controls in a cybersecurity framework. Provide one example of each.
7. What are the five stages of the NIST Cybersecurity Framework, and how do they contribute to an organization's cybersecurity posture?
8. Differentiate between encryption-in-transit and encryption-at-rest. Why are both important for protecting client data?
9. Provide an example of how administrative controls can complement logical and physical controls in a law firm setting.
10. What is a firewall and how can it contribute to an organization's security?

CHAPTER 4

Cryptography, Blockchain, and Smart Contracts

Cryptography is the practice of hiding a message so that only the intended recipient can read it. Depending on the strength of the encryption, this goal can be circumvented by individuals other than the intended recipient. The actual act of encoding a message so that it cannot be read by anyone except the intended recipient is called using a cipher, which is where we get the term decipher meaning to understand. Many of the oldest ciphers were used by political leaders and generals to disguise correspondence with troops in order to hide military strategy in case a messenger was captured with orders.

One of the oldest ciphers is the Caesar cipher. The Caesar cipher is reasonably straightforward and easy to understand. Imagine you have a set of dials with twenty-six faces, each face with a letter of the alphabet on it in descending alphabetical order. You begin with your message; we'll use "Hello World" for fun. Once the message is in place, you decide what's called a shift value. This is the number of spaces up or down that you will rotate the dials. In our example, we will use a shift value of three. All of our dials are rotated three places so that "Hello" becomes "Khoor" (see Figure 4-1). To a random person seeing our encrypted message, it is nonsense, but for someone who knows the shift number, they are able to rotate their own set of dials in reverse order three places to arrive at our original message.

The Caesar cipher is an exceedingly simple one and not very secure. It only has 25 possible shift values in English and could easily be broken by a "brute force attack" that we discussed in the previous chapter. It also does not protect against frequency analysis, as the patterns of the letters

Figure 4-1: Visualizing a Caesar cipher.

remain intact. This means that all of the characters shift the same number of spaces, and it is relatively easy to look at the word "Khoor" and scan through the possible combinations to find the initially translated word "Hello."

As systems became more complex, cryptographers typically took advantage of the advances to increase the complexity of ciphers. Another famous example of a cipher was the subject of the 2014 film *The Imitation Game*. The film portrays the efforts of World War II code breakers, led by Alan Turing, in combating the German Enigma machine (see Figure 4-2), a complex mechanical device used to encrypt and decrypt military communications. The Enigma machine was a type of substitution cipher machine that scrambled messages into a nearly unbreakable code. At the heart of the machine were several rotating disks called rotors, each wired to substitute letters in different ways. So, rotor one might associate the letter "A" with the letter "G," while rotor two might associate it with the letter "M." So with each key pressed, the machine would shift to a different rotor that had different key mappings, which limits the efficacy of frequency analysis that we talked about with the Caesar cipher. Further complicating the cipher was a plugboard that could swap letters before and after they passed through the rotors, adding another layer of encryption. So even though the rotor might be set to have the letter "A" associated with "G," the plugboard could alter that association to say that the letter "A" was the letter "X." So, each letter was encrypted individually, and there were at least two potential layers of encryption that changed

Figure 4-2: An Enigma machine.

with each character that was input. Finally, operators used a daily code sheet to change the initial positions of the rotors and plugboard connections, ensuring the sender and receiver used the same settings. This means that anyone trying to break the code had one day to do so before the settings were altered, and work had to begin anew.

With our previous example of Caesar's cipher, the key is the number of places to shift letters, and there are 26 possible shifts, one of which is the original message, which is equivalent to saying it has roughly 5-bit encryption. The Enigma machine is a polyalphabetic substitution cipher, meaning that it encrypts the message by substituting each letter with another, but the substitution pattern changes frequently based on the rotation of its rotors, making it more complex than a simple substitution cipher. It has roughly 159 quintillion possible combinations, which is equivalent to a roughly 76-bit encryption. Today's secure communications, however, are transmitted using 256-bit encryption, which means that malicious actors are contending with approximately 115 x 1075 combinations. For those like me who went to law school to escape scientific notation, that equates to 115,792,089,237,316,195,423,570,985, 008,687,907,853,269,984,665,640,564,039,457,584,007,913,129,639,936 combinations. Further complicating matters for our malicious actors is the implementation of public key encryption.

States of Encryption

An important concept to understand with encryption is the different states of data when it is encrypted. This is especially important when dealing with cloud-based services, as discussed in Chapter 3. Depending on where the data is and how it's being handled, encryption can be categorized into three states: at rest, in transit, and in use. This is important with cloud-based services since they are in possession of confidential and possibly sensitive client data for which you are responsible. If the data is unencrypted there is no way of proving that the cloud-based service hasn't accessed it.

Encryption-at-rest refers to information that is stored on a device or server, such as a hard drive, cloud storage, or database. Encryption-at-rest ensures that this stored data is unreadable to anyone who doesn't have the decryption key. Think of a locked filing cabinet. Even if someone gains access to your office, they can't read the documents inside without the key to open it. The process works by encrypting the data before it is stored using a secure algorithm, like the 256-bit encryption we discussed earlier. An authorized user or system must decrypt it with the appropriate key to read that data.

Encryption-in-transit refers to information moving between systems or devices—like emails, file uploads, or messages sent over the internet. Encryption-in-transit protects the data from being intercepted or tampered with during this transfer. Imagine sending a confidential letter through the mail. You seal the letter in a tamper-proof envelope so no one can read it or change it while it's en route to the recipient. Encryption-in-transit frequently makes use of public key encryption to secure communications. This type of security protects against "man-in-the-middle attacks" discussed in Chapter 3.

Finally, encryption-in-use refers to information being actively processed by an application, program, or user. Encryption-in-use focuses on protecting sensitive data while it's being accessed, manipulated, or analyzed. Imagine you are reading a sensitive document on your desk. Encryption-in-use ensures that even if someone is peeking over your shoulder or gains temporary access, they can't decipher the contents. In this situation, data is decrypted only momentarily for processing and then re-encrypted immediately. This type of encryption is advantageous when processing sensitive client data in a secure cloud environment.

Public Key Encryption

Both the Caesar cipher and the Enigma machine were symmetric ciphers, meaning that the same key is used to both encrypt and decrypt messages. Public key encryption is known as an asymmetrical cipher and is used to encrypt communications on the internet. With symmetric ciphers, the parties communicating with one another have a key agreed upon in advance that will allow them to send and interpret messages. This doesn't work with internet communications as the communications are primarily spontaneous, and the parties aren't known to one another prior to engaging in communications.

Imagine you are practicing and working on a sensitive matter, and you need to send a highly confidential document to a client. How can you ensure that only your client can open and read the document, even if it is intercepted along the way? With public key encryption, each person has a unique "mailbox" with a special lock. The twist is that this mailbox comes with two keys. A public key acts like a lock that anyone can use to "secure" messages sent to the mailbox, and a private key is the only key that can unlock the mailbox and read the messages. The public key takes care of the need for senders and recipients to have a shared key for encrypting communications; the private key ensures confidentiality in decrypting them. While anyone can get a copy of your public key, only you have access to the private key that unlocks your mailbox.

So, we have decided to use public key encryption to send that confidential document to your client. Your client shares their public key with you. This public key is like a lock that, when attached, will seal the document so that only the person with the correct key can open it. By using their public key to encrypt the document it is entirely secure. Even if it is intercepted, the meaning cannot be *deciphered* (see what we did there?) because it is encrypted. Your client then uses their private key to decrypt the document (unlock it). The document will now be legible to them as their private key was the one needed to open the lock. The genius of public key encryption is that you don't need to send your private key over the internet; only the public key is shared, and the private key never leaves the owner's control.

Digital Signatures and Hashing

Digital signatures and hashing are ways to authenticate both the source and contents of a message. A digital signature acts as a form of nonrepudiation and identification; it clearly identifies the sender of a message and allows that message to be traced back to the sender. Hashing acts as a form of authentication, proving with mathematical certainty that the message has not been altered. So digital signatures assure the recipient of the sender's identity, and hashing assures them of the contents of the message. To be clear, digital signatures and hashing do not affect the contents of the original message. These are tools to ensure authenticity. The contents of the message itself should be encrypted to ensure confidentiality.

Let's say that you have a critical and time-sensitive document that needs to go to a client—a settlement offer with a tight deadline. The stakes are high, so you need to be assured of two things: that the client can trust the document came from you and not a malicious actor and that the document hasn't been tampered with while in transit. Think of the digital signature as a special pen; instead of using a regular pen to sign the document, you use this special pen—your private key. This private key creates a digital fingerprint of your document, called a hash. More on this shortly, but for now, think of the hash as a super-specific code representing your document that comes from an algorithm. The resulting hash is then encrypted using your private key. Your message is then sent to your client where the digital signature is examined. The recipient's device then runs a second hashing; the results of the recipient's hashing are compared against the hash value that was decrypted from the original message; if it returns an identical value, we know that the message has not been altered and that your private key was used in the hashing process of the message, thereby allowing us to presume that you sent the message.

The process of hashing is more complicated. Hashing is a process to convert any data—like a document, password, or message—into a fixed-length string of characters. This string is called a hash, or sometimes a digest, and it's unique to the original data. Even changing a single letter or number in the original data will produce an entirely different hash. To demonstrate, let's walk through a simple hashing algorithm step-by-step. Let's say the message you want to send to your client says, "Settlement offer $10,000 by 5:00 pm." We'll convert the message to ASCII (American Standard Code for Information Interchange) so that we can plug it into an algorithm. ASCII values are standard numerical representations of characters in computers. Consult Table 4-1 for the values:

S = 83	e = 101	t = 116	t = 116	l = 108	e = 101
m = 109	e = 101	n = 110	t = 116	o = 111	f = 102
f = 102	e = 101	r = 114	$ = 36	1 = 49	0 = 48
, = 44	0 = 48	0 = 48	0 = 48	b = 98	y = 121
5 = 53	: = 58	0 = 48	0 = 48	p = 112	m = 109

Table 4-1: Corresponding ASCII values

Next, we add up these numerical values; for clarity, we will calculate the value for each word and then add them together:

Total Sum (Settlement): 83(S) +101(e) + 116(t) + 116(t) + 108(l) + 101(e) + 109(m) + 101(e) + 110(n) + 116(t) = 1,061

Total Sum (offer): 48(o) + 102(f) + 102(f) + 101(e) + 114(r) = 467

Total Sum ($10,000): 36($) + 49(1) + 48(0) + 44(,) + 48(0) + 48(0) + 48(0) = 321

Total Sum (by): 98(b) + 121(y) = 219

Total Sum (5:00): 53(5) + 58(:) + 48(0) + 48(0) = 207

Total Sum (pm): 112(p) + 109(m) = 221

Total Sum: 1061 (Settlement) + 467 (offer) + 321 ($10,000) + 219 (by) + 207 (5:00) + 221 (pm) =2,496

In our example, the actual algorithm/formula is unimportant since there are standardized algorithms that exist for different contexts and are much too complex to explain here. A prime example is SHA-256 (Secure Hash Algorithm), which is an algorithm that renders hashes of 256 characters and is primarily used in conjunction with the Bitcoin blockchain. So, for our example, we'll focus on keeping it simple and say we want the result to be the remainder after division by 256 (modulus operation). This will allow us to keep the value between 0 and 255.

Hash Value = (Total Sum ASCII values) mod 256

Hash Value = (2496) mod 256

Hash Value = 2496 /256 = 9 with a remainder of 192

In our example, the hash value of the message "Settlement offer $10,000 by 5:00 pm" is 192. Hashing is highly effective at preventing tampering because even a slight change in the original message alters the hash value. For instance, if the message is modified to "Settlement offer $10,001 by 5:00 pm," the hash value changes to 193. This happens because the new message value, 2,497, leaves a remainder of 193 when divided by 256.

This demonstrates how even a minor input change (from "0" to "1") produces an entirely different hash value. Regardless of the message length, our algorithm ensures that hash values always fall between 0 and 255 by using the remainder after division by 256. As this example shows, hashing transforms input data of any size into a fixed-size value. The process relies on simple math to generate a hash that remains consistent for identical inputs but shifts significantly when the input changes, ensuring data integrity.

The concepts of digital signatures and hashing help establish the foundation for blockchains. While blockchains are associated primarily with cryptocurrencies, they have other applications, especially in the legal world.

Blockchains and Distributed Ledger Technology

The concept of blockchains, chains of digital records secured by digital signatures and hashing, precedes cryptocurrencies, though the two have developed very closely. In 2008, amid the global financial crisis that shattered faith in traditional banks, an individual or group under the presumed pseudonym Satoshi Nakamoto created the most recognized cryptocurrency: Bitcoin. Cryptocurrencies are built around the concept of trust. For thousands of years, trust in financial transactions was mediated by central authorities—whether through banks, governments, or other third parties. While these systems worked, they were flawed and vulnerable to corruption, inefficiency, and, as the 2008 crisis proved, catastrophic collapse.

Nakamoto's whitepaper, "Bitcoin: A Peer-to-Peer Electronic Cash System,"[1] outline a vision for a decentralized system where trust would no longer depend on a central authority. Instead, it would be distributed across a network of participants, maintained through cryptographic algorithms and immutable records. Blockchain was the skeleton of this vision—a public, digital ledger designed to record transactions in a way that made them tamper-resistant and transparent.

At its core, a blockchain is a chain of blocks, where each block contains a body of transactions. These blocks are cryptographically linked to one another, forming an unbroken chain that serves as a record of every transaction ever made. Once data is added to a blockchain, it is meant to be virtually impossible to alter without altering every subsequent block—a feat requiring an infeasible amount of computational power. This system allowed for what Nakamoto called "trustless" transactions—trust was no longer needed because the technology itself guaranteed security and reliability.

While the discussion of blockchain often revolves around cryptocurrencies like Bitcoin, the technology's potential extends far beyond digital money. Blockchain is, at its core, a distributed ledger technology (DLT)—a system for recording transactions securely, transparently, and immutably across a network of participants. Let's break this down further.

The key characteristics of blockchain are that it is decentralized, immutable, transparent, and secure through consensus. Unlike traditional databases maintained by a central authority (e.g., a bank or government agency), blockchains are maintained by a decentralized network of computers known as nodes. Every node has a copy of the blockchain, ensuring that no single entity has control over the system. In the blockchain associated with Bitcoin, anyone can be a node and host the chain. Depending on the source, it is estimated that there are over 10,000 reachable nodes currently on the Bitcoin blockchain.

Once data is recorded in a blockchain, it becomes incredibly difficult to alter. This is because each block in the chain contains a list of transactions or data entries, a timestamp, and a hash value that links it to the

---

1. Satoshi Nakamoto, Bitcoin: A Peer-to-Peer Electronic Cash System (2008), https://bitcoin.org/bitcoin.pdf.

previous block. Changing the data in one block, as we saw with our simple hashes, would mathematically alter the hash value of the subsequent block. So, depending on how far back in time the block is that we are trying to change, every subsequent block would have to be recalculated along the chain, which is a computationally prohibitive task, especially in an extensive, distributed network.

Public blockchains, like Bitcoin, are open for anyone to inspect. Every participant can see the transaction record on the chain, promoting transparency. However, while the data is visible, it is also anonymized, ensuring privacy. Transactions on the blockchain are validated through a process called "consensus." In the Bitcoin blockchain, this is achieved via proof of work (PoW), where nodes compete with one another to solve complex mathematical puzzles. Other blockchains use alternatives like proof of stake (PoS) or delegated proof of stake (DPoS) to achieve consensus more efficiently.

Proof of work requires "miners" (participants in the network) to compete in solving a cryptographic puzzle; think back to our elementary hashing example, only instead of our sum of all characters being divided by 256 to get a remainder, the formula is vastly more complicated. The first miner to solve the puzzle "wins" the right to add the next block of transactions to the blockchain. After a miner solves the problem, their solution is sent out to the rest of the network, where other nodes check their work to see if it is accurate. Once confirmed correct, the block is added to the chain, and the winning miner receives a reward (often in cryptocurrency).

Instead of requiring miners to solve a puzzle for the right to validate transactions, a proof of stake system is based on how much miners "invest" in the system. Validators invest a certain amount of cryptocurrency as a stake in the network. The system then selects a validator to propose the next block in the chain based on the size of their stake (e.g., the more they stake, the higher their chances of being chosen). This also serves to deter potential fraudulent transactions. Other validators confirm the proposed block, but if a validator attempts to validate fraudulent blocks, they lose the amount they have staked in the network. Delegated proof of stake works similarly but involves delegates representing larger groups that are voted on to propose and validate blocks.

The decentralized nature of the blockchain increases its tamper resistance. To break it down, not only would a malicious actor have to engage in a computationally prohibitive process to alter the data associated with the established blocks, but it would have to find a way for a majority of the nodes on the chain to accept their proposed solution as valid. If we take the 10,000 reachable nodes figure as accurate for Bitcoin's blockchain, then the actor would have to convince 5,001 nodes to accept their proof of work as valid in order to alter the chain. This is the genius of the blockchain; validation rests not just in one trusted intermediary but in an increasing number of nodes depending on how large the blockchain grows. Effectively, a malicious actor would have to convince not just a single authority figure but thousands of node hosts in addition to the mathematical difficulty associated with altering a block in the first place.

Blockchain's attributes, beyond its applications in cryptocurrency, make it particularly helpful in legal contexts, offering solutions to long-standing issues of authenticity, tamper-resistance, and efficiency. Namely, it has the greatest potential with smart contracts, evidence chain of custody, intellectual property protection, and real estate and land registries.

Smart Contracts

Smart contracts are often described as self-executing agreements in which the terms and conditions between parties are translated into computer code. Once deployed, this code automatically enforces the contract's stipulations when triggered by specific events. The term "smart contract" is a misnomer as they do not technically contain legal language or actual agreements. Instead, they are scripts that contain code that executes actions between two or more parties when certain conditions are met. In addition to not technically being contracts neither are they smart, as they may continue to execute even if a loophole is found in the coding and is being exploited.

Much of the transformative power of smart contracts lies in their reliance on blockchain technology. As we discussed, the blockchain is designed to be extraordinarily difficult to alter retroactively. Once information is added to the blockchain, changing it would require manipulation of not just one record but also its reference in subsequent records across the network, typically an infeasible endeavor if the blockchain is sufficiently large and decentralized. Consequently, the terms of a smart contract that "lives" on the blockchain become resistant to unauthorized modification. If you imagine a traditional contract's text etched into stone and witnessed by many impartial observers at the same time, you have a rough sense of the permanence and transparency that a blockchain-backed smart contract can achieve.

In practical terms, the reliability of blockchain confers significant advantages on smart contracts. First, it offers a robust form of immutability. The code cannot be tampered with unless a majority of the network agrees to initiate changes—something that rarely, if ever, happens without a compelling reason and the knowledge of the participants. Removing unilateral power from any single party helps ensure that contractual terms remain intact, free from after-the-fact meddling. Second, blockchain technology promotes transparency, allowing authorized participants to view the smart contract code and all transactions tied to it, thereby offering reassurance that the agreement unfolds as designed.

The most frequent example is that of a fictitious vending machine. Existing with instructions to verify the existence of an offer of sufficient value, the machine executes the transaction without additional instruction once the predetermined amount has been received. This is a simple example and other real-world examples exist that illustrate the prevalence and value of smart contracts.

In the entertainment and publishing industries, creators often face delayed or opaque royalty payments. A smart contract can be designed so that whether a song is streamed or digital artwork purchased, an automatic payment is triggered to the creator's account. The blockchain records each transaction, providing clarity on how often a piece of content was consumed and ensuring the artist is compensated in real-time. A company might use a smart contract to automate payment to a supplier once the supplier uploads digital proof of shipment. An insurance carrier could rely on a smart contract to release funds to a policyholder as soon as external data—perhaps weather data indicating a natural disaster—confirms that the specific catastrophic event occurred. At a fundamental level, any time a condition-based event can be reliably verified through digital means, smart contracts provide a mechanism to automate the resulting obligations.

This is where lawyers come into the picture—and in a crucial role. While the idea of an automated, self-executing agreement might suggest that legal expertise is less necessary, quite the opposite is true. At their heart, smart contracts must still align with conventional legal principles for them to be recognized and enforced in courts or arbitration. A smart contract's code might handle payment automatically, but that code is still based on an underlying offer, acceptance, and consideration. So, while the actual coding of these contracts might be beyond the technical skill of most attorneys, the logic behind their enactment and adherence to established principles of contract law are best informed by the expertise of an experienced attorney.

Moreover, not all contractual conditions can be neatly translated into binary code. While a clause that "transfers a certain amount of money when a document is verified" is relatively straightforward, more nuanced provisions—especially those involving human judgment—can be tricky to encode. Lawyers are therefore needed to collaborate with developers to identify which aspects of an agreement lend themselves to automation and which require conventional legal drafting or alternative dispute resolution methods. The old adage "garbage in, garbage out" rings true in this situation: if the logic embedded in the smart contract is flawed or incomplete, no amount of technological innovation will prevent undesirable outcomes.

From a broader perspective, smart contracts also implicate theories of private international law. Blockchains and smart contracts do not inherently adhere to national borders; a party in one jurisdiction might enter an agreement with a party halfway across the globe. Identifying which laws govern such an agreement can be a challenge, as can determining how any dispute would be resolved. Contracts benefit from clarity regarding governing law, venue, and applicable regulations, yet these frameworks can be murky when contracts are executed in a decentralized network that is not anchored to a single country. Additionally, depending on the jurisdiction, there may be a significant lack of precedent regarding the legal enforceability or interpretation of smart contracts.

One of the significant drawbacks of smart contracts is the coding complexity and the potential for catastrophic expenses from errors. This problem would be exacerbated in a decentralized context since there may be no single entity to fix or roll back problematic code. Picture a situation where a smart contract fails to account for the scarcity of a given product. Without a limit to the number of transactions that can be completed, a situation arises where an unlimited number of transactions can occur as long as specific criteria exist, even though there may be a finite number of products to fulfill those transactions. Add to that situation the need to achieve a consensus among a majority of the nodes on the chain to edit the code, and you have the potential for a serious mess.

Also, while the underlying blockchain technology provides robust protection against many cyber threats, the software powering a given smart contract might be susceptible to hacks and exploits. In these situations, a smart contract's autonomy might work against it since a lack of the oversight typically dedicated to traditional contracts might allow malicious actors to continue siphoning assets from a smart contract for a significant time period before anyone is alerted to the issue. In addition, there is the oracle problem, where smart contracts rely on external data feeds (oracles) to confirm that real-world events have taken place. If an oracle provides inaccurate or tampered data, the smart contract will execute actions based on faulty information.

Chain of Custody

Blockchain technology also offers lawyers a reliable means to maintain an unbroken, verifiable chain of custody for evidence. As we've discussed, blockchain provides a decentralized ledger that timestamps and records every transaction or update in a series of interconnected blocks. When a piece of digital evidence—for instance, a photograph or audio file—is first entered into a blockchain-based system, it is assigned a unique cryptographic "fingerprint;" its hash value. Any subsequent alteration, even as minor as changing a single pixel in an image, generates a different hash that alerts the system to the discrepancy. If the evidence is physical (such as a blood sample), its associated metadata—time of collection, location, handling officers—can be similarly recorded in the ledger to track custody transfers and key observations. Because all parties with the requisite permissions can view and verify this ledger, it becomes significantly easier to demonstrate that the evidence has remained intact throughout the investigative and pretrial processes.

By automating the creation of these tamper-resistant records, blockchain reduces the administrative burden of manually logging every piece of evidence at each stage. It also strengthens the attorney's ability to counter claims that a crucial exhibit has been edited or mishandled. In a courtroom setting, presenting blockchain records can help establish an unassailable chronology of events and bolster the credibility of the evidence, making it less vulnerable to challenges regarding authenticity.

Ultimately, the immutability and transparency of blockchain-based systems align closely with the imperative to preserve and protect the integrity of evidence, positioning blockchain as a valuable tool in the discovery process.

IP Protection

Blockchain also provides a significant boon to time-based inquiries such as intellectual property claims and real estate registries. The logging of transactions on a tamper-resistant timestamped ledger immediately calls to mind legal processes requiring verification of ownership and establishment of credible documentation.

In the area of intellectual property, disputes often center on proving who created a work first, when it was created, and whether it has been altered. These questions are especially relevant when multiple parties claim rights to the same idea, invention, or piece of content. Blockchain's immutable ledger can securely store time-tamped evidence of authorship and ownership. For a writer who completes a novel, a musician who records a new piece, or a software developer who codes a unique algorithm, recording this work on a blockchain effectively places a digital seal on the work's existence at a specific time. From a legal standpoint, this means that whenever the issue of originality arises in a dispute, the party who recorded their work on a blockchain would be able to present a verifiable record that is highly resistant to manipulation.

One of the greatest strengths of this approach is that it reduces the need to rely on centralized registries or third parties, which can face backlogs or human error when processing information. In high-stakes intellectual property disputes where time is of the essence, having a quick automated mechanism for establishing when a work was produced or transferred can be critical. A large enough blockchain would essentially act as a notary, but on a global scale and without the risk of paper documents going missing or official stamps being forged. This creates a layer of certainty that benefits content creators who want to establish the provenance of their work quickly and in a manner that courts are increasingly willing to recognize as credible evidence.

Real estate and land registries present a similarly vital use case for blockchain technology. The transfer of property rights, especially across borders or in places with historically weak recordkeeping practices, can be riddled with delays, fraud, or overlapping claims of ownership. Blockchain-based property records have the potential to bring order to this chaos by offering a system where each plot of land or piece of real estate is assigned a unique entry that tracks every transaction from one owner to the next. When someone purchases a property, the transaction is recorded on the blockchain, and any subsequent changes—whether a mortgage, lien, or conveyance of partial interests—are also logged. Because every change is linked to the block before it, forging a property deed would require rewriting the history of all subsequent transactions.

A key advantage in this context is transparency for stakeholders. Buyers can confirm the chain of title without having to rely solely on government bureaucracies or private databases that might be prone to hacking or clerical mistakes. Officials too, ranging from local registrars to judicial authorities, can see that each step is documented consistently. This capability can significantly reduce the time and legal expense often associated with property disputes, which can stall development projects or force buyers and sellers into protracted negotiations. The blockchain, in a sense, makes the ledger of property rights a public good rather than a fragmented series of individual files.

One of the drawbacks to this approach lies in the tension between immutability and evolving legal frameworks. Laws change over time, and in certain circumstances, legal agreements might require amendments or rescissions. While blockchain's permanence is one of its most significant selling points, it can become a liability when parties need to alter recorded information to comply with updated regulations or to rectify a mistake discovered after the initial entry. This challenge highlights the need for carefully designed smart contracts and governance mechanisms that allow authorized modifications without undermining the overall trustworthiness of the ledger.

Costs and technological competency barriers remain additional concerns. Setting up a robust blockchain solution, including training staff and developing user-friendly interfaces, can be expensive and complex. Attorneys and clients may also worry about interoperability between different blockchain platforms, especially if each jurisdiction or agency endorses its own version. Such fragmentation can limit blockchain's potential impact and lead to confusion over which records should be considered authoritative in court.

Still, the possibilities for intellectual property and real property registries are undeniable. Blockchain technology addresses some of the most pervasive legal issues—proof of ownership, sequence of transactions, and the security of records—by providing a transparent, tamper-resistant repository. Attorneys who understand how to integrate blockchain tools into their practice can offer clients a strong, modern safeguard. As with any emerging technology, careful consideration of potential pitfalls and a thoughtful approach to implementation can pave the way for more efficient legal systems, giving clients peace of mind in an increasingly digital world.

Corporate Filings

Unlike traditional systems that rely on a central authority to validate and store data, blockchain operates on a peer-to-peer network where every participant holds a copy of the ledger. The combination of decentralization, transparency, and immutability makes blockchain a compelling tool for corporate filings, where accuracy, accountability, and accessibility are paramount.

One of the most significant advantages of blockchain technology in corporate filings is its ability to enhance transparency. In the traditional filing process, documents are typically stored in centralized databases maintained by regulatory bodies such as the Securities and Exchange Commission (SEC). These databases, while secure, are not immune to tampering or unauthorized access. Moreover, their centralized nature makes them susceptible to single points of failure, such as hacking or system outages.

Blockchain, by contrast, ensures that all stakeholders—including corporations, regulators, and investors—have access to the same, tamper-resistant records. For example, a company's financial disclosures or shareholder reports could be uploaded to a blockchain network, where they would be instantly visible and verifiable by all authorized parties. This transparency not only reduces the risk of fraud but also builds trust among stakeholders, particularly investors who rely on accurate information to make decisions.

Corporate compliance is often a resource-intensive process, involving multiple layers of checks, audits, and reporting. Blockchain technology can streamline this process by automating many of the routine tasks associated with filings. Through the use of smart contracts blockchain can trigger actions based on predefined conditions. For instance, a smart contract could automatically file a report with regulators when certain financial thresholds are met or when a board decision is finalized. This automation not only reduces administrative burdens but also minimizes human error, which is a common cause of non-compliance.

Moreover, blockchain can significantly cut costs associated with corporate filings. Traditional systems often require intermediaries, such as auditors and escrow agents, to verify and facilitate transactions. With blockchain, these intermediaries can be eliminated or their roles reduced, leading to substantial cost savings. Additionally, the decentralized nature of blockchain means that companies do not need to invest heavily in maintaining centralized databases or proprietary software for compliance purposes.

The immutable nature of blockchain is particularly valuable for ensuring the integrity of corporate filings. As we have discussed, once data is recorded on the blockchain, it cannot easily be altered without leaving an auditable trail. This feature addresses one of the key vulnerabilities of traditional filing systems: the potential for tampering or unauthorized modifications.

Because of the advanced cryptographic techniques employed by blockchain, it is highly resistant to cyberattacks. This level of security is especially critical for sensitive corporate filings, such as those related to mergers and acquisitions, intellectual property, or executive compensation. By ensuring that these documents are both accurate and secure, blockchain can help companies avoid legal disputes and regulatory penalties.

Despite its potential, the adoption of blockchain for corporate filings is not without challenges. One of the primary barriers is the lack of a unified regulatory framework. Blockchain operates across jurisdictions, but corporate filing requirements vary significantly from one country to another. This regulatory fragmentation can create legal uncertainties and hinder the widespread adoption of blockchain technology.

Moreover, blockchain is still a relatively new and complex technology. Many corporations and regulatory bodies lack the technical expertise required to implement and manage blockchain-based systems effectively. This skills gap may slow adoption, particularly in industries that are traditionally resistant to technology change.

Despite these challenges, several initiatives demonstrate the feasibility and benefits of blockchain in corporate filings. The approach that comes most readily to mind is that of the state of Delaware. In 2018, Delaware signed an agreement with IBM for $738,000 to develop a blockchain-based corporate filing system.[2] As a hub for business incorporations in the United States, Delaware's adoption of blockchain could set a precedent for other jurisdictions.

Conclusion

The interplay of cryptography, blockchain, and smart contracts represents a transformative shift in how data security, authenticity, and trust are managed across industries, particularly within the legal field. From ancient ciphers to modern cryptographic algorithms, the evolution of encryption has laid the groundwork for secure communication and data handling in an increasingly digital world. Blockchain technology builds on these principles, offering an immutable, transparent, and decentralized solution to longstanding challenges in evidence management, intellectual property disputes, and real estate transactions.

The advent of smart contracts further extends the utility of blockchain, automating transactions and enforcing agreements with precision and reliability. These innovations reduce reliance on intermediaries, streamline processes, and provide robust protections against fraud and tampering. However, as with any technology, challenges such as coding vulnerabilities, jurisdictional uncertainties, and integration barriers highlight the importance of careful implementation and continuous oversight.

For legal professionals, understanding and leveraging these technologies is no longer optional but essential. Cryptography and blockchain are not just tools for securing information—they are instruments for building trust, preserving evidence, and enabling innovative legal solutions. As the legal landscape evolves alongside technological advancements, those who embrace and adapt to these changes will be best posi-

2. Phil Goldstein, *What Is Behind Delaware's New Blockchain Deal with IBM?*, State-Tech, Jul. 28, 2018, https://statetechmagazine.com/article/2018/07/what-behind-delawares-new-blockchain-deal-ibm.

tioned to serve their clients and navigate the complexities of a digital future. By combining traditional legal expertise with an informed approach to emerging technologies, lawyers can ensure both integrity and efficiency in their practice.

Review Questions

1. Describe the Caesar cipher and explain why it is considered insecure in modern cryptography.
2. Define encryption-at-rest, encryption-in-transit, and encryption-in-use. Why are these distinctions important for legal professionals?
3. How does public key encryption differ from symmetric encryption? Provide a practical example of its application.
4. What is a digital signature, and how does it ensure the authenticity of a message?
5. Explain the concept of hashing. How does a hash value demonstrate the integrity of a document or file?
6. What is a smart contract, and how does it utilize blockchain technology?
7. How can blockchain technology enhance the chain of custody for evidence in legal cases?
8. Explain the "oracle problem" in the context of smart contracts. How might it impact the execution of a contract?
9. Reflect on the potential drawbacks of blockchain's immutability. How might this feature complicate compliance with evolving regulations?

CHAPTER 5

Artificial Intelligence

What Is AI?

Artificial Intelligence (AI) is a multifaceted field of computer science dedicated to creating systems capable of performing tasks that typically require human intelligence. These tasks include learning, reasoning, problem-solving, perception, and language understanding. At its core, AI seeks to simulate human cognitive processes using algorithms and dynamic computing environments. The history of AI dates back to the mid-twentieth century, with foundational concepts rooted in the aspiration to develop machines capable of mimicking human thought processes. This endeavor has evolved from simple algorithms to complex machine learning and deep learning techniques powered by data and sophisticated neural networks. Machine learning, a subset of AI, enables systems to learn and improve from experience without being explicitly programmed by identifying patterns and making decisions based on data. Deep learning, a further subset of machine learning, utilizes layered neural networks to analyze various factors in data, learning to interpret and process information in a way akin to the human brain.

AI's applications are diverse and have transformative implications across various sectors. In the legal field, AI can significantly streamline processes by automating document analysis and legal research, thus reducing the time and cost associated with these tasks. Additionally, AI-driven predictive analytics can aid in anticipating case outcomes,

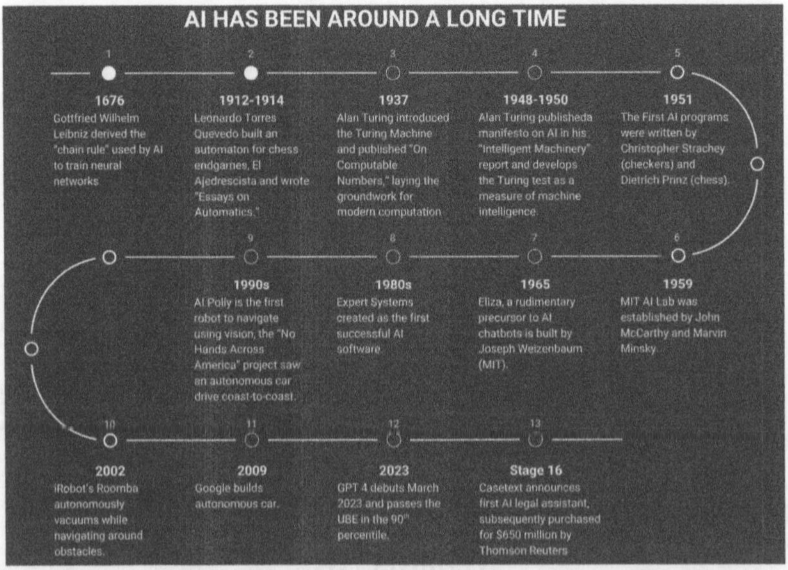

Figure 5-1: A timeline of artificial intellegence development.

assisting lawyers in formulating more informed strategies and decision-making. However, the advancement of AI also raises ethical and societal concerns, such as the impact on employment, privacy issues, and the potential for biased decision-making. The field continues to evolve with ongoing research focused on creating more explainable, ethical, and transparent AI systems, ensuring that these powerful tools are used responsibly and for the benefit of society.

The preceding two paragraphs were drafted by Open AI's ChatGPT platform. ChatGPT is possibly the most well-known platform in the recent wave of generative AI technology. Throughout this chapter, we will be examining the basic concepts of AI and its application in the legal field, concluding with a look at some practical applications. The pace at which AI is currently developing is staggering. By the time this book is published, many of the specific applications discussed in this chapter will likely have evolved or be obsolete. It is important to understand that despite how quickly new tools enter the field, at its core, AI is used to find patterns in data. The format, purpose, and application of the data may change, but at its most basic level, AI seeks to discern patterns in massive quantities of data; with generative AI, it goes a step beyond and attempts to replicate those patterns.

The simplest definition of AI is computer systems being trained to perform tasks traditionally associated with human intelligence. These fields generally include the ability to reason, self-correct, and learn through visual input, speech recognition, and translation. So, what do you think of when you hear the term AI? A computer program playing chess? Your Roomba vacuum? High-end eDiscovery platforms? ChatGPT? The Terminator? The great thing is no matter which item on the list your brain conjured first, you were right!

The most current trend in AI is in the field of generative AI, though other forms of traditional AI have impacted the legal field for decades. Much of the anxiety associated with the integration of AI into various industries stems mainly from a lack of understanding regarding how long the field of AI has existed. Figure 5-1 provides a non-exhaustive look at some of the historical milestones in the development of AI.

While it may seem like the news reports on a new development in AI every week, the field of study has followed a gradual evolution through stages. The number of stages varies, but certain similarities exist in its observable evolution. I introduce my students to the following overviews of development, one with very broad categories and the other more granular. See Figures 5-2 and 5-3.

In the three-stage model, the first category is extensive and addresses AI capabilities relative to human capabilities. AI Narrow Intelligence (ANI) is rated as being inferior to human capabilities as it is limited in scope to the specific tasks for which it was trained. Within those particular domains, it is deemed as functioning at or exceeding human capa-

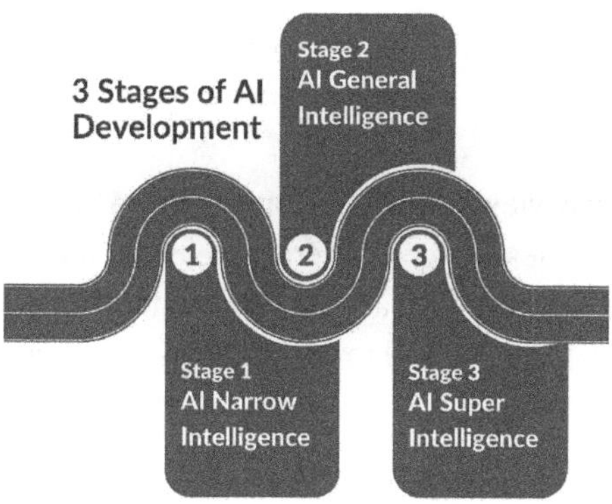

Figure 5-2: Three broad stages of AI development.

bility; however, outside of its realm of training, it is unable to function or meaningfully perform tasks. To put it simply, ANI is extremely good at what it does, but what it does is not very expansive compared to a person's ability to apply their skills across different areas. This first stage is the only type of AI that has been achieved so far, and the remaining categories are theoretical at this point.

Artificial General Intelligence (AGI), once achieved, would be comparable to human intelligence. It would have the ability to act autonomously to solve problems across multiple domains. This form of AI would have the ability to understand, learn, and apply its intelligence broadly, allowing it to perform tasks in new domains without the need for new programming for each new field. It would in effect be programming itself.

Finally, Artificial Super Intelligence (ASI) would exceed human capabilities in all fields, including those not normally associated with technology, including emotional intelligence and creative arts.[1]

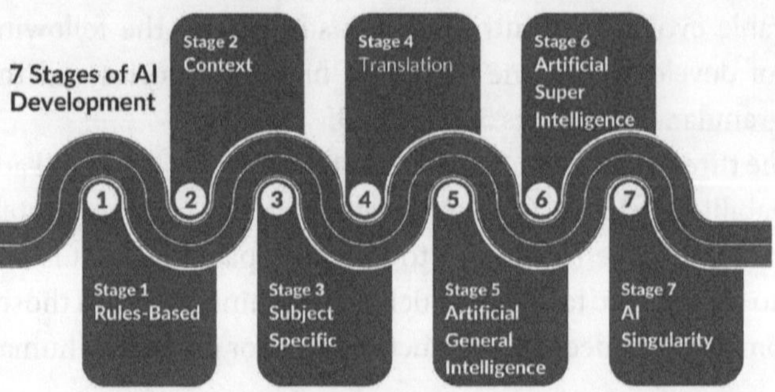

Figure 5-3: Seven more granular stages of AI development.

A more granular view of the development of AI is the seven stages of AI development. These stages generally refer to the progression from basic, rule-based algorithms to advanced systems capable of human levels of reasoning, with the potential to greatly surpass human capabilities.

---

1. *See* Andreas Kaplan and Michael, *Siri, Siri, in my hand: Who's the fairest in the land? On the interpretations, illustrations, and implications of artificial intelligence*, 62 Business Horizons 15 (2019).

Rule-Based Systems: This initial stage involves AI systems that operate based on explicitly programmed rules. These systems make decisions based on a set of predefined rules and are limited to the data on which they are initially trained. A prime example is a computer playing chess; the program can use its programmed algorithms and coded rules to determine the best next move after evaluating changes in the board state. In the legal field, form and contract automation are prime examples, as well as relevancy rankings in legal research. These tools are highly consistent and accurate in the tasks they have been trained to do. However, they are unable to adapt to new situations for which they are not explicitly programmed.

Context Awareness and Retention: At this stage, AI systems begin to understand and retain contextual information across tasks. This includes basic recognition of patterns and the ability to use historical data to inform future decisions, meaning they remember past interactions and can respond to new situations while recalling user preferences. The most prevalent examples of this stage would be virtual assistants like Siri or Echo and the recent wave of AI Chatbots like ChatGPT. Contract analysis software that can review contracts and identify or suggest clauses typifies this stage in the legal technology field.

Domain or Subject-Specific Expertise: Here, AI systems specialize in particular domains, demonstrating expert-level knowledge and decision-making in specific fields. This stage is a significant step from the preceding steps as it exhibits a deeper subject awareness in narrowly defined subject areas. The AI in this context is trained on vast quantities of subject-specific data and can use deep learning to recognize complex patterns that are not apparent to humans or simpler AI systems. These systems do not replicate human adaptability and are limited to the specific domain in which they are trained, but they are powerful tools in their particular domains. Some of the more complex eDiscovery software and Lexis+'s AI-assisted research platform use this type of system.

Reasoning Systems: This is the stage where AI begins to reason in unfamiliar subject areas and can solve novel problems. This involves making informed decisions by considering various factors and outcomes, much like human reasoning. It includes probabilistic reasoning and decision-making in complex, unpredictable environments. This stage is where the AI begins to exhibit something closely akin to creative thinking as opposed to the formulaic application of rules.

Artificial General Intelligence, Artificial Super Intelligence, and AI Singularity: Similar to the three stages of AI development discussed earlier, these stages are theoretical and sound a bit more like the stuff of science fiction. They involve AI gaining self-awareness and emotional intelligence, and a debatable point is where AI surpasses the sum of human intelligence in all aspects. It is important to remember that AI development has been limited to the first three stages. The later stages, particularly from stage five onwards, are primarily theoretical and subjects of debate in their fields.

As we discussed in the first chapter, a useful practice for moving towards mastery of a tool is understanding how it functions at its most basic level; with AI this is how it receives data, how it is trained on that data, and what it can do with the finished product.

How AI Receives Data

Without data, AI systems would be inert sets of mathematical equations. Think of algorithms, architecture, and parameters as the car, while data is the fuel. A can of gas on its own is about as useful as a car without fuel. Many AI models have enormous capabilities, but all start as ignorant as a newborn. The classic example is training an AI model to identify a dog by feeding it a large set of images and allowing the algorithms to identify patterns in the data. In supervised machine learning, which we will discuss in more depth shortly, the model returns images of what it has determined to represent dogs. The human supervising the training provides feedback by acknowledging the model's selections or correcting them, just like showing pictures or flashcards to children and helping them to identify shapes, colors, or animals. Eventually, after having been trained on enough data and feedback, the model can consistently distinguish between dogs and cats, raccoons, or opossums.

Teaching a model to distinguish between a dog and other animals, while an impressive feat, is relatively simple compared to many of the applications that AI is assuming. Let's expand a bit and use the example of self-driving cars. Imagine a world where cars navigate bustling streets without a human at the wheel. How do these vehicles make split-second decisions? With these AI systems, we are talking about volumes of data exponentially more extensive than that required to teach an AI to recognize a dog. These autonomous vehicles receive terabytes of data from their various sensors. Without being trained, these vehicles would not distinguish between a pedestrian and a pothole and would treat them the same. With the training data, these systems take the basic task of identifying dogs and expand it to recognize patterns and distinguish dogs from people, people from potholes, and potholes from other vehicles. Consider what might happen if that vehicle were confronted with the choice between avoiding either a pedestrian or a pothole and it had not been trained to distinguish between the two.

So, what is AI training data and where does it come from? AI training data is data that has been carefully curated and cleaned. Cleaning data refers to the process of preparing the dataset for analysis by correcting or removing inaccuracies, inconsistencies, redundancies, and irrelevancies. Training data is generally image, video, audio/speech, or text depending largely on the intended purpose of the model.

Knowing the source of the data that the model being used was trained on is vital to avoid inaccuracies, but equally important to avoid bias. For example, in 2017, Amazon decided to scrap its AI-powered employment screening platform. The tool was trained to sort through batches of resumes and return the top applicants. Unfortunately, there was a problem. The model had been trained on 10 years' worth of resumes submitted to the company, and the program began discriminating against certain applicants. Remember that AI tools look for patterns in data; sadly, an underlying overrepresentation of men in the tech industry had led the AI tool to conclude that male candidates were preferable to females. The tool began to downgrade resumes that included references to women's activities or graduates from all-women's colleges.[2]

---

2. Jeffrey Dastin, *Insight—Amazon scraps secret AI recruiting tool that showed bias against women*, REUTERS, Oct. 10, 2018, https://www.reuters.com/article/idUSKCN1MK0AG/.

Below are some examples of datasets that might be used in AI training.

URL	Sources	Description
https://data.gov	U.S. Government	Datasets published by federal agencies including census data.
https://open-data.europa.eu/en/data	European Union	Similar to data.gov but based on data from the European Union
https://www.healthdata.gov/	U.S. Department of Health & Human Services	125 years of U.S. healthcare data. Including, Medicare, epidemiology, and population statistics data.
https://aws.amazon.com/datasets	Amazon Web Services	Variety of datasets, including the 1000 Genomes Project and NASA's database of satellite imagery of Earth.
https://www.ncdc.noaa.gov/data-access/quick-links#loc-clim	National Climatic Data Center	Collection of environmental, meteorological, and climate datasets.
https://pewresearch.org/internet/datasets	Pew Research Center	Datasets collected by the Pew Research Center on its various studies conducted.
https://datasetsearch.research.google.com	Google	Publicly available structured and unstructured datasets.

Table 5-1: Large Training Datasets

Models of Machine Learning

Machine Learning (ML) uses algorithms and statistics to find patterns in data sets that would dwarf human comprehension. Where human beings can discover patterns in dozens, or perhaps hundreds, of points of data, AI is deployed to find patterns in thousands or millions of data points. The data points can include anything from the words in a corporate filing to the last video that you watched on Netflix. In a very superficial sense, the whole ordeal can be boiled down to a relatively simple concept: "Find the pattern, apply the rule."

The primary difference between AI and traditional programs is their flexibility. Traditional programs are sets of instructions created by programmers for a computer to follow explicitly to reach a specific outcome. With AI, an algorithm is trained using a large set of data to identify patterns and relationships within the data. If you contrast programming and ML with traditional human development, it is the difference between giving a child simplistic step-by-step instructions to accomplish a specific task and that same child being presented with a familiar situation and drawing on past experience to discern the correct response. ML is generally classified into three categories: supervised machine learning, unsupervised machine learning, and reinforcement learning.

Going back to our example of training AI to recognize dogs, let's take a look at the three types of ML. Try not to be distracted by wondering how ML happens and focus instead on what is happening; think of these methods simply as teaching methods for training computers.

Supervised Learning

Imagine that you're teaching a child to identify animals. Holding up pictures of various animals, you clearly state to the child, "This is a cat" or "This is a dog." In this situation, users are providing examples with obvious labels. This is a rough approximation of supervised learning. Large amounts of data are fed to the learning algorithm, but equally important is that the data is labeled. So, if you want a machine to recognize an animal as either "dog" or "not a dog," you give it lots of pictures of dogs that are clearly marked as either "dogs" or "not dogs." Remember, AI's primary strength is identifying patterns, so with each successive picture, its accuracy will increase as it identifies not only what makes a dog a dog but also how to distinguish other animals as "not dog."

Supervised ML provides a high degree of accuracy and predictability when trained with large, well-labeled datasets. Additionally, this type of ML is relatively easy to evaluate with clearly defined metrics such as accuracy, recall, and precision. It is most commonly used for regression analysis (e.g., stock price forecasting), classification (e.g., email spam detection), anomaly detection (e.g., fraud detection), and recommendation systems (e.g., Spotify).

Be aware that this type of ML has particular limitations. Namely, it is limited by the size of the dataset and the efficiency of the labeling. If an item is mislabeled, like labeling a gerbil as a dog, it will carry that label forward in its application. Additionally, it is going to be limited to known patterns, which can result in overfitting to the data, similar to a student who memorizes facts for a test but fails to grasp the underlying concepts and will have difficulty applying the concepts to new facts.

Unsupervised Learning

Now, think about giving a different child a box filled with photographs of other animals without any labels or instructions. They start sorting them out on their own, maybe by color, shape, or size. In unsupervised learning, the machine is given data with no labels, and it begins searching for patterns or relationships. A great example of unsupervised learning is market segmentation. Suppose that you have a database of customer information, but you aren't really sure what to do with it or what value it may have. Unsupervised learning can identify patterns, like grouping customers with similar buying habits, without being told explicitly what to find.

Unsupervised ML is much more flexible than supervised ML. It can explore large data sets and identify hidden patterns in the data without the extra step of labeling each data point. It excels at grouping similar documents together (e.g., eDiscovery), discovering relationships between variables (e.g., legal analytics), and anomaly detection (e.g., fraud detection).

Unsupervised models' ability to detect hidden patterns, however, makes it difficult to come up with metrics for how well the model is performing. If the developer doesn't know what the algorithm is looking for, how can they evaluate how well it performed in finding it? The lack of a clear objective also tends to make unsupervised models less accurate for tasks like classification relative to supervised models.

Reinforcement Learning

Finally, suppose you have a third child who also has a box filled with unlabeled photographs of animals. Only this time, the child is instructed to find a picture of a dog, even though they are unfamiliar with a dog. If the child holds up a picture of a dog, you give them a candy. If not, no candy. The child begins to learn to identify dogs by noticing patterns in the pictures where they receive candy. Video games are classic examples of this. The algorithm tries various strategies to win the game, getting "rewards" for successful actions and "penalties" for unsuccessful ones. Over time, it learns the best methods to maximize its rewards.

Reinforcement models specialize in change. They are powerful in environments where trial and error are feasible and decisions based on changing scenarios are necessary. These models learn from interacting with the environment and can adapt to changes, make decisions, and exercise control. Supervised and unsupervised models are more prevalent in the legal field. Reinforcement learning, however, is still used in relevancy determinations for legal research searches as well as legal chatbots (e.g., Lexis+ AI) and virtual legal assistants (e.g., Casetext CoCounsel).

These models tend to be very complex and require substantial computational resources. Additionally, it is paramount that the reward structure be carefully crafted to reinforce the appropriate decisions, which can be challenging to design depending on the model's purpose.

Each learning style has its strengths and weaknesses and is useful for particular tasks. Supervised learning is great when you have clear examples and labeled data to teach from, unsupervised learning is useful for exploring unknown patterns in data, and reinforcement learning excels in environments where you can simulate actions and learn from feedback. For quick reference and see the strengths of the different types of learning, consult Table 5-2.

Machine Learning

Comparison

1 Supervised ML	2 Unsupervised ML	3 Reinforcement ML
High accuracy	Discovers hidden patterns	Decision making and learning from interaction
Predictability	Functions without a clearly defined objective	Adaptability
Dependent on labels	Handles unlabeled data	Complex and resource hungry
Limited to known patterns	Difficult to interpret	Difficult to design reward structure

Table 5-2: Comparing types of machine learning.

Traditional AI v. Generative AI

The primary difference between traditional AI and generative AI lies in their purpose and output. Traditional AI is primarily tasked with understanding, processing, and making decisions based on existing data. Generative AI is typically about creating new data that is similar to its training data. Think about the difference between categorizing a group of artworks as compared to creating tracings or sketches. Generative AI seems intimidating when we look at its ability to generate conversation, artwork, or audio/visual media, and the underlying architecture processes are definitely impressive, but ultimately, it follows the same general rule as traditional AI: "Find the pattern, apply the rule."

In his book, Stephen Wolfram describes the process as seeking to "produce a 'reasonable continuation' of whatever text it's got so far." All law students can breathe a sigh of relief as he doesn't require you to read a host of cases to define reasonable, instead, he provides a very succinct definition: "what one might expect someone to write after seeing what people have written on billions of webpages."[3] So if you think back to the methods in which AI is trained you should be able to identify the "billions of webpages" as the training data set, what's left to accomplish a basic understanding of generative AI is to identify the type of machine learning taking place.

Generative AI uses a process known as Deep Learning, which involves the use of complex networks of computers structured to imitate the neural pathways of the human brain. Consider deep learning as an analog to machine learning; it can be applied across all three major types of machine learning. Traditional machine learning leverages preprocessed data, while deep learning focuses on the ability to process unstructured data. It isn't easy to consider any part of AI simple, but it is helpful to view deep learning as the method reserved for more complex tasks like virtual assistants or chatbots.

Historically, there has been a tension between legal education and legal practice over the development of practical knowledge. The distinction between traditional AI and generative AI can be summarized by comparing the paragons of this tension: the book-learned law graduate

3. Stephen Wolfram, *What Is ChatGPT Doing … and Why Does It Work?*, Stephen Wolfram Writings (Feb. 14, 2023), writings.stephenwolfram.com/2023/02/what-is-chatgpt-doing-and-why-does-it-work.

and the experience-laden seasoned attorney. The recent law graduate (i.e., traditional AI) is razor sharp in terms of the knowledge base they have cultivated to pass the bar. They can recite precedent (training data), statutes, and court rules (i.e., algorithms and architecture) but may struggle with entirely new cases where the law is not clear because of a lack of experience. The seasoned attorney (i.e., generative AI) compliments their legal knowledge with adaptability (i.e., skill with unstructured data) and experience (i.e., neural networks refine and improve with exposure to more data) to form intuitive reasoning that makes connections in datasets that may not be immediately obvious.

LLMs and Prompt Engineering

Large language models (LLMs) are sophisticated artificial intelligence systems built on deep learning architectures that have been trained on massive quantities of text from diverse sources. For example, ChatGPT was trained on extensive collections of textual data such as books, news articles, manuals, and web pages. A large portion of the training data came from the Common Crawl, a publicly available dataset with petabytes of data collected from the web since 2008. The curation of the dataset directly affects its utility towards a given purpose. Lexis+ AI, for example, doesn't rely on a single LLM, even though GPT is included, but it is fine-tuned with data from the Lexis legal databases, making it ideal for legal research but a poor fit for general knowledge queries. What makes LLMs extremely interesting is that by ingesting these large volume data sets, they are able to discern statistical patterns within language: how words frequently co-occur, which terms often appear in similar contexts, and what logical or rhetorical structures underlie paragraphs or even whole documents. Having been exposed to legal memos, briefs, cases, and contracts, you can see how an LLM trained on legal material might find different patterns in language than one trained on the Internet in general. Through this training, LLMs develop a remarkable capacity to generate coherent, contextually relevant text, whether the prompt is a request for a summary of legal opinion, a short story set in medieval times, or an elaboration on a technical topic like quantum computing.

Despite their ability to generate impressively human-like responses, LLMs do not "think" or "reason" like humans. Their knowledge comes from identifying correlations in vast data sets rather than understanding content in a conceptual or experiential manner. When a model like this receives an input—often called a prompt—it draws on the patterns it has internalized to produce an answer that seems plausible and contextually aligned with the question. This means that much of the model's output quality depends on how well the user formulates the initial prompt.

This is where the concept of "prompt engineering" becomes important. Prompt engineering contains elements of both artistry and science dedicated to crafting instruction that guides the model's response toward the user's goals. Without a well-structured prompt, even a highly trained LLM can produce text that is vague, off-topic, or peppered with inaccuracies. However, by deliberately designing the prompt, users can coerce the model to provide specific types of output, whether it's coding help, creative writing, or the synthesis of something approaching legal analysis by replicating the textual patterns of treatises, cases, and statutes.

The first step in prompt engineering typically involves establishing a clear *intention*. If the user wants a concise summary of a case, for instance, the prompt might begin with a statement clarifying the desired length, tone, or detail level. The user could explicitly request an overview suitable for someone with minimal legal background, or conversely, they might need a technical legal memorandum that references case law and statutory authority. By articulating these requirements up front, the user helps the model filter through the vast pool of possible resources and focus the response on a specific format and style. Bear in mind that the training data is going to limit the resources available for consultation. Lexis+ AI or Thomson Reuters's CoCounsel is going to have proprietary resources like treatises, formbooks, and information from Shepherds and West's Key Number system respectively. These resources are denied to the training data of other platforms like ChatGPT or Claude by a paywall.

Context is another critical element. LLMs excel when the user includes relevant background information in the prompt itself. If the model is being asked to analyze a complex contractual dispute, simply writing "Explain this contract dispute" probably won't suffice. Instead, the user should supply key facts—perhaps excerpts from the contract, the nature of the alleged breach, any existing case law that might be relevant—and state what specific analysis is desired. The prompt might say, "Based on the following clauses from a service agreement, please identify potential breaches and suggest possible legal remedies, assuming this dispute is governed by the laws of [a particular jurisdiction]." While it's not a good idea to rely solely on the analysis of an LLM, this type of specificity helps the LLM model anchor its response in the provided context rather than generating a general or tangential discourse on contracts.

Tone and style further shape the final output. LLMs can switch between conversational and formal registers or provide short answers versus lengthy analyses, depending on user instructions. If a user wants an elevator pitch to present to an executive who only has a few minutes to spare, the prompt could request precisely that. If, on the other hand, a user requires a white paper level of detail, the prompt needs to specify that. By predefining the tone—casual, persuasive, neutral, scholarly, and so forth—the user can avoid receiving an output mismatched to the intended audience.

A beneficial technique in prompt engineering is iteration. Rarely does the perfect prompt emerge on the first attempt, especially in complex tasks. Instead, the user examines the initial response from the LLM and makes note of areas where the answer might not respond to the user's desires, such as it being too vague, too broad, or confusing. Then, the user refines the prompt by adding clarifications or instructions. You might say, "Expand on the explanation of punitive damages. Provide examples from at least three relevant cases." By creating subsequent iterations like this, you can gradually guide the model to produce text that aligns more closely with your desired outcome.

These considerations also highlight potential pitfalls. Because LLMs aren't "thinking" in a traditional sense, they are designed to generate text that appears coherent; they can easily produce statements of fact that sound convincing but are ultimately fabricated. This phenomenon has come to be referred to as "hallucinations," where the model invents legal precedents, historical events, or other data, usually fact-oriented when its training data lacks relevant information on the point. Lawyers, researchers, or any professional user must, therefore, treat the model's responses with caution. Prompt engineering can mitigate the risk by instructing the model to cite sources that can later be verified, but vigilance and thorough review of the LLM's product remains indispensable.

Moreover, privacy and confidentiality issues loom large. Some tasks require the user to feed sensitive or proprietary information into the LLM. In such cases, users need to consider how their prompts may be stored or processed by the underlying systems. Lexis+ AI, for example, creates a new session after the preceding prompts have been closed out, purging any user-supplied information between sessions. ChatGPT, on the other hand, may use anonymized user data to train future iterations, though there is an option to opt-out. Whatever system is being used, and as with any third-party platform, knowing how the data you supply is used is of crucial importance. Users in the legal field must be diligent about redacting or anonymizing any sensitive client data. That process can itself become an element of prompt engineering: deciding precisely how much detail to share so the model can be helpful without exposing confidential data.

My favorite descriptions of LLMs derive from conversations had with colleagues, speculating on generative AI's place in legal academia. One states that LLMs are excellent first-draft generators. They will give the bones of a solid response, but they need someone to verify the facts and refine the presentation. The other compares LLMs to brilliant but scattered and needy coworkers. They have incredible depths of knowledge but are easily confused and cannot admit when they don't know the answer. Ultimately, LLMs are a useful tool, but you are responsible for the work you submit. Much like Wikipedia might be a valid starting point for researching a new topic, it's generally not something you are going to cite in a court filing.

AI in the Legal Industry

With most things that are technology-related, the law itself is slow to adapt. The business side of the legal industry, however, has branched into the field of AI and adopted many tools to alleviate the workload of attorneys and streamline many tasks for firms. Many of the latest tools are targeted at larger firms and businesses, but avenues are opening for access for non-profits and the public sector (e.g., Everlaw For Good, Fast-Case bar association partnerships, and the HotDocs partnership with Pro Bono Net.). Legal industry forays into AI have been traditionally targeted at five areas: document automation, legal research, eDiscovery, due diligence, and the more recent advent of AI legal assistants (see Figure 5-5). These tasks share similar attributes in that they are repetitive or routine, data-intensive, or have clearly defined rules and parameters.

Figure 5-4: How AI is typically used in the legal industry.

Legal Research

AI-powered legal research tools focus on language processing, document analysis, citation checking and updating, and organizing and summarizing massive legal databases. AI boosts the relevancy of search results through repeated exposure to the user's habits, saving time that would otherwise be spent on traditional legal research. In the past, searching large legal databases was an art and sometimes a mystery. Queries were crafted with exacting precision, lists of synonyms, and archaic, magical words in a mystical language called Boolean. Many times, the act of crafting a search resembled an algebra problem more than a legal question. With the advances in AI, the search box has become much more forgiving and can intuit meaning based on the behaviors of specific users and users across the platform.

Advances in language processing from AI allow platforms to mine massive quantities of text and seek out patterns to better organize documents and make connections. These connections enable the platforms to summarize entries and provide simplified explanations of complex legal jargon that can be relayed to clients. Many of the newer tools, like

Lexis's Brief Analysis and West's Quick Check, can even take a user-drafted document and seek out legal authority users may have missed by focusing on the language used in the draft and making connections to similar frequently cited laws or precedents, which is very handy for checking your work or when looking for precedent damaging to your opponent's arguments.

Additionally, legal citators, that before could only identify explicitly invalidated cases, can now identify situations where a case may have been implicitly overruled. Tools like Westlaw's KeyCite can evaluate cases and employ AI's pattern-seeking expertise to identify cases standing for similar premises that have been overruled. More simply, the citator does not have to rely on direct citation of bad law to alert the user of potential adverse treatment. The AI can identify when there is negative treatment of cases standing for similar points of law and pass that insight on to the researcher.

Generative AI, while still relatively new to the scene, is already positioned to make massive changes in the traditional legal research context. As of the writing of this book, Lexis+ AI is the most recent player in AI-powered legal research, with Thomson Reuters purchasing Casetext for $650 million after it debuted a similar product. In the legal research context, Lexis+ AI acts as a chatbot that cites its sources, thus minimizing the hallucinations that have plagued fact-oriented questions presented to ChatGPT. In addition to answering simple questions, Lexis+ AI can generate simple drafts of memoranda, clauses, and arguments. These tools eliminate a large portion of the false starts and time-consuming first drafts associated with traditional legal research and writing.

Much of the work done over the past to facilitate legal research has made it a field that is ripe for AI adoption. Due to the chronological publication of cases, finding aids have been necessary to enable research. West and Lexis have expended considerable effort in generating systems like Headnotes and the West Key Number system that draws connections between individual cases and broad legal concepts. The work already put in to draw these connections can act as a roadmap when training new AI models, making the legal field ripe for deploying generative AI programs.

EDiscovery

Perhaps no field in the practice of law lends itself so intuitively to AI assistance than eDiscovery. EDiscovery involves handling massive amounts of data while searching for documents that share specific characteristics that make them relevant. Many eDiscovery projects involve sorting gigabytes or even terabytes of data to locate relevant documents. Technology-assisted review, or TAR, refers to deploying these AI-powered systems to comb through produced discovery documents, focusing the legal team's attention on potentially relevant documents, thereby expediting the team's review and saving the firm money.

EDiscovery platforms make use of predictive coding to return potentially discoverable documents. Recall the section on supervised machine learning; this is a prime example. Predictive coding uses machine learning algorithms to classify documents as relevant or irrelevant to a case based on a set of training documents reviewed by legal experts. Some platforms even employ a user interface similar to Spotify, where review teams simply give returned documents a thumbs up or thumbs down to indicate their relevance, thus further training the algorithm.

Natural language processing (NLP) is another AI technology that plays a crucial role in eDiscovery. NLP enables computers to understand, interpret, and generate human language in a way that is valuable for legal analysis. It allows for more sophisticated searches of electronically stored information (ESI) by understanding the context of words and phrases rather than just performing simple keyword searches. This improves the relevancy determinations of AI models by allowing them to return documents whose context makes them relevant and not just the use of specific keywords and phrases.

Anyone who has ever been involved in a traditional document review will understand the sheer relentless nature of wading through thousands of documents searching for specific details and the nature of the human mind to wander in such monotonously plodding tasks. A significant benefit of AI over human review of eDiscovery is the consistency with which these machine tools seek out relevant documents. These AI models automate tasks that are repetitive and time-consuming for humans. This automation not only speeds up the eDiscovery process but also helps to minimize human error, ensuring that the review process is relatively less time-consuming, more thorough, and more accurate.

It is important to note, however, that human oversight of the eDiscovery process is still crucial. Legal professionals exercise a degree of nuanced understanding and ethical consideration that is simply not present in AI models. For example, determining the relevance of documents in the training set as well as subsequently returned documents requires a knowledge of complex legal doctrine as well as an understanding of the nuances of human communication. One is not necessarily better than the other; it is the complimentary synergy between human expertise and AI capabilities that ensures the technology-assisted review process is both efficient and effective.

Due Diligence

Traditionally, due diligence in the legal industry involved paralegals, interns, and entry associates sifting through large volumes of documents—contracts, financial reports, and correspondence—seeking inconsistencies, liabilities, or critical deal points. AI-driven solutions streamline this process by applying algorithms to categorize, summarize, and identify anomalies in documents at a fraction of the time it would take a human reviewer.

The key advantages of AI over human reviewers in this context are speed and consistency. As we have covered, AI can be trained on examples to identify patterns in vast quantities of data. In a due diligence situation, this might include clauses indicating regulatory noncompliance or specific termination provisions that pose a heightened risk. By scanning tens of thousands of pages or data points, the AI model flags relevant passages, drawing attention to certain documents for attorney reviewers to focus on. Additionally, unlike human reviewers, who can grow fatigued or distracted by such monotonous tasks, AI models apply uniform criteria to every page or data set. If well-trained, they excel at spotting repeated patterns or deviations—like a missing signature block or an unusual provision in an agreement. When unusual terms appear, the system alerts the legal team, who can then examine those documents more closely to confirm whether a genuine issue exists or it is just a false alarm. This hybrid human-machine approach ensures that results are thoroughly vetted while offloading the rote, high-volume tasks to the algorithm.

AI due diligence solutions also reduce costs by allowing firms to reallocate staff time to higher-value work. Instead of devoting hundreds of hours to document reviews, attorneys can focus on advanced and more nuanced strategies that elude AI systems. By increasing efficiency and consistency, these platforms ultimately strengthen client confidence in a firm's diligence and help identify potential risks early, laying a stronger foundation for informed decision-making in mergers, acquisitions, or other high-stakes transactions.

Document Automation

Artificial Intelligence can significantly streamline document automation in the legal field by transforming the way contracts, pleadings, and other standardized materials are created and managed. At the heart of this transformation is the ability of AI algorithms—particularly large language models—to quickly generate or adapt text based on templates, clauses, and user-provided inputs, thereby reducing repetitive manual labor and decreasing the likelihood of human error. Instead of drafting a contract from scratch every time, an attorney can rely on an AI-powered platform to assemble boilerplate text and add in relevant variables such as party names, dates, and jurisdictional requirements. This process not only speeds up initial document creation but also maintains consistency, especially in large firms that regularly reuse standard clauses for compliance or business objectives.

AI's natural language processing capabilities go beyond single template filing. Modern systems can analyze existing documents in a law firm's database, identify commonly used clauses, and recommend their inclusion in new contracts based on criteria like deal size, industry, and risk tolerance. For firms without established databases of agreements, vendors exist with prebuilt databases of form agreements or that access publicly available agreements to suggest commonly used terms or boilerplate for inclusion. Lawyers can then review these suggestions, ensuring that the final product aligns with both the client's needs and the latest regulatory requirements. This form of dynamic, data-driven document assembly helps maintain uniformity in style and substance, all while reducing the time attorneys spend on mechanical tasks. As a result, legal professionals can allocate more energy to higher-level strategic analysis or negotiations requiring a level of nuance that isn't available in AI systems.

In addition to suggesting terms or clauses, AI can help detect inconsistencies, missing sections, or contradictory language in a draft. By comparing each version of a document to known standards or best practices, the system can highlight problem areas that might require an attorney's attention. This reduces the risk of errors that could otherwise go unnoticed until after a contract is signed, thus minimizing client exposure to unfavorable terms. It also enables more thorough internal reviews without adding extra rounds of manual proofreading.

From a business perspective, the enhanced efficiency and reliability provided by AI-powered document automation yield distinct competitive advantages. Firms can offer faster turnaround times, better quality assurance, and potentially lower costs. For clients, this often translates to more predictable legal fees and quicker resolution of transactional matters. At the same time, attorneys gain the freedom to focus on substantive legal issues rather than retyping standard boilerplate language over and over.

While AI can suggest the initial structure and content, human oversight remains crucial. Tools may generate flawed or inapplicable language if they are trained on flawed or irrelevant data. Like many of the applications discussed and to be addressed, confidentiality is an issue when attorneys feed sensitive information into AI-powered platforms that could store or inadvertently repurpose it elsewhere. Careful review and scrupulous data-handling policies are thus vital to ensure that AI-driven document automation serves as a complement to, rather than a substitute for, legal skill and professional judgment.

Legal Analytics

Legal analytics refers to the application of data analysis techniques—often aided by artificial intelligence and machine learning—to the vast quantities of legal information generated by courts, law firms, and regulatory agencies. The process traditionally involves the use of machine learning, natural language processing, and data mining to process large datasets and provide analysis of trends in the legal field. Rather than relying solely on traditional research methods, attorneys who use legal analytics draw upon structured data to gain insights into patterns, trends, and probabilities that inform how a case might progress or conclude. This data-driven approach goes beyond keyword searches; it delves deeper into nuances such as the historical behavior of judges, the average duration of certain case types, and common outcomes in specific practice areas or jurisdictions.

At a practical level, legal analytics often begins with collecting and organizing large datasets that might include judicial opinions, dockets, motions, briefs, and other court filings. For example, if a commercial litigator is researching how a particular judge has ruled on summary judgment motions in contract disputes, legal analytics tools can quickly sift through thousands of relevant cases, revealing patterns of leniency or strictness in granting those motions. This type of insight helps attorneys tailor their arguments or strategies to that judge's known tendencies. In the same vein, corporate counsel may examine an opposing party's litigation history to evaluate how frequently that party settles, how aggressively they litigate, or whether they have a track record of going to trial for specific types of disputes. Armed with this data, a lawyer can develop a more precise negotiation strategy, make more informed decisions about when to push for settlement, and provide data-driven strategy advice to clients. Lawyers can supplement their professional judgment with data-driven forecasts, providing clients with a more comprehensive view of their legal position and potential results. This shift toward an empirically grounded practice also resonates with clients who demand greater cost predictability and strategic direction, particularly for high-stakes or high-volume litigation. The ability to tell a client with a degree of certainty that a particular court traditionally takes three months to rule on a particular motion provides a sense of stability appreciated by clients.

For law firms seeking to improve their operational efficiency, legal analytics can reveal internal metrics, such as where time is most profitably spent, which types of cases consume the most resources, and how long matters typically last from start to finish. Managing partners and practice group leaders can use this information to allocate staff, refine billing practices, and identify where additional training or support might be needed. A firm might also highlight its success rates or specialized expertise by drawing on empirical performance data, offering prospective clients more concrete evidence of the firm's capabilities and track record.

Still, the adoption of legal analytics carries its own challenges and ethical considerations. Accuracy depends on the quality and completeness of the underlying data; gaps or errors in the dataset can skew predictions and misinform legal strategies. The most glaring example of this pitfall is the effect of the COVID-19 pandemic on litigation timelines. Many courts, at least temporarily, stopped hearing cases until safeguards were implemented. The pandemic creates roughly an entire year of statistical outliers on timelines to the completion of a matter or judicial rulings on different matters. These outliers are going to skew the dataset until enough data has been gathered to offset their impact. An effective legal analytics user is going to look at the broad picture to understand where the data is coming from and its consistency, as well as be aware of anything that may distort the analysis.

Furthermore, attorneys must remain cautious when relying on statistical models to guide real-world decisions, ensuring they interpret and communicate the results responsibly to clients and colleagues. Confidentiality concerns also loom large: while many analytics platforms rely on public records, some seek to incorporate internal firm documents or discovery materials. As we discussed previously, use of sensitive client data to inform these systems, many of which would be cloud based, should trigger concerns about data security and the need to establish encryption standards from the outset.

Conclusion

Artificial intelligence has emerged as a transformative force in the legal industry, reshaping how legal professionals conduct research, manage documents, and streamline workflows. By automating repetitive tasks, uncovering patterns in data, and even generating insights, AI tools enable lawyers to work more efficiently and focus on higher-level strategic thinking. However, with these advancements come responsibilities—ensuring ethical use, maintaining client confidentiality, and exercising informed oversight.

While AI's applications in the legal field continue to expand, it is essential to approach these tools with a balanced perspective. They are powerful allies but not replacements for human expertise. By combining the precision and speed of AI with the critical thinking and ethical judgment of skilled legal professionals, the potential for innovation is boundless. As we look to the future, cultivating a deeper understanding of AI's capabilities and limitations will be key to navigating this evolving landscape and leveraging these technologies responsibly and effectively.

Review Questions

1. What are the differences between supervised, unsupervised, and reinforcement learning?
2. How can AI improve efficiency in legal research and document analysis?
3. Explain how AI is used in eDiscovery. What are its benefits, and why is human oversight still critical?
4. What distinguishes traditional AI from generative AI, and how does deep learning contribute to generative AI capabilities?
5. Discuss the significance of training data in generative AI. What are the potential consequences of biased or incomplete data?
6. What is prompt engineering, and why is it critical when using large language models (LLMs)?
7. What insights can legal analytics provide to attorneys, and how can these insights improve case strategies?
8. What are some ethical concerns associated with AI use in the legal field, particularly regarding confidentiality and data security?

CHAPTER 6

EDiscovery: Practices and Tools

Introduction

In your civil procedure courses, you should have gained a general understanding of the structure and processes of discovery. In this chapter, we will focus specifically on eDiscovery, a subset of discovery, while acknowledging areas of overlap between the two. EDiscovery, or electronic discovery, involves the identification, preservation, collection, and review of electronically stored information (ESI) for use as evidence in legal proceedings. ESI can include a wide range of digital data, such as emails, documents, databases, social media posts, audio files, video recordings, and other information stored in electronic formats. One of the most significant challenges you will encounter in eDiscovery is the sheer volume of ESI that must be managed, far surpassing the physical documents traditionally handled in discovery.

In response to the growing prevalence of ESI in litigation, the Federal Rules of Civil Procedure (FRCP) were amended in 2006 to address the unique challenges posed by the increasing prevalence of digitally created information. These amendments introduced the concept of ESI and established guidelines for its management during the discovery process. Key concerns included ensuring the reliability and relevance of ESI while balancing issues related to data privacy, security, and the vast quantities of information involved. Since these amendments, technological advancements—such as predictive coding, data mining, and AI-powered eDiscovery platforms—have revolutionized the process. These tools are specifically designed to quickly and efficiently sift through massive datasets, helping legal professionals identify relevant materials in the age of "big data."

In this chapter, we will begin with a review of some of the key rules from the Federal Rules of Civil Procedure (FRCP) and the practices they inform, like the discovery conference, the litigation hold, relevance and proportionality, and accessibility as they relate to eDiscovery. This review is not intended to be exhaustive and will only cover key concepts before we move on to technology-oriented topics. Next, we will cover the characteristics and locations of electronically stored information (ESI) and the Electronic Discovery Reference Model (EDRM) before moving on to the specifics of technology-assisted review (TAR).

Preceding the 2006 eDiscovery-oriented amendments to the FRCP, two organizations pioneered the field of eDiscovery with detailed research publications and conceptualized models. For a profound dive into both the theory and concepts behind many contemporary eDiscovery practices, I would recommend exploring the publications from the Sedona Conference[1] and the Electronic Discovery Reference Model group.[2]

Relevant Federal Rules and Practices

The *Zubulake* line of cases are largely considered foundational for the practice of eDiscovery because of their attention to detail and thorough examination of the challenges facing ESI and its use in discovery.[3] In this case, there were claims of foul play, with electronic records being intentionally deleted and the cost required to extract the data from backup tapes being held up as prohibitive for production. In a very even-handed judgment, Judge Shira Scheindlin ordered the production of the ESI from the backup tapes with one hand and then required the requesting party to assist in offsetting the cost of production with the other. Pertinently, Judge Scheindlin enumerated a seven-factor test for determining

1. *See* specifically, *The Sedona Principles, Third Edition: Best Practices, Recommendations & Principles for Addressing Electronic Discovery Production*, 19 Sedona Conf. J. 1 (2018), https://thesedonaconference.org/.

2. Electronic Discovery Reference Model, https://edrm.net/.

3. *Zubulake v. UBS Warburg LLC*, 229 F.R.D. 422 (N.Y. 2004).

whether ESI was to be considered so inaccessible that the cost of production should either be shared or born by the party seeking discovery. This test evaluated:

1. Whether or not the request is specifically tailored to demand the production of relevant data.
2. Whether or not the electronically stored information is available from other sources.
3. The cost of production relative to the resources of each party.
4. The cost of production relative to the total amount in controversy.
5. The relative benefit of the electronically stored information to the requesting party.
6. The importance of the issues at stake in the case.
7. The relative ability of the producing party to control its discovery costs.

Since this decision, the FRCP have been updated to reflect the growing relevance of ESI in discovery practices. For our purposes, we will be looking briefly at Rules 26 and 37. FRCP 26(b)(1) now includes a proportionality determination originally established in Judge Scheindlin's seven-factor test, requiring parties to look beyond just what is relevant to the case and also to what is proportional to the needs of the case. Precisely, proportionality is measured by:

> Considering the importance of the issues at stake in the action, the amount in controversy, the parties' relative access to the relevant information, the parties' resources, the importance of the Discovery in resolving the issues, and whether the burden or expense of the proposed Discovery outweighs its likely benefit. Information within the scope of Discovery need not be admissible in evidence to be discoverable.[4]

Additionally, Rule 26(f) and its application have established common practice that this pre-trial meet and confer be the place where issues surrounding eDiscovery between parties be discussed and settled. The 26(f) conference is required before any discovery can occur, and a written report outlining the agreed-upon discovery plan must be submitted to the

4. Fed. R. Civ. P. 26(b)(1).

court within two weeks after the conference. This conference is crucial as it helps establish the scope of the litigation hold we will be discussing. Finally, Rule 37(e) establishes the standard for allowing unfavorable assumptions about unintentional deletion of ESI. In the *Zubulake* string of cases, the court determined that Warburg had willfully spoiled evidence, and the jury was permitted to make an adverse inference regarding what the evidence would have shown. With the amendments to the FRCP, this negative inference option was curtailed to requiring a finding of intent to deprive opposing parties of the evidence.

Relevance and Proportionality

A crucial concept emphasized by the FRCP in the context of eDiscovery is proportionality. Under Rule 26(b)(1), the scope of discovery is limited to what is "proportional to the needs of the case," reflecting the recognition that the vast quantities of ESI generated by modern organizations require careful management. This proportionality principle helps ensure that eDiscovery remains efficient and manageable, avoiding the excessive costs and delays that could result from the indiscriminate production of large volumes of ESI.

Proportionality in eDiscovery is primarily a balancing test, with one side of the scale containing the likelihood of uncovering evidence relevant to the case at hand and the other the burdens relative to the party of whom discovery is being requested. It is interesting for our purposes that the majority of the factors weighed against the likelihood of recovering relevant information have to do with cost and access. The access factor will make more sense as we move through an explanation of ESI and the Electronic Discovery Reference Model (EDRM). The factor of cost is interesting because the cost associated with entirely unfettered eDiscovery would far outweigh the amount in controversy of most cases many times over. An article by Everlaw estimated that the document review process alone has ballooned to roughly $42 billion per year in the legal industry, not to mention costs for data storage, processing, or security.[5]

5. Justin Smith, *Ediscovery Costs in 2024*, EVERLAW (Jan. 9, 2024), https://www.everlaw.com/blog/ediscovery-best-practices/ediscovery-costs-in-2024/#:~:text=Data%20Type%20and%20Size&text=A%20more%20complex%20file%20might,money%20to%20process%20as%20well.

For a much more in-depth exploration of the concept of proportionality in eDiscovery I would recommend taking a look at the Sedona Principles. The Sedona Conference is a nonprofit research institute that has drafted some of the most informative content on eDiscovery available, including the Sedona Principles, which are drafted very similarly to a Restatement.[6]

Discovery Conference

Federal Rule of Civil Procedure 26 requires that parties meet together and essentially hash out the details of discovery in the case at hand before it proceeds. The moment a case begins, both parties have to start preparation for the discovery process. As we will continue to discuss, the sheer volume of ESI maintained by organizations can be overwhelming unless an appropriate scope is set, which is where the Rule 26(f) conference comes in. Think of this conference as a strategy meeting that just happens to be required by the Federal Rules of Civil Procedure. The purpose is to help both sides get on the same page about how discovery will proceed, especially when it comes to eDiscovery. The Rule 26(f) conference is your chance to work with opposing counsel to outline the rules of engagement for eDiscovery. Imagine playing a board game with the Rule 26(f) conference being where you and your opponent meet and agree on house rules before starting.

Rule 26(f) is framed in such a way as to encourage cooperation between parties regarding the eDiscovery process. Additionally, the Sedona Conference issued a cooperation proclamation, which would carry the weight of sense but little else, except that many members of the judiciary have signed on endorsing the concept of cooperation in eDiscovery.[7] The proclamation advocates for a shift toward cooperative and transparent discovery practices in legal proceedings, particularly in managing ESI. It highlights the burdens and inefficiencies of adversarial discovery, emphasizing that cooperation aligns with ethical advocacy

---

6. *The Sedona Principles, Third Edition: Best Practices, Recommendations & Principles for Addressing Electronic Discovery Production*, 19 Sedona Conf. J. 1 (2018), https://thesedonaconference.org/sites/default/files/publications/The%20Sedona%20Principles%20Third%20Edition.19TSCJ1.pdf.

7. *The Sedona Conference Cooperation Proclamation*, https://thesedonaconference.org/cooperation_proclamation.

and benefits everyone involved. The proclamation's ultimate goal is to reduce the costs of discovery, minimize costly disputes, and uphold the principles of justice and efficiency in the legal system. The Rule 26(f) conference, therefore, is the perfect venue for discussing the scope of the litigation hold, ESI custodians and data sources, the scope of discovery, and the process for producing ESI to discovery requests.

The Litigation Hold

Most large organizations have a policy in place that governs information retention. As you will see when we discuss the EDRM, these information governance policies involve setting a process for deletion of ESI. There is nothing nefarious about the routine deletion of ESI; while the storage costs have decreased greatly over time, they can still be significant, not to mention the expertise required to maintain ESI in any meaningful format or keeping it usably organized as the amount increases.

A litigation hold (also called a legal hold) is a directive within an organization to preserve all data that might be relevant to a potential lawsuit or regulatory investigation. In practical terms, once an organization has been made aware of possible legal proceedings, it is under an obligation to save an unaltered set of data, including metadata, of all information relevant to the scope of the hold request. The discovery conference will help narrow the scope of what must be preserved, but initially, it is advisable to opt for broad preservation.

At the outset, IT professionals and legal teams identify which data sources—such as email servers, cloud platforms, or physical devices—could contain relevant information. After those sources have been identified, instructions must be provided to suspend any routine deletions that might be included in the organization's information governance policies and implement access controls. Access controls are the policies, mechanisms, and technologies an organization uses to regulate who can view, modify, or interact with its data, systems, and physical or virtual resources. They help isolate evidence from broad access and help ensure that no one will inadvertently alter or destroy critical evidence.

As soon as data is placed under legal hold, each item's path is carefully tracked. Any copy or transfer—from a user's mailbox to a secured repository, for example—is documented to show precisely when and where the data moved. This documentation becomes part of the audit trail, often including date and time stamps, information about the individuals handling the data, and the specific systems involved. Throughout the process, tamper-evident or read-only storage solutions should be used so the evidence remains in its original state. These practices should render it extremely difficult for the data to be modified unnoticed. Each step in the evidence's lifecycle—initial preservation, subsequent review by the legal team, any third-party processing or storage, and eventual release from the hold if applicable—should be recorded in detail, tying the data back to the original collection point. This careful logging provides the necessary transparency if a court later questions whether data was altered or misplaced. It should be noted that if employees use personal devices for work, those devices can also fall under the scope of a litigation hold, and employees should be made aware of this possibility prior to engaging in any bring-your-own-device practices.

Many enterprise systems provide options for implementing a litigation hold setting. An enterprise system merely refers to a large-scale software platform designed to support and coordinate numerous business processes across an entire organization. This setting suspends normal retention or deletion rules for specific users or datasets. This ensures that even if a policy is set to delete emails older than six months, those belonging to users under hold will be kept intact for however long the hold remains in effect. In cloud-based services, the litigation hold feature typically locks down user accounts so that no files or messages can be permanently removed until the hold is lifted, thereby preventing spoilation.

In Microsoft 365, for example, the litigation hold feature is designed to preserve potentially relevant data in Exchange and Sharepoint. When the litigation hold is enabled, Microsoft 365 essentially suspends routine purging or modification of emails, chat logs, or files that match the parameters you specify. Typically, this type of process is enabled from the Microsoft Purview (Compliance) portal or Exchange Admin Center, depending on your license and administrative permissions. This is not a feature that the majority of employees are going to have access to. When a litigation hold is created, deleted items are retained in a Recoverable Items folder in the user's mailbox, and items deleted from this Recoverable Items folder are retained for the duration of the hold. Additionally, identified users' primary and archived mailboxes are retained, and storage quotas are dramatically increased to accommodate the influx of data to the Recoverable Items folder.[8]

After the hold is in place, IT teams typically generate "snapshots" or targeted exports of critical data for counsel to review. These snapshots might be stored in a secure, read-only repository (like many eDiscovery platforms) to ensure further edits do not compromise the evidence. Larger organizations often rely on eDiscovery software that automates the process of collecting data, tagging it for relevance, and providing search and review capabilities for attorneys while still keeping an audit trail for each piece of information. Smaller entities may undertake a more manual process, such as creating archival copies of relevant mailboxes or network folders. Either way, logging the specific dates, file paths, and users encompassed by the hold is essential to demonstrate compliance and avoid later disputes about the thoroughness of the process. A litigation hold may need to be maintained for months or years. The audit trail associated with the initial preservation of the data all the way until its eventual release from the legal hold and all documented interactions with that data in between is referred to as the chain of custody. If a hold is not correctly implemented or if the organization allows critical files to be deleted or changed after it should have been aware of the potential litigation, courts can impose sanctions or adverse inferences against the offending party.

ESI Custodians and Data Sources

ESI custodians are the individuals or entities (e.g., cloud platforms) who possess or control ESI that could be relevant to the potential dispute or regulatory investigation that triggers the legal hold. In practical terms, these custodians are often employees, contractors, or departments responsible for data—such as email, documents, databases, or intranets—that may become evidence in a case. A senior manager involved in key decisions might be a custodian of key emails stored in her mailbox. An IT employee could be a custodian if they maintain system

8. Robert Mazzoli and Stephanie Savell, *Create a Litigation hold*, Microsoft Learn (Jan. 12, 2025), https://learn.microsoft.com/en-us/purview/ediscovery-create-a-litigation-hold.

logs or other records. Even outside vendors can serve as custodians if they handle relevant corporate data.

One of the first steps in the legal hold is determining which people or systems are likely to have created, received, or stored information pertinent to the issues in question. This process can involve reviewing organizational charts to find out which employees oversaw a particular project or interviewing department heads and managers about who was most involved in key decisions. In more complex scenarios, IT and legal teams collaborate, mapping out possible data repositories to track where digital information resides and which employees have control over it. Once these custodians have been identified, their data becomes subject to the legal hold. By preserving the content in those custodians' mailboxes, drives, or applications, the organization demonstrates due diligence in protecting potentially relevant evidence through the legal hold and chain of custody.

Electronically Stored Information

ESI encompasses any data created, stored, or utilized in electronic format. If you consider this seemingly simple definition, it will begin to dawn on you just how vast a universe it encompasses, especially if you take it outside of a personal context and consider it in light of the day-to-day activities of an organization of even modest size. Consider the following list of potential sources of ESI:

1. Emails: Both sent and received, along with attachments. Also, consider email chains between members within an organization would each generate ESI unique to that person's email account, increasing the copies of each message in an email chain exponentially.
2. Text and instant messages: SMS texts, Messenger, Teams, GroupMe, and so on.
3. Social media posts: Public and private messages, comments, and shared media on social media platforms and the pertinent metadata associated with it.
4. Electronic documents: Spreadsheets, Word documents, presentations, and all of the associated metadata.
5. Databases and all of their contents.

6. Digital photograph, audio, and video files.
7. Web browser history and bookmarks for devices associated with all relevant members of an organization.
8. System logs and audit trails: Logs from applications or servers showing user activities or security events.
9. Deleted files: This would likely require the involvement of computer forensics to recover inadvertently deleted data.
10. Cloud-stored data: Information stored on cloud services like OneDrive, Google Drive, or Dropbox.
11. Information on mobile devices like smartphones or tablets associated with members of the organization.
12. Backup files and device images.
13. Collaborative documents: In this situation, a copy of the document for each member of the collaboration would be produced.
14. Network and IT systems data: Logs, security events, and security configurations.
15. Geolocation data for devices that track location through apps or GPS.
16. Metadata: Hidden data embedded in files, such as timestamps, author information, document revisions, or geolocation data.

Aside from the sheer volume of data created in electronic format, two of the other troubling qualities of ESI are its volatility and ease of duplication. To illustrate, imagine a group e-mail between four parties. The initial message would generate the sent message from the initial message and three copies, one in each inbox. Moving forward from that conversation, the duplication of messages would continue as long as the conversation lasted, ending with four copies of every message sent in that conversation. Additionally, metadata from duplicated documents can become very confusing. A relevant example from the Sedona Principles highlights the potential problems associated with this sort of duplication:

> A native format file contains application metadata that may not always be contextually accurate. For example, when a Microsoft Word document is created, the computer on which that document is saved may automatically assign the document an "author" based on the information stored on that computer. That document subsequently may be used as a tem-

> plate by other persons, but the original "author" information may not change. Thus, subsequent iterations of the document may carry as an "author," a person with no knowledge of the document's content. Similarly, if a Microsoft Word document is created on one machine and transferred to and saved to a second machine without being altered, the copy on the second machine (erroneously) will show the date the document was saved to the second machine as the date created.[9]

Regarding volatility, compare the fluid nature of digital files with that of hard-copy documents in the past. Once a document has been printed, it is more difficult to alter than if the file is still in its native format on a computer. This seems like a simple concept, but consider the need to collect ESI from organizations while they continue operating. The number of people creating and deleting data daily, coupled with the need to preserve helpful evidence and not inadvertently run afoul of rules governing evidence preservation, can result in quite the convoluted puzzle without a comprehensive information governance plan; this brings us to the Electronic Discovery Reference Model.

Electronic Discovery Reference Model

The EDRM refers to both a framework for conceptualizing the eDiscovery process and the community and advisory group responsible for maintaining it. Along with the Sedona Conference, EDRM is one of the most informative organizations on eDiscovery there is. They provide tools for measuring the degree of preparedness of a given organization, security and audit lists, and budget calculators for eDiscovery. If you consult Figure 6-1 you will see the EDRM model that conceptualizes the eDiscovery process.[10] We will be focusing primarily on the EDRM, but Figure 6-2 also provides an enhanced view of the Information Gover-

---

9. *The Sedona Principles, Third Edition: Best Practices, Recommendations & Principles for Addressing Electronic Discovery Production*, 19 Sedona Conf. J. 1, cmt. 12.a (2018), https://thesedonaconference.org/sites/default/files/publications/The%20Sedona%20Principles%20Third%20Edition.19TSCJ1.pdf.

10. *Electronic Discovery Reference Model 2.0, Simplified Model*, 2023, https://edrm.net/edrm-model/current/.

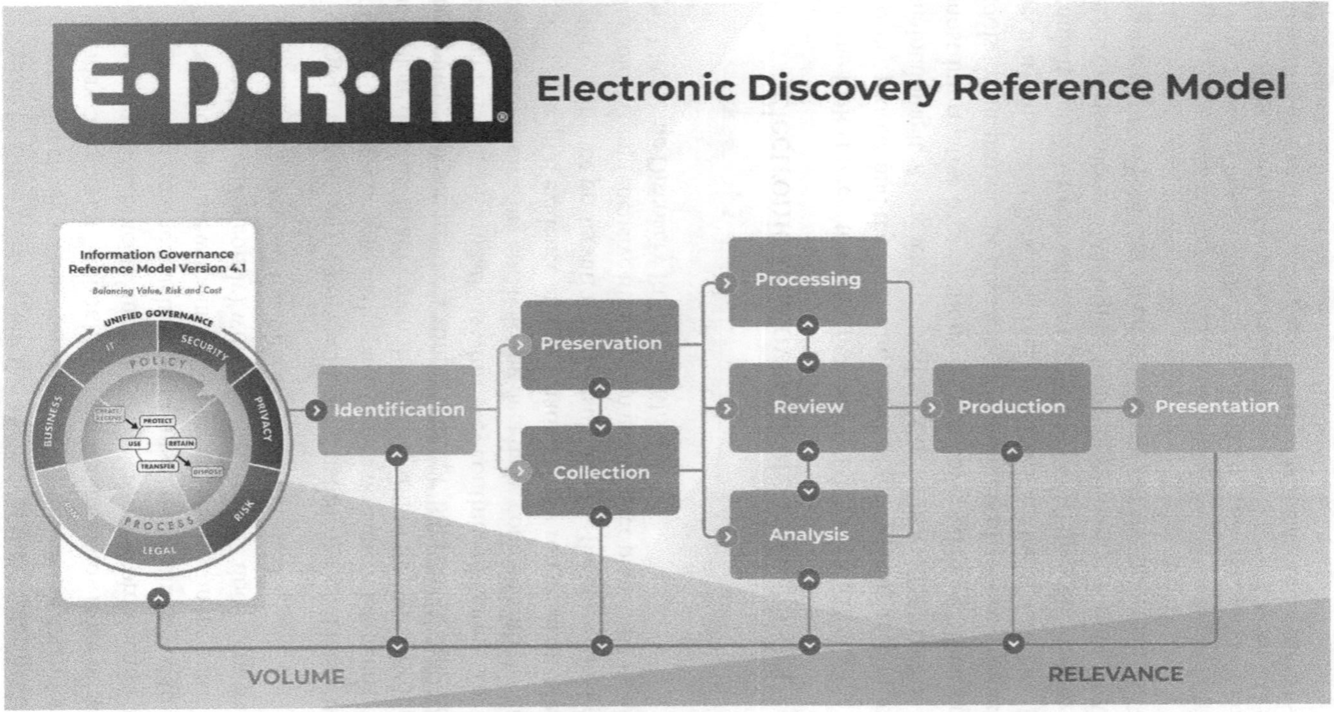

Figure 6-1: Electronic Discovery Reference Model (EDRM). Copyright 2023 EDRM. Creative Commons Attribution 4.0 International (EDRM.net).

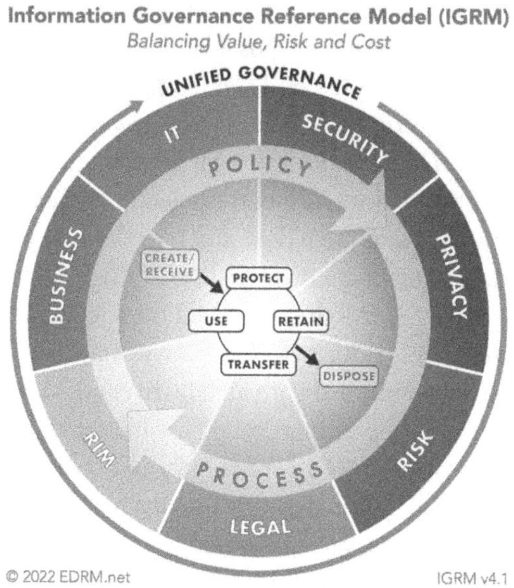

Figure 6-2: Information Governance Reference Model (IGRM). Copyright 2023 EDRM. Creative Commons Attribution 4.0 International (EDRM.net).

nance Reference Model (IGRM).[11] A well-established IGRM is key to developing responsive policies for responding to litigation holds and acceptable document retention policies.

You can see at first glance at the EDRM that the volume of data decreases and relevance increases as an organization moves through and processes its ESI for eDiscovery. Through this process it is, among other things, eliminating duplicative or irrelevant data and isolating privileged data from the starting mass of information.

An exhaustive discussion of the stages of eDiscovery is beyond the scope of this text. Instead, we will briefly cover the stages to provide an overview before moving into the various technologies currently involved in the eDiscovery world. The EDRM emphasizes identifying, collecting, and producing ESI for legal proceedings. You'll notice that the process begins with the IGRM; however, it is probably best to view the IGRM as the natural state in which an organization operates. It is a unified concep-

11. *Information Governance Reference Model*, 2023, https://edrm.net/resources/frameworks-and-standards/information-governance-reference-model/.

tual framework directing an organization on how to handle data throughout its lifecycle from creation to disposal with the goal of complying with relevant legal and industry standards and with an eye towards reducing any potential eDiscovery costs. These policies are often put together through consultation between IT and legal departments to balance practicality and ensure the ability to respond efficiently to eDiscovery requests.

The first step away from the IGRM and into the EDRM would be the identification stage. This stage involves identifying potential sources of relevant ESI that may need to be preserved for a legal matter. This step would engage once an organization has been notified of a possible lawsuit. You'll notice, however, that with an effective IGRM operating as the status quo, there would be a retention policy in place that would act to prevent accidental deletion of relevant information leading up to that legal action. The focus of the identification stage is on recognizing the scope of potentially discoverable information. At this stage, legal teams work closely with IT departments to understand where data is stored (e.g., emails, databases, cloud storage) and what types of information may be relevant. An example might be a company facing a patent infringement suit identifying all emails, documents, and engineering reports pertinent to the design and development of the product in question. The identification stage involves not only identifying the sources and locations of information but also those individuals within a company responsible for that information: the custodians.

After the relevant information has been identified, we move to the preservation stage, where steps are taken to preserve the data to ensure it is not destroyed or altered. Recall that ESI is volatile, and its susceptibility to change correlates directly with the number of organizational actors who have access to it. Preservation involves issuing a litigation hold to custodians of the relevant ESI, instructing them not to modify or delete it. Failure to preserve relevant data can run afoul of the FRCP and result in sanctions, including adverse inference instructions or fines.

Next, the collection stage involves gathering the relevant ESI from its various containers for review and analysis. Collection needs to be done in a manner that ensures the integrity of the data (no alterations or corruptions) and maintains the chain of custody. It's vital that the data remains admissible in court and can be easily authenticated. This is the stage where eDiscovery professionals begin to take a more prominent role as they coordinate with IT professionals and the legal team to retrieve data from servers, cloud storage, and mobile devices in such a way as to ensure all relevant documents are captured for review but ensuring that the chain of custody is preserved.

The processing, review, and analysis stages are primarily where the technologies we will be discussing come into play. The processing stage involves removing duplicative or irrelevant information from the collected data, making it easier to review. Processing reduces the volume of data, normalizes file formats, and ensures that the remaining information is structured in a way that facilitates effective legal review. The review stage involves attorneys examining the processed data to determine what is relevant, privileged, or confidential. The goal is to review the ESI for relevance to the case and identify any privileged information that should be withheld from production. Legal teams often use technology-assisted review (TAR) or predictive coding to speed up the process while ensuring accuracy. The analysis stage involves digging deeper into the ESI to identify patterns, uncover critical facts, or assess the context of the documents. Analysis can help attorneys identify key documents, relationships between parties, and gaps in the evidence. It often involves creating timelines or conducting keyword searches to uncover insights from the data.

Finally, the production and presentation stages involve the output of the data after it has gone through the previous processes. The production stage consists of the delivery of relevant, non-privileged ESI to opposing counsel or regulatory authorities in a format that would be useful to them. The goal is to provide the requested information in a usable and accessible format, adhering to the court's or agency's specifications or the specifications agreed to in any pre-trial discovery conferences between parties. Data may be produced in native formats (e.g., .xlsx, .docx) or as image files (e.g., PDFs or TIFFs) with accompanying metadata. The presentation stage, as its name implies, involves presenting ESI to the factfinder in a way that is understandable to the audience. It ensures that the data retained from the previous stages has been preserved in such a way that it is formatted and readily authenticated for trial. This stage also involves elements from Chapter 7, on courtroom technology. It is necessary to format data in a way that makes complex information more digestible for non-technical audiences.

Technology-Assisted Review

Technology assisted review (TAR), also referred to as computer-assisted review (CAR), refers to the process of implementing machine learning concepts and AI to assist lawyers and other legal professionals in sifting through large volumes of ESI for the purpose of eDiscovery and document review. Historically, the review process demanded extensive manual examination of emails, documents, system logs, and other forms of digital content to locate items relevant to litigation, regulatory inquiries, or internal investigations. The advent of TAR has significantly changed the landscape of discovery by offering faster, more accurate, and more cost-effective ways to sort, prioritize, and categorize massive datasets. While TAR is not a single, monolithic product—instead, it is an umbrella term encompassing various components and approaches—certain core technologies recur across different implementations. These include machine learning algorithms, predictive coding, natural language processing, clustering and concept grouping, email threading, de-duplication, and even privilege detection. Each of these facets contributes to an integrated framework that can dramatically reshape how legal and compliance teams approach document review.

Although TAR solutions can vary from one vendor to another, most share foundational underpinnings in machine learning. As you will remember from Chapter 5, machine learning describes a branch of artificial intelligence where algorithms learn from sample data, identifying patterns that they can later apply to new, unseen data. In a document review scenario, the software might be shown a set of documents the legal team has coded as relevant or irrelevant. By analyzing the text within these sample documents and detecting patterns—repetitive phrases, certain keywords, the presence of specific types of metadata—the algorithm trains itself to predict which other documents in the broader corpus might also be relevant or irrelevant. Over time, as users confirm or correct the software's predictions, the algorithm refines its model, improving accuracy in classifying documents. The continual interaction between the human reviewer's feedback and the machine's evolving model exemplifies the central role that machine learning plays in TAR. Rather than manually sorting hundreds of thousands or millions of documents, the legal team can focus on verifying and refining the model's decisions on smaller subsets, thereby achieving high levels of precision without exhaustive human review of every single page.

A common term frequently associated with machine learning in eDiscovery is "predictive coding." Predictive coding can be viewed as a specialized application of machine learning algorithms, typically designed for the classification and prioritization of documents in a review workflow. The process often begins by having human reviewers examine a "seed set" of documents, carefully labeling them as relevant or irrelevant to the matter. The software then analyzes the text, metadata, and any other structured information within these documents to form a statistical model. This model can assign probabilistic relevance scores to unreviewed documents, effectively ranking them from most likely to be relevant to least likely. With this ranking in place, attorneys or paralegals can prioritize the top-scoring items, which the model suggests should be reviewed first. As the reviewers confirm or reject these predictions, that feedback is fed back into the software, allowing it to iteratively refine its classification rules. Eventually, the legal team can reach a point of diminishing returns where the software demonstrates high confidence in its labeling of remaining items, allowing the bulk of irrelevant documents to be bypassed after minimal manual inspection. Predictive coding, therefore, has become a potent cost-saving and time-saving tool, especially in cases that involve voluminous ESI where months of manual review might otherwise be necessary.

Natural language processing (NLP) is another integral element of technology assisted review. NLP focuses on enabling machines to interpret and "understand" human language in a way that goes beyond simple keyword matching. Using advanced computer methods, NLP can analyze sentence structures, understand relationships between words, and even figure out emotions in specific situations. In the eDiscovery setting, NLP can help identify documents that discuss certain concepts or entities even when the particular keywords used in a search query do not appear directly in the text. For example, an email might contain language describing an individual's job function, or referencing a corporation's subsidiary, without using the precise name or label an attorney might initially have in mind. The NLP algorithms can detect these connections by analyzing the context, synonyms, and relationships within the text. This approach reduces the risk of missing important content simply because the dataset uses unexpected phrasing. Additionally, NLP can be applied to categorize documents by topics and concepts, detect duplicative discussions across different documents, and highlight unusual language usage that may warrant closer scrutiny. Such capabilities can significantly enhance the thoroughness of the review and reduce the burden of sifting through mountains of irrelevant data.

While predictive coding and NLP are primarily concerned with classification and interpretation, another vital dimension of TAR is the clustering and concept grouping process. Clustering is a technique where the system groups documents that share similar features—whether those features come in the form of textual similarity, metadata markers, or even authorship. For instance, if there is a significant conversation thread among employees about a product recall, one can anticipate that many documents will repeatedly cite similar language, dates, or references to the same set of people. Clustering algorithms can detect these similarities automatically, creating logical groupings. Reviewers can examine a representative sample from each cluster to quickly ascertain what those documents are about and how relevant they might be. Meanwhile, concept grouping extends beyond strict textual overlap and attempts to identify thematic or conceptual overlaps, even when the identical words are not used. For example, a cluster might contain documents discussing "marketing budgets," and another cluster might contain documents discussing "advertising funds," which, at a broad conceptual level, are closely related, even if the keywords do not match exactly. By grouping such documents, TAR platforms empower lawyers and reviewers to gain a bird's-eye view of the topics under discussion in the dataset, allowing them to prioritize clusters or concepts that align with the matter's legal issues.

Email threading is another feature that significantly reduces duplication of effort and confusion during a review. In most corporate environments, emails rarely exist as single, standalone messages; instead, they evolve into threads that can span multiple participants, times, and iterations. Without a robust threading mechanism, a reviewer might end up reading the same text over and over. Email threading algorithms piece together the chronology of a conversation, identifying which message is a reply or forward of a prior message and which segments of text are quoted carry-overs from older messages. By recognizing that certain content is repeated from an earlier point in the chain, the system can display to the reviewer only the unique portions of each message. This not only saves time but also reduces the likelihood that important context is missed. Instead of rummaging through multiple near-duplicate emails to figure out the final state of the conversation, the reviewer can see a single-threaded view that depicts the entire storyline. From a legal perspective, thorough comprehension of an email chain is often crucial in discerning who knew what and when and how instructions or information may have changed over the course of a series of communications. Email threading thus directly supports a more accurate understanding of the facts while drastically reducing redundant reading.

A natural companion to threading is de-duplication, another key function within technology assisted review platforms. Large corporate datasets frequently contain multiple versions of the same document, whether due to employees sharing attachments, saving drafts, or forwarding copies to different parties. De-duplication uses hashing algorithms, metadata comparisons, and textual similarity checks to identify files that are effectively identical or so highly similar that they can be regarded as duplicates for review purposes. Once the system flags these duplicates, an attorney or reviewer can designate one "master" version for thorough review while skipping or automatically tagging the duplicates as non-reviewable duplicates. The system will still maintain links indicating that these duplicates existed if they become relevant for verifying the authenticity or completeness of the data. However, from a workflow standpoint, the reviewer is spared from reading the same 200-page policy document half a dozen times. Over large datasets, de-duplication alone can result in a substantial reduction in review time, not to mention a significant decrease in costs for the client or organization in question.

Privilege detection further exemplifies how these TAR capabilities can extend into more specialized legal tasks. Privileged documents, often those that contain attorney–client communications or attorney work product, must be identified and separated from the main batch of discoverable content. This step is critical because inadvertent disclosure of privileged information can lead to serious legal consequences, including the potential for waiver of privilege. Traditional review methods might involve applying search terms like "legal advice," "attorney–client," or "confidential," but these simple text-based filters are notoriously imperfect and can produce many false positives or negatives. With TAR techniques—especially predictive coding, NLP, and concept analysis—the system can learn from examples of truly privileged documents what legal communications tend to look like in an organization. For instance, the presence of counsel's email domain and specific language structures or references to a legal matter might be strong indicators of privilege. Once the system identifies a document as likely to be privileged, it flags it for specialized handling by attorneys who can confirm whether it should be withheld, redacted, or produced with privilege exceptions. This approach reduces the chance of accidental disclosures and streamlines the often painstaking process of privilege review.

To appreciate the full scope of technology assisted review, it helps to envision how these tools integrate in an actual eDiscovery workflow. At the beginning of a matter, counsel or a litigation support team collects data from relevant custodians. This dataset might be enormous, containing hundreds of thousands or even millions of documents. The next step involves ingestion into a TAR platform where machine learning, NLP, and clustering help categorize the data, identify major topics, and highlight documents that appear to have high relevance. Meanwhile, email threading and de-duplication keep the review from being cluttered by endless copies or repetitive threads. Attorneys can then use predictive coding to rank documents by likelihood of relevance or privilege. High-value documents—those the system flags as being critical—are pushed to the top of the review queue, ensuring that attorneys see them as early as possible. Lower-ranked documents might be sampled periodically to confirm that the system's classification is still accurate. This iterative cycle continues, with humans guiding the technology and the technology reducing the burden on humans until counsel can confidently say they have identified and reviewed all documents that truly matter for the case.

Despite the broad benefits of TAR, it is essential to acknowledge that it does not entirely replace human expertise. While the technology excels at pattern recognition and can drastically reduce the volume of documents that require direct human oversight, attorneys remain responsible for the final decisions about relevance, privilege, and strategy. Courts and regulators generally accept the use of TAR, and in many jurisdictions, judges have allowed or even encouraged parties to use predictive coding to handle massive datasets. Still, lawyers must ensure that their use of TAR satisfies legal standards. That typically involves documenting how the process was carried out, maintaining logs of training and validation, and sometimes providing statistical measures of accuracy or recall. If the opposing side challenges the methodology, the party using TAR must be ready to show that their approach was fair, transparent, and thorough.

Nevertheless, implementing a TAR solution does come with potential pitfalls. One issue is the risk of over-reliance on the model's early predictions. If the seed set used to train the model is not representative of the data as a whole—perhaps it omits a significant category of documents related to the dispute—the model can develop blind spots. This is why iterative training and sampling are essential: the legal team must continually evaluate whether the tool is capturing all the relevant issues. Another challenge involves the sophisticated infrastructure required to handle large datasets. TAR generally demands robust computational resources and a well-designed platform that can efficiently process documents, store metadata, and offer intuitive review interfaces. For smaller firms or organizations lacking strong IT support, implementing such technology can be daunting. Lastly, not every jurisdiction or opposing counsel is equally comfortable with machine-driven review; while attitudes have evolved, there are still contexts in which the parties or the bench might insist on more traditional or at least heavily audited manual approaches.

One of the underlying reasons TAR has gained acceptance is that it aligns with fundamental principles of proportionality and reasonableness. Discovery is supposed to be thorough but also not so burdensome as to be impossible in scope or cost. TAR makes it feasible to handle enormous volumes of data without resorting to either highly superficial skimming or letting litigation balloon into a protracted war of attrition over discovery. By employing predictive coding and other advanced review techniques, parties can prove to courts that they used state-of-the-art methods to identify relevant documents effectively, thus meeting their discovery obligations. Moreover, courts recognize that in many modern cases, manual review of every single document would be prohibitively expensive. Consequently, many judges see well-documented TAR approaches as a preferable solution, as long as the process is transparent and the parties meet their obligations in good faith.

What emerges, then, is a pattern in which technology and human oversight complement one another. The TAR software automates the laborious and repetitive aspects of review—spotting patterns, grouping similar items, and assigning predictive relevance scores—while the attorneys focus on final decision-making, verification, and strategizing. Email threading and de-duplication keep the review streamlined, reducing costs and ensuring that content is not overlooked. Privilege detection algorithms highlight potentially sensitive documents, preventing unwarranted disclosures. NLP-based concept grouping and clustering help attorneys visualize the thematic shape of the dataset, uncovering trends or issues they might otherwise overlook. Over the course of this process, the machine learning model improves with feedback, continually refining its ability to separate relevant from irrelevant items. By the end of the review, the legal team can be confident in the completeness of their production, having minimized the odds that crucial evidence lies buried in the archives.

Conclusion

EDiscovery has revolutionized how legal professionals navigate the discovery process, allowing for the efficient handling of vast quantities of electronically stored information (ESI). From foundational case law such as *Zubulake* to the integration of advanced technologies like technology-assisted review, the evolution of eDiscovery reflects the legal field's response to the complexities of the digital age.

Key concepts such as proportionality, relevance, and the litigation hold have become indispensable tools in managing ESI. The Electronic Discovery Reference Model (EDRM) offers a structured approach to the eDiscovery process, ensuring that the identification, preservation, collection, review, and production of data adhere to both legal standards and practical constraints. Meanwhile, technological advancements, including predictive coding, natural language processing, and clustering, have reduced the time, cost, and human effort required to sift through massive datasets.

However, the effective use of eDiscovery tools requires more than just technical knowledge. Collaboration between legal teams, IT professionals, and opposing counsel is essential to maintain transparency, comply with ethical standards, and ensure that discovery obligations are met. Legal practitioners must also stay vigilant about potential challenges, such as data privacy, over-reliance on algorithms, and maintaining a defensible chain of custody.

Ultimately, eDiscovery exemplifies the power of combining human judgment with technological innovation. By embracing these tools and processes, legal professionals can navigate the complexities of modern litigation more effectively, ensuring both fairness and efficiency in the pursuit of justice. As the legal landscape continues to evolve, staying informed about best practices in eDiscovery will remain critical for success in the digital era.

Review Questions

1. What is eDiscovery, and how does it differ from traditional discovery?
2. List three examples of electronically stored information (ESI) commonly encountered in legal proceedings.
3. What are the key components of the proportionality test under Rule 26(b)(1)?
4. What is the role of Rule 26(f) in eDiscovery, and why is the discovery conference critical?
5. What is a litigation hold, and why is it essential in preserving relevant ESI?
6. Explain the concept of chain of custody and its significance in eDiscovery.
7. Describe the stages of the EDRM and their purpose in the eDiscovery process.
8. How do predictive coding and natural language processing (NLP) enhance document review in TAR?
9. What is email threading, and how does it improve the efficiency of document review?
10. Explain the role of de-duplication in eDiscovery and how it reduces review time and cost.

CHAPTER 7

Courtroom Technology

The effective use of legal technology compared to the effective use of courtroom technology is the difference between watching a movie in your office and performing a show before a live audience. While managing the lighting. Sound. Cameras. And set. There are steps you can take in advance to minimize the chances of unforeseen and embarrassing errors. Still, there is always an element of the dreaded law school cold call when managing technology before a judge or jury at trial.

To optimize your chances of an effective presentation, you should rehearse as many aspects of your case as you can in advance. As with any production, the actors' performance can be made or broken by the work of the techies. If feasible, consider employing a hot seat operator or trial technician to handle the technical side of your presentations. This will not only prevent you from splitting your attention between the technology employed in your case and making an effective case before the court, but also allow for a more professional and seamless presentation of evidence, demonstratives, and slides. Additionally, it is essential to be familiar with the technical assets and liabilities available in the court where you will present your case.

In this chapter, we will focus primarily on improving your knowledge of courtroom technology. However, a critical practice to understand is the employment of a hot seat operator or trial technician. If you are the director of your case, consider the trial technician to be the stage manager, coordinating the timing and execution of the presentation, responding to "cues" from the attorney-director, making sure that each piece of evidence appears at the precise moment it is needed, and quickly troubleshooting any unforeseen technical difficulties to ensure the show goes on.

NITA's *The Trial Presentation Companion*, by Shannon Lex Bales, does a beautiful job of describing best practices for effectively integrating a trial technician into the trial team. Namely, she points out that effective trial teams:

1. Involve the trial tech in the early stages of the case.
2. Plan effective workflow for receiving, processing, and storing exhibits.
3. Plan for redundancy in equipment, software, and storage mediums.
4. Avoid overburdening their trial tech with superfluous tasks.
5. Include the trial tech as a contributing member of the team and not as a glorified button pusher.
6. Include the trial tech in the trial plan and allow them time to become familiar with the physical site of the trial.[1]

Failure to ensure that (1) your trial technician is an integral part of your trial team from the beginning or (2) you, as the attorney deploying the technology on your own, have correctly estimated your skills and, through practice, found them up to the task, can result in catastrophic consequences to your case. Indeed, the fiascos that have resulted from practicing attorneys either baselessly overestimating their skill or underestimating the impact of excessive technical issues on their credibility have led many courts to establish rules for technology-assisted presentations in their courtrooms. For example, the U.S. District Court of the Eastern District of Tennessee provides the following checklist for attorneys wishing to use courtroom technology in proceedings before the court.[2]

As members of a profession that studies the law, we know that rules don't arise in a vacuum and are usually prompted by the actions of individuals that cause rule-makers to pause and say, "There oughta be a law." It is easy to imagine each of the interactions that occurred numerous

1. Shannon Lex Bales, The Trial Presentation Companion: A Step-By-Step Guide to Presenting Electronic Evidence in the Courtroom 12–13 (2018).

2. U.S. District Court for the Eastern District of Tennessee, *Courtroom Checklist*, https://www.tned.uscourts.gov/sites/tned/files/courtroom_checklist.pdf.

Courtroom Checklist

- ☐ Bring sufficient copies of your witness and exhibit lists for the Judge, Courtroom Deputy, and Court Reporter.

- ☐ Bring sufficient pre-marked copies of exhibits. Check your scheduling order or contact the Courtroom Deputy as to whether exhibits should be numbered sequentially or if duplicative numbers can be used (ex. – Pl. 1, Def. 1).

- ☐ Make sure you know how to use the Court's Digital Evidence Presentation System (DEPS) equipment by scheduling a training session with the Courtroom Deputy and/or practicing with your exhibits. Do this *before* the day of your trial or hearing.

- ☐ Make sure that all audio or video exhibits are in the correct format to play on the DEPS equipment. On the Court's website, the Courtroom Technology link will identify the available technology for each courtroom in the district and the technical information for that technology. You can also contact the Courtroom Deputy or the Information Technology department with any questions.

- ☐ Make sure you know how to connect your laptop to the DEPS equipment and send video to the Court's equipment. You need to check this *before* the day of your trial or hearing.

- ☐ Remember that there is no internet connection in the courtrooms.

- ☐ On the day of your trial or hearing, arrive early enough to set up and retest the equipment.

- ☐ Have a backup plan for the presentation of your evidence in case the technology doesn't work.

- ☐ Remember that the DEPS equipment will not alter the quality of your evidence, *i.e.*, the DEPS equipment will not sharpen a blurred photo and an unintelligible audio recording will not be clarified.

- ☐ If you need assistance, bring your computer expert with you. The Court's IT personnel will gladly offer any guidance, but cannot work on *your* equipment.

- ☐ If you have a special request or needs for the presentation of your evidence or for a witness, please provide the Court with 1-2 days advance notice so we can find a solution.

Figure 7-1: An example preparation checklist for the use of technology in the courtroom.

times that prompted the adoption of each of these rules. Every technical mistake or blunder diminishes your credibility with the factfinder and interrupts your primary task when presenting in the courtroom—representing your client and telling their story. This chapter is not meant to be exhaustive; it only serves to highlight common issues that arise and that you should be prepared to address before for trial. Every situation is going to be slightly different, and any guidance provided should take into account the circumstances in which you find yourself.

The Value Behind Visuals and Good Storytelling

One of the theories behind juror decision-making suggests that jurors construct stories based on evidence, prior knowledge, and expectations about what constitutes a complete story.[3] These stories help jurors make sense of the trial by organizing events in a causal and intentional sequence. In summary, jurors construct narratives from the trial evidence, which involves organizing facts into a cohesive story that explains the events. Then, they learn the definitions of legal verdicts, including specific attributes like mental state, circumstances, and actions that define the crime. Finally, they classify their constructed story in the best-fitting verdict category by matching the story's features with the attributes of the verdicts. Their confidence in the verdict often aligns with how well the story aligns with the legal criteria for the verdict.

Effective use of visuals in the courtroom will benefit your storytelling ability by increasing the information retention rate of the jury, reducing evidence complexity, increasing engagement, and preventing the jury's attention rate from deteriorating. As you can see from Figure 7-2, lecture alone provides for the lowest retention rate. Even adding reading of text from a PowerPoint slide increases retention significantly. Taking this a step further, using visuals increases the retention rate even more. Including auditory, visual, and kinesthetic senses in the presentation of information increases retention rate remarkably. A theory of cognition was proposed by Allan Paivio of the University of Western Ontario in 1971, who postulated that both visual and verbal information is used to represent information.[4] Visual and verbal information, however, are

---

3. Nancy Pennington and Reid Hastie, *A Cognitive Theory of Juror Decision Making: The Story Model*, 13 Cardozo L. Rev. 519 (1991).

4. James M. Clark and Allan Paivio, *Dual Coding Theory and Education*, 3(3) Educ. Psychol. Rev. 149 (1991).

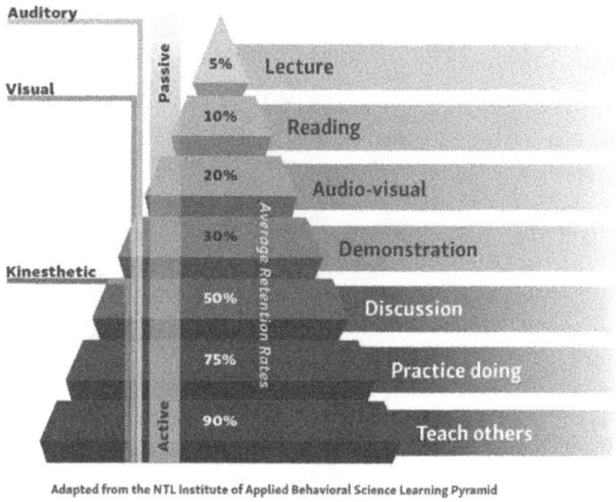

Figure 7-2: A pyramid illustrating the retention rate of various techniques, from least to most effective.

both processed differently by the brain and are processed along very distinct channels, which creates separate representations for information that has been processed in each channel. To break it down to basics, representing information in two formats increases the chances of the jury remembering it, which implies that rising to a third (i.e., kinesthetic) may increase potential retention even further.

When discussing reducing evidence complexity with my students, my favorite example is the following. I can stand in front of the class and tell them that 11 companies control everything that they buy. I could list all of the subsidiaries and the products, and eventually, it's going to be a list that loses their attention and thereby loses its impact, since each of the companies has dozens of sub-brands, and each of those sub-brands has dozens or hundreds of products. Or I could show them the following figure and convey that long list of mind-numbing facts in a bright, colorful, easily digestible graphic.[5]

Finally, effectively using graphics, videos, models, and so on keeps the jurors' attention active and engaged. You are presenting the same information but in a way that keeps their attention from degrading and wandering. Bear in mind that changing rapidly between different

5. I should premise this graphic with the statement that I am not presenting it for its veracity. I have not conducted independent research to verify that. I am presenting it as a demonstration of the effective reduction of information complexity.

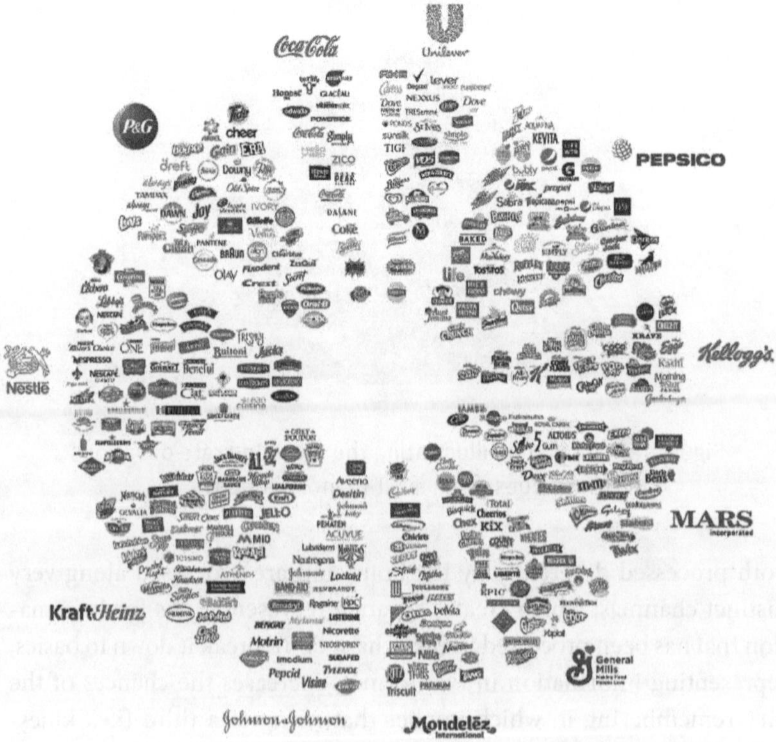

Figure 7-3: Using a graphic to memorably convey information for a jury. These eleven brands have remarkable diversification and market penetration.

modes of presentation can lead to overload or cause the jurors' attention to wander during transitions between presentation types. Additionally, with the inclusion of supplemental presentation media, you increase the necessary preparatory work needed and run the risk of distracting your audience from your point with too many bells and whistles. It is essential to balance the use of courtroom technology to enhance and not override the information you are conveying.

Courtroom Equipment and Systems

Increasingly, courts are updating the technology available in their physical spaces to accommodate more technology-driven presentations and trials, with judges weighing in on what tech should be available in today's courtroom.[6] Despite a minimum threshold of technology offerings developing in the courts, the responsibility of presenting your client's case falls squarely on your shoulders. Being a zealous advocate includes ensuring that the appropriate tools are available to tell their story to the best of your ability. It is essential to acquaint yourself with the systems available in the location where you will be presenting your client's case and to prepare to supplement technology as necessary.

One of the most efficient methods of ascertaining the tools available in a given location is to reach out to the appropriate court personnel and request an opportunity to conduct a tech inventory of the courtroom where you will be presenting. A tech inventory involves an initial assessment of a courtroom's available technology, reviewing required technology from the legal team's perspective, conducting security checks, creating backup and redundancy plans, conducting a final test, and a final-final test (day of trial preparation). The goal of a tech inventory is to compare your team's technology needs against what is available in the courtroom and supplement the shortcomings as necessary. Additionally, putting together a trial kit will ensure that your equipment can connect to the systems you encounter, let you test your equipment to ensure that it is all compatible before trial, and help you determine what backup equipment you should keep on hand.

I want to reiterate the invaluable nature of having a trial tech consulting with your trial team as you prepare; however, I know that this isn't an expense that can be justified for every trial or conveniently absorbed into overhead by every business model. If faced with the prospect of conducting a technology inventory on your own, there are some key items that you should review when doing so. The following list of tips and guidance is meant to be representative of items you should review when conducting your technology inventory. Each trial is unique and

---

6. Judge Herbert B. Dixon, Jr., *The Basics of a Technology-Enhanced Courtroom*, 56 Judges J. 36 (2017), https://www.americanbar.org/content/dam/aba/publications/judges_journal/vol56no4-jj2017-tech.pdf.

has different technology requirements based on the types of evidence presented, and you should customize and expand on this list to fit the needs of your situation.

Audio/Video

Each courtroom is going to have a slightly different method for displaying graphical content, whether that be presentations, videos, imagery, or demonstratives. Some opt for a projector and screen setup, while others have dedicated monitors for courtroom display. The important thing in conducting your technology inventory is to be aware of which combination is employed in the courtroom where you will be presenting. The majority of modern displays utilize either HDMI or USB-C connections (see Figure 7-4). These connections allow the transmission of both video and audio signals and reduce background distortion in both audio and video signals.

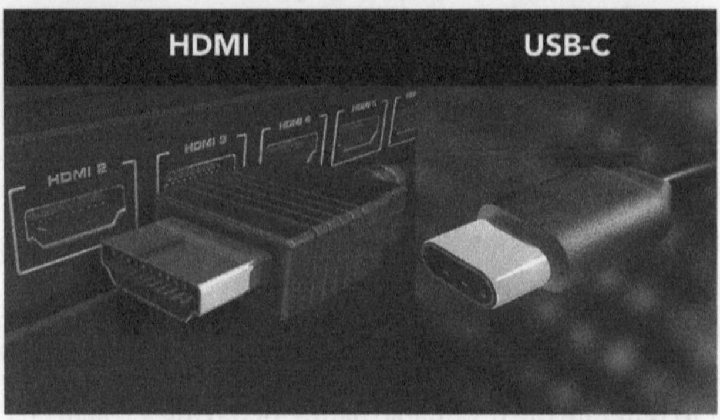

Figure 7-4: A comparison of HDMI and USB-C plugs.

Another prevalent video connection that is rapidly being replaced is VGA. VGA connections do not transmit audio but are often supplemented with an audio jack (see Figure 7-5). HDMI and USB-C are supplanting VGA because they support higher resolutions and refresh rates, transmit audio and visual over a single cable, and are less susceptible to signal degradation.

While you should be aware that some courts still employ VGA/audio jack connections, it is probably unnecessary to include those cables in your trial kit. You should make sure that you have multiple HDMI or

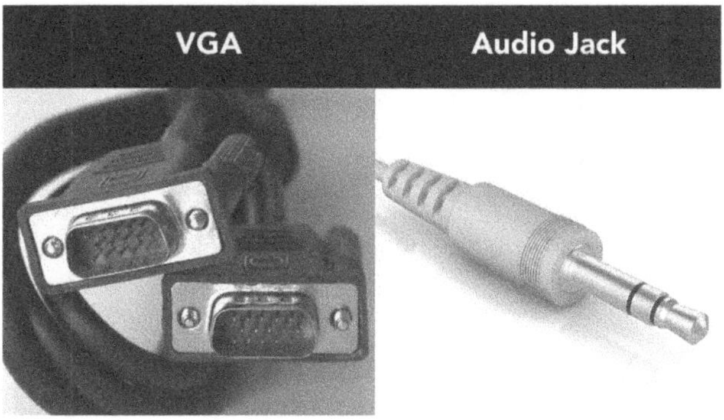

Figure 7-5: The common combination of VGA and an audio jack is being rapidly replaced by USB-C and HDMI connections.

USB-C cables of varying lengths (3', 6', 10' and 25' are standard). Additionally, to avoid a tripping hazard, keep a roll of gaffer's tape in your kit to secure loose cables.

Many courts have integrated systems allowing counsel to connect to their system from a counsel table, a podium, or both. You should note the types of connection or ports, as discussed above (e.g., HDMI, USB-C, VGA), but also note the number of connections and the presence or absence of a switch. A switch has different uses depending on the context, but with an A/V system, an input switch will allow you to connect multiple devices to a system and control which device is displaying at a given time. A four- or six-port switch is a valuable addition to your trial kit, as it will allow you to connect multiple devices to a single input in the courtroom.

As an example of why this is useful, imagine you are presenting before the jury, and in the middle of your presentation, your primary laptop is struck down by the infamous blue screen of death. You have fastidiously backed up your files, so you haven't lost any data, but your backup laptop is tucked snugly in its carrying case, and it will take you at least 10 minutes to turn it on and get it hooked up, assuming that there are no malfunctions, since this will be the first time today that it has been connected to the court system. Would you rather beg the jury's indulgence while opposing counsel quietly revels in the delay to your case? Or would you prefer to have your backup laptop connected and presenting concurrently with your primary device on your handy four-

Figure 7-6: A duplicated display.

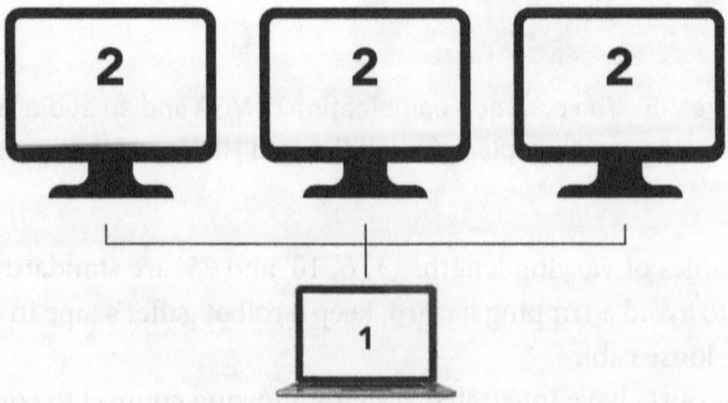

Figure 7-7: An extended display.

port switch, so that with a push of a button, your presentation continues from the same slide with barely a hiccup? This example is a bit extreme, but hopefully it illustrates the benefits of both running a backup laptop alongside your primary and of having multiple devices connected through a video switch.

Whether or not a video switch is present, you should have your laptops set to extended desktop mode instead of duplicating your display. This will create an improvised staging area that allows you or your team to review visuals before they are presented to the factfinder. When you duplicate your desktop (Figure 7-6) any display that your device is connected to will display exactly what is happening on your screen in real time.

With extended desktop (Figure 7-7), the connected screens only display the windows you drag to them. The connected displays and your device's screen function independently of one another, giving you a makeshift staging area. This allows you or your trial technician to preview exhibits and content prior to publishing them to the jury. In so doing, you retain a modicum of control so that if there is some dispute about the evidence you intend to present to the jury, you can have it up for reference on your device without inadvertently publishing it to the jury. Additionally, even though trial presentation software provides the flexibility to edit content before publishing it to the jury (e.g., cropping a video to a relevant section), it may be necessary to make changes to exhibits and content before they are presented to the jury, which can be done privately by your trial technician in extended desktop mode while you are still engaging the jury.

Aspect Ratio and Resolution

Aspect ratio refers to the proportional relationship between the width and height of a display or screen. It is expressed as a ratio, with the most common being 4:3 or 16:9. The aspect ratio is critical to bear in mind when planning your presentation so that you can be aware of how your graphics and slides will appear on the screen. Think of 4:3 as a square and 16:9 as a rectangle. Determining the aspect ratio of the screens in the courtroom will allow you to customize your presentation to be the most effective. When in doubt, opt for creating your presentations and graphics in 4:3 over 16:9 to avoid any nasty surprises, since a 4:3 will be displayed on a 16:9 screen, but a 16:9 graphic will have pieces cropped out when displayed on a 4:3 screen.

Screen resolution refers to the number of pixels displayed on a screen, often described as the width by the height (e.g., 1920 x 1080). The resolution defines the clarity and detail of an image, with higher resolutions containing more pixels, which generally produce sharper images. The screen resolution will give you an idea of the detail you will be able to display on a given screen in the courtroom; the higher the clarity, the more detail and sharper the image will be. For example, a 720p screen with 1280 x 720 pixels will have 1280 pixels along the width and 720 pixels along the height, resulting in 921,600 pixels total, whereas a 4K screen with 3840 x 2160 pixels will have 3480 pixels along its width and 2160 along its height resulting in 8,294,400 pixels total. Aspect ratio defines the shape of the image, while resolution determines the number of pixels contained within that shape. If you can determine the resolution of the screen in the courtroom, you can divide both the width and height by their greatest common divisors (GCD) to discover the aspect ratio.

You can more strategically deploy your trial graphics and presentations by being aware of these concepts. A higher screen resolution ensures that your visuals appear sharp, detailed, and easy to understand. If a resolution is too low, text or images may become pixelated or blurry, which can hinder comprehension and distract from the point being made, thus reducing the impact of the presentation. Ignoring the aspect ratio of a screen can result in your content appearing stretched, squished, or cropped, reducing your credibility before the factfinder.

In summary, aspect ratio affects the shape of your content, while resolution affects how clearly it appears. Before you finalize your presentations, double-check both to make sure your visuals will display correctly.

Court Systems and Procedures

Ensuring that your systems are functioning from the comfort of your office or meeting room is excellent; it allows you to work through all the bugs on your end and ensure all of your systems are backed up and functioning the way they should. Unfortunately, despite many advancements in virtual meeting technology, you will still most likely be presenting in a courtroom, which means your devices have to play nicely with the courtroom's systems. It helps if you are able to make a rough sketch of the courtroom's layout for reference—it doesn't have to be a masterpiece; aim for basic geometric shapes in the same general layout of the courtroom. On this sketch include placement of power outlets relative to where your systems will be setup, location of key screen placement orientation and distance relative to the relevant parties (jury, judge, opposing counsel), system access points (VGA, HDMI, USB-C), and their location (counsel table or shared podium), and the presence and location of a document camera. While artistry is not necessary, distance is.

Distance between key locations in the courtroom will help determine the length and number of cables you will need. Bear in mind, just because something like a power outlet is only three feet from your counsel table doesn't mean a three-foot cable will be sufficient. Frequently, you will need to lay cables along an indirect route to avoid having them in high-traffic areas where they present a tripping hazard. So, plan in advance and adjust your cabling needs to the situation based on your courtroom layout. Make sure that once you have your cabling configured, you deploy gaffer's tape to hold it in place and avoid any tripping hazards.

After you have conducted your tech inventory, you may need to supplement the equipment available in the court where you are presenting. If this is the case, familiarize yourself with the court's procedures for this process. More importantly, make sure you are familiar with the stakeholders at the court who determine these policies and grant exceptions to them. Don't assume that you are free to bring in your own equipment. Some courts have limited IT staff or contract out to third-party support, which means the support staff may not be on site. It would be a nasty surprise indeed to have done months of prep work only to find a key piece of evidence cannot be presented because you aren't able to connect something as small as an adapter to the court's system. In addition to court IT support, you must consider security, both the court's and that of your equipment. Are you going to have to bring the equipment with you every day? Is there a special entrance, or will you have to go through security checkpoints? Can equipment be left in the courtroom? Is the courtroom secured every night?

Finally, make sure that you check your equipment every day before the session begins. This may take a bit of time to complete. You should check that all of your cabling is undisturbed and still connected and taped down. Start-up and log in to your devices and ensure they are operating normally. Open any software you are going to need and let them complete their start-up process (PowerPoint, Trial Presentation Software, Video Players, and so on). Recall from Chapter 1 that the storage sizes of RAM and your CPU registers are significantly smaller than the non-volatile storage of your hard drive. In the context of our current discussion, this means that having too many programs attempting to open at the same time, especially trial presentation software, can lead to a sluggish or unresponsive device as your CPU is overwhelmed, so make sure you open programs consecutively, giving each ample time to complete start-up. Also check to make sure that your system settings have not been changed by any intervening security patches or software updates.

Your system settings should be configured to avoid any unnecessary downtime or jarring transitions. You don't want your system settings to take attention away from the information you are presenting. You should disable sleep mode, remove all icons from your desktop and configure the background to be a solid neutral color (black is preferable), ensure your screen doesn't shut off, and test your system volume while connected to the court's systems to make sure it isn't too loud or soft. These options can be configured from the "System Settings" (in Windows) or "System Preferences" (in Apple) menus.

File Organization, Retention, and Security

There are specific tech skills you should be familiar with if you are planning on using technology to enhance your presentations in a courtroom. These skills are relatively basic, but it is important to bear them in mind when preparing for trial so that you are mindful of them during your presentation and can quickly respond to potential issues.

File Organization

First off, while not limited to a techy skill, it is important to review your organizational skills. In preparation for trial, review the file organization on your device. If possible, determine a data organization plan at the onset of trial preparation and stick to it; otherwise, review your file structures to maximize accessibility. Effective file management involves creating a logical and structured system that makes it easy to find, access, and present your materials. Efficient file management allows for quick retrieval of evidence, minimizes the risk of errors, allows for easy integration with trial presentation software, simplifies backup and recovery, and helps ensure that files are stored in the formats and with labels that will enable them to be easily shared with the court or opposing counsel if required.

Although generalized, Figure 7-8 on the following page provides a good starting point for organizing your case files, specifically your trial presentation materials.

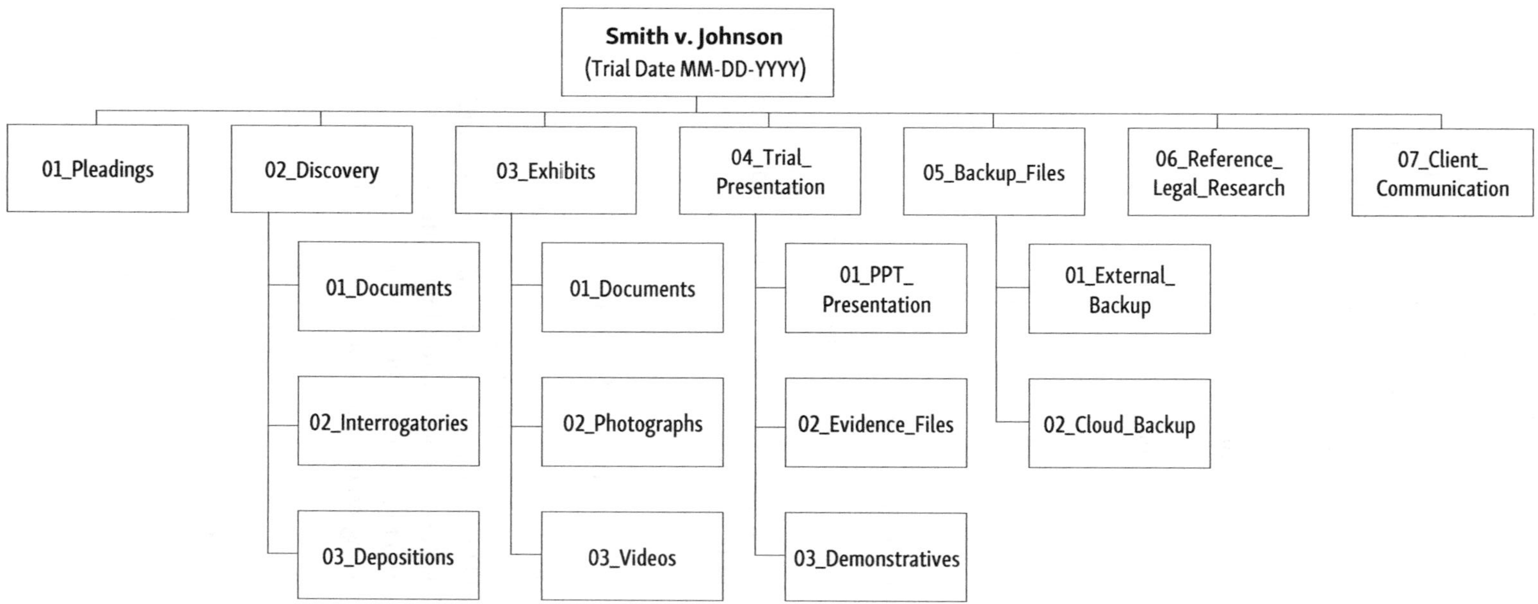

Figure 7-8: Suggested organization of case files for trial presentation.

You will notice that each file has a self-explanatory name and that the naming tends to be consistent throughout the diagram. Continuing deeper into the file organizational system, be sure to include identifiers that allow you to recognize files by their type, date, and subject matter. For example:

- Pleadings: Pleading_[Type]_[FilingDate]_[ShortDescription]
  - Example: Pleading_MotionToDismiss_2024-09-01.docx
- Exhibits: Exhibit_[ExhibitNumber]_[Description]
  - Example: Exhibit_12_SecurityCameraFootage.mp4
- Depositions: Deposition_[Name]_[Date]
  - Example: Deposition_JohnDoe_2024-08-15.pdf
- Presentation Slides: TrialPresentation_[Date]_[Version]
  - Example: TrialPresentation_2024-09-19_v2.pptx

Data Backup and Security

In addition to having your files organized, in preparing for trial you must also formulate a backup strategy and a method for keeping your files secure. It is a good strategy to have both a physical and a digital backup of your trial laptop.

Imaging and Cloning a Laptop

When imaging a hard drive, it is vital that you ensure that your backup storage device has sufficient free space available for the task. Best practice would be to have an external hard drive dedicated to storing the contents of each device, thereby avoiding confusion. The hard drive will typically connect to your device via USB cable. As the process is different for each operating system, I will walk through the process for Windows.

Windows

There are multiple ways to navigate to the menu that you need; the most direct is to either use the search bar at the bottom of the screen or to press Windows + R to bring up a dialog box. In either case simply type in "Control Panel" and press enter. From the control panel you will want to select the "File History" icon.

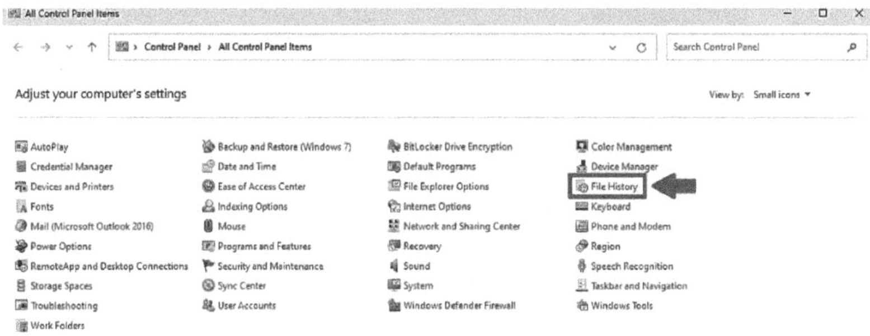

Figure 7-9: The control panel and "File History" icon.

From this window, you will need to locate the "System Image Backup" option, which is located in the lower left of the "Control Panel" window.

From the "System Image Backup" window, you will be presented with options to create either a system image or a system repair disc.

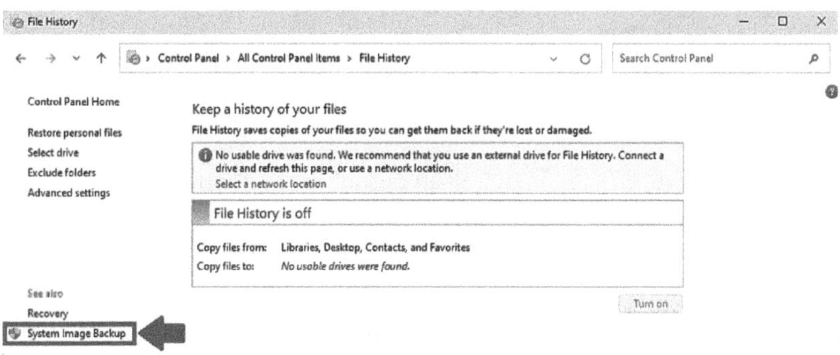

Figure 7-10: Locating the "System Image Backup" button.

A system image is a complete backup of your entire system, including the operating system, settings, installed programs, and all personal files. If your system fails or becomes corrupted, you can use a system image to restore your computer to the exact state it was in when the image was created. It is important to note that the recovery state will be from the point when you created the backup, so if you have made any significant changes to your settings or files, or added software in the interim, they will not be captured unless you create a new system image after adding

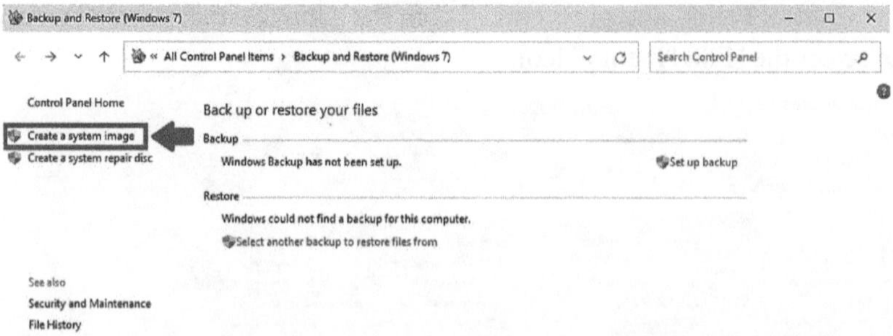

Figure 7-11: Locating the "Create a System Image" option.

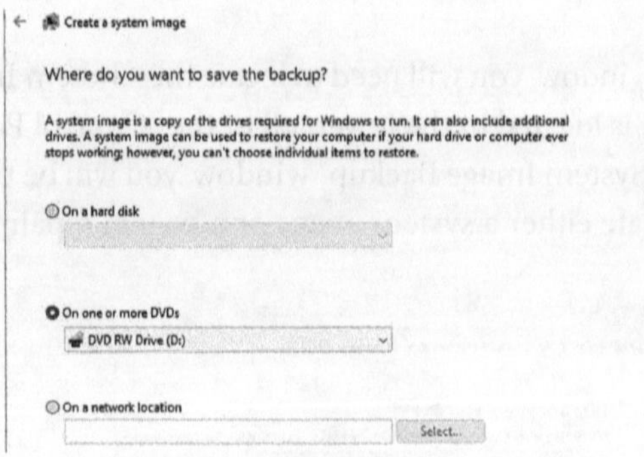

Figure 7-12: Selecting an output destination for a complete backup.

them to your device. The system image is ideal for full system recovery, while a system repair disc contains system recovery tools to help you troubleshoot and fix problems with Windows, such as start-up issues. It doesn't include your files or programs. The system repair disc has its place in system recovery, but for our purposes, we are only covering creating a system image.

When you click on "Create a System Image," your device will begin the process by searching for storage options available to back up your system. Since many devices have foregone including CD/DVD drives, and creating a system image across a network is a bit beyond our focus, you will want to select the option to create a system image on a hard disk.

After you select the output destination for the system image you will begin the backup process. Be aware that this process backs up an immense amount of information and will probably take hours to complete. Keep your device connected to a power source during the process so you don't lose your progress.[7]

Trial Presentation Software

In the modern legal environment, trial presentation software (TPS) has become an essential tool for litigation. These programs go beyond the basic capabilities of general presentation software, like PowerPoint, allowing attorneys to present evidence in a dynamic and organized manner. Below, we explore the features and capabilities of TPS platforms in general and the system requirements of three of the more popular TPS solutions—OnCue, TrialDirector, and TrialPad.

TPS is a specialized category of technology designed to assist attorneys in organizing, managing, and presenting evidence and exhibits during courtroom proceedings. Unlike preparation-intensive software, like PowerPoint, TPS is built specifically for the needs of legal professionals, offering features that streamline the presentation of complex case materials clearly and compellingly. That is not to say that PowerPoint should be disregarded altogether. Each type of presentation software has its pros and cons. PowerPoint lends itself to more scripted and rehearsed presentations, like opening and closing arguments, where it shines, whereas TPS has built-in tools to edit and create content on the fly, making it more suitable for situations calling for more flexibility, like witness examination, where it may be necessary to pivot your line of questions or even impeach a witness. Additionally, TPS tends to be much more expensive than PowerPoint, and the learning curve for the user interface is pretty steep.

Common Features of TPS

There are a variety of TPS platforms available; however, they tend to share some standard features and differ primarily in how they support those features. TPS platforms allow for document and exhibit manage-

---

7. For a walkthrough of the process for MacOS, *see Disk Utility User Guide*, https://support.apple.com/guide/disk-utility/create-a-disk-image-dskutl11888/mac.

ment within the platform. Where a PowerPoint presentation only has the information that you put into it in advance, TPSs either have a file database attached to them or draw files directly from cloud storage, allowing you to import and manipulate your case files as the need arises. This flexibility further enforces the need for good file management techniques so that you or your trial technician can quickly and efficiently access your files through the TPS platform to respond to your needs in the courtroom. Each piece of evidence can be tagged with metadata, bates numbers, or other relevant information for quick access.

Also, unlike PowerPoint slides, TPS offers dynamic interaction with your exhibits. For example, attorneys can zoom in on particular sections of a document, highlight important points, or draw annotations directly on the screen while addressing the court. These real-time tools help to focus the attention of the factfinder on the most critical parts of the evidence. Given enough notice, it is possible to duplicate these illustrations in PowerPoint. The significant advantage here is the flexibility to create these illustrations in real time as the need arises. Working in tandem, a good attorney/trial technician team working with TPS can create a rebuttal or cross-examination that looks like it has been ready to be deployed for weeks even though it was spliced together while opposing counsel was still speaking.

One of the key features that distinguishes TPS platforms from general presentation software is its ability to manage video depositions. Many of the available platforms allow attorneys to synchronize video deposition clips with the text of a written transcript. This makes it easy to play back specific sections of a deposition, display the transcript as the video plays, and quickly search for essential segments to highlight. With the advent of machine learning and AI, it is likely that TPS platforms will begin to release tools to generate transcripts from uploaded deposition video clips.

Finally, in trial presentations, it's often necessary to zoom in on or call out specific parts of a document. This process can be accomplished on general presentation software by a combination of screenshotting, zooming, cutting and pasting, but TPS allows users to make these adjustments during the trial, highlighting sections of contracts, medical records, or other documents to make them easier for the factfinder to understand. This real-time ability to manipulate evidence enhances clarity and keeps the factfinder engaged.

The aforementioned capabilities of TPS highlight some additional features that are worth noting. The ability to dynamically edit, call out, and annotate exhibits, videos, and transcripts illustrates the robust multi-media support of these platforms. General presentation software can include images, videos, text, and so on. However, once it is saved, it is in the format of that software. TPS platforms support various file formats, including PDFs, Word documents, Excel spreadsheets, images, videos, and audio recordings, all in their native formats. This versatility allows attorneys to manage all types of evidence from a central platform. Additionally, these platforms offer advanced search functions that enable attorneys to search through hundreds or thousands of documents quickly using keyword searching, dates, or exhibit numbers to pull up relevant evidence on the spot. Finally, a feature worth noting in both TPS and PowerPoint is the availability of presenter mode. Remember back when we mentioned the difference between extended desktop vs screen mirroring? The use of presenter mode coupled with extended desktop mode allows you as the presenter to control the flow of information and provides you with a staging area where your notes and tools will remain private while displaying only the relevant evidence to the audience.

System Requirements

One thing to note about the system requirements before we dig in is that of the three major platforms mentioned, two of them are designed to operate on the Windows operating system. Despite advancements in software as a service (SaaS) products, there are areas of legal technology that are still very much dominated by Windows-based devices. If you are a Mac user, this bias is important to remember when selecting the laptop and backup laptop for your trial kit. You have the option to run Windows on your Mac laptop, but if the terms "partitioning your hard drive" or "virtual desktop" give you anxiety, it may behoove you to take a look at TrialPad or look at getting a Windows-based laptop. Ultimately, if you are the one selecting your own TPS, you will be best served by surveying all of them and seeing which one most closely matches the requirements of your organization.

These programs can be demanding on a device, and even though they can be run at minimum specifications to minimize chances of lag or freezing, you should try to secure a device that meets the recommended specifications. For TrialDirector, this would include a device that has 16GB of RAM, a Quad-Core CPU with 2.4GHz or higher speed, 500GB of disk space, and a graphics cards with 4GB dedicated display graphics memory.[8] According to its documentation, OnCue seems to be a less strenuous installation, requiring only 8GB of RAM, though it would not boggle the mind for 16GB to be recommended. The disk space requirement is significantly lower at 250MB + the size of your case files.[9] Finally, TrialPad was originally designed as an iOS-based app specifically for the iPad, meaning its focus was on portability. However, in 2022, Lit Software (which makes TrialPad) released apps accessible by the MacOS.[10]

Overall, there are solutions across multiple platforms to deploy a TPS in your trial arsenal. Many of the features are very similar, and if you are part of the decision-making process you should look at upfront cost and subscription cost, file storage solution employed (local or cloud based), and complexity of the user interface along with the needs of your specific practice.

Video Conferencing Technology

Video conferencing technology has become a staple in modern legal practice, reshaping how judges, lawyers, litigants, and witnesses connect within the courtroom environment. On one hand, the advantages can be significant. Courts and counsel often benefit from reduced travel expenses and streamlined scheduling, as witnesses, parties, and experts located in distant regions no longer need to physically attend every stage of a proceeding. This efficiency can be especially pronounced in preliminary or administrative hearings, where appearing virtually allows everyone involved to conserve resources and focus on the substantive issues at hand. For courts struggling with crowded dockets or geographically dis-

---

8. Trial Direction Help Center, *System Requirements: TRIAL DIRECTOR* (Nov. 20, 2024), https://my.ipro.com/help/Desktop/Content/Product_Resources/System_Requirements_TD.htm.

9. OnCue Technology, *OnCue Facts and Specifications* (January 2, 2025, 11:17:49 AM), https://www.oncuetech.com/articles/oncue-facts-and-specifications.

10. LitSoftware, *Mac Apps Are Amazing!*, https://www.litsoftware.com/blog/mac_apps.

persed caseloads, video conferencing offers a means to clear backlogs and optimize limited time and personnel.

Another notable benefit is expanded accessibility. Remote appearances eliminate barriers faced by those who find it challenging to travel, such as the elderly, disabled, or financially constrained. By simply logging into a secure platform, these individuals can fulfill their legal obligations without enduring the ordeal of long-distance trips or navigating unfamiliar environments. Even for more routine matters, the convenience of a remote hearing can make legal processes more user-friendly, potentially encouraging greater civic participation and adherence to court schedules. Moreover, many lawyers report that remote proceedings help them manage multiple matters in different venues more efficiently since they can quickly connect from one virtual court appearance to another, avoiding wasted transit time.

However, the drawbacks of video conferencing can be just as pronounced. Foremost among these challenges is the quality of participation, which hinges on stable internet connections and precise audiovisual setups. When technology glitches—when video freezes, audio lags, or connections drop—meaningful communication can break down in a matter of seconds. A jury or judge might miss critical facial expressions, subtle vocal cues, or emotional reactions that would otherwise shape their assessment of credibility and trustworthiness. Lawyers themselves may find it more difficult to establish rapport with clients and witnesses when forced to rely on a screen rather than the intimacy of face-to-face interaction.

In addition, there are procedural concerns about witness authenticity and unauthorized coaching. In-person court appearances offer a measure of certainty that the person speaking is, in fact, who they claim to be and that they are not receiving assistance from anyone who is out of sight. In a video setting, covert prompting through text messages or a silent observer off-camera becomes more plausible. Courts may need to adopt stricter verification protocols—such as requiring a wide-angle camera shot of the entire room or a court-certified individual to confirm the witness's identity—to counteract these risks. Even these measures are not foolproof if a witness is intent on subverting the system.

Finally, some argue that video conferencing changes the dynamic of a courtroom, potentially eroding the ceremony and gravitas that in-person proceedings can confer. Critics note that part of the deterrent to frivolous litigation or evasive testimony arises from physically stepping into a courtroom with a judge, jury, and counsel arrayed in a formal environment. Remote proceedings, by contrast, may feel less imposing, leading to concerns about lower levels of decorum or seriousness. The challenge for legal systems going forward is to integrate video conferencing in a balanced manner, preserving the efficiency it brings while remaining vigilant about technical and procedural safeguards. Through measured policies, robust training, and careful oversight, courts can continue to evolve this technology in ways that bolster access to justice without compromising the core values of a fair trial.

Demonstratives

In legal proceedings, real evidence is a tangible object directly involved in the events of a case—such as a weapon allegedly used in a crime, a piece of clothing bearing forensic traces, or physical property in dispute. Because real evidence is the object itself, it is typically offered for direct inspection or testing by the factfinder (jury or judge). Courts often treat it as particularly trustworthy if it has been preserved and authenticated correctly since it can allow jurors to examine the physical characteristics and conditions for themselves.

By contrast, demonstrative evidence consists of items created to illustrate or explain the facts of a case or the testimony of a witness—such as charts, graphs, models, simulations, or diagrams. These items are not the original objects from the event in question but rather tools to help the jury or judge visualize or understand the issues at hand. For example, a scale model of a crime scene, a timeline of events, or a computer simulation of how an accident might have occurred are all forms of demonstrative evidence. Their value lies in clarifying or confirming information introduced by testimony or other evidence rather than serving as direct proof in their own right.

In essence, real evidence is the actual thing that was part of the incident or transaction, whereas demonstrative evidence is an aid that depicts or explains something about the incident. Both types can be pivotal at trial but serve distinct functions: one offering a direct look at the original items involved, the other helping jurors better understand or interpret the circumstances surrounding those items.

Technologically advanced demonstratives—such as interactive 3D animations, virtual reality reconstructions, or data-driven simulations—can dramatically enhance clarity for judges and jurors by providing vivid, intuitive depictions of complex issues. However, the very qualities that make these tools so compelling also pose questions about fairness and the potential for undue prejudice. These concerns often revolve around whether such visually engaging materials may skew the factfinders' perceptions or disadvantage one party compared to another.

One important fairness consideration arises from the resource gap between litigants. Sophisticated digital demonstratives can be expensive to produce; they often require specialized software, technical expertise, and professional design. Well-funded parties—frequently large corporations or government entities—may commission animations or simulations that visually reinforce their theory of the case. By contrast, less-resourced parties, such as pro se litigants or smaller firms, may not have the budget to create high-caliber graphics. In cases where visuals strongly influence juror perception, this disparity in presentation can tilt the playing field, potentially overshadowing the substance of the evidence itself.

Even setting aside economic inequality, advanced visualizations inherently risk overemphasizing their own narrative power. Jurors might perceive a meticulously rendered accident scene or sophisticated data visualization as an indisputable fact rather than as an argument constructed by a party seeking a particular outcome. Any demonstrative is, to some degree, a curated interpretation of events, but high-tech exhibits can appear more "objective" simply because they leverage modern tools. Attorneys may inadvertently (or intentionally) conflate an animation's persuasiveness with its factual accuracy, leaving jurors susceptible to persuasion by visually attractive but ultimately selective or incomplete portrayals.

Closely related to this issue is the potential for psychologically potent imagery to overshadow critical analysis. Studies suggest that vivid visuals can trigger emotional responses and memory retention more strongly than textual or spoken testimony alone. While the goal of a demonstrative is often to engage the factfinder, a risk emerges when emotional reactions overshadow logical deliberation. For instance, a hyper-realistic simulation of an injury incident could evoke strong sympathy or horror, distorting jurors' capacity to weigh the technical evidence objectively.

The same danger applies if a computer-generated re-enactment purports to show the "definitive" sequence of events when, in reality, it rests on contested assumptions about speeds, angles, or timelines.

Courts have begun to address these concerns by subjecting advanced demonstratives to heightened scrutiny. Judges typically require the proponent to show that the exhibit is relevant, reliable, and not unduly prejudicial under evidentiary rules. Expert testimony can help validate the underlying methodology—for instance, explaining how accident data, sensor readings, or medical imagery informed the animation's creation. Some courts also allow the opposing side to cross-examine the designer of the demonstrative or present their own counter-visualizations. These measures serve to highlight the exhibit's potential limitations or alternative interpretations, giving jurors a clearer sense of the line between what is genuinely fact-based and what is illustrative speculation.

From an ethical perspective, attorneys are obliged to ensure that technologically advanced demonstratives do not mislead. Even well-intentioned enhancements, such as color-coded diagrams or reconstructed vantage points, can subtly shift the narrative if they distort proportions or emphasize specific evidence over other salient details. Defense counsel or plaintiff's counsel might unintentionally magnify key moments while minimizing contextual factors. Recognizing this, many legal ethics guidelines and bar association commentaries advise practitioners to take particular care in balancing the persuasive force of demonstratives with their duty of candor.

Finally, fairness also involves ensuring that jurors have sufficient explanation to navigate digital evidence. Detailed instructions or curative statements from the judge can remind jurors that simulations or reconstructions are representations based on selected data, not infallible truth. In some instances, judges may even order disclaimers—such as watermarks or textual on-screen notices—that indicate specific parameters or assumptions underlying the technology. By fostering transparency, the court attempts to maintain focus on the strength of the testimony and physical evidence rather than the allure of state-of-the-art graphics.

In sum, while technologically advanced demonstratives can significantly enhance comprehension of intricate facts, they raise critical fairness and prejudice concerns. Resource disparities, the persuasive power of immersive visuals, and the potential to blur lines between interpretive artistry and objective reality underscore the need for robust judicial oversight. When properly vetted and contextualized, these high-tech exhibits can be transformative aids to factfinding. However, they must be balanced against the core legal principle of fairness, ensuring that no party gains an undue advantage solely from superior presentation methods or emotionally charged imagery. As legal practice continues to embrace cutting-edge technology, navigating the tension between innovation and impartiality remains a central challenge.

Conclusion

The effective use of courtroom technology is no longer a mere advantage—it is an essential aspect of modern legal practice. From ensuring smooth presentations with trial technicians and well-organized files to mastering courtroom systems and leveraging advanced demonstratives, attorneys must adopt a holistic approach to their technological preparations. Each step, from conducting a comprehensive tech inventory to optimizing trial graphics and presentations, underscores the importance of preparation and adaptability.

Courtroom technology serves as a bridge between complex legal narratives and the decision-makers who must understand them. Whether through dynamic trial presentation software, precise file management, or visually compelling demonstratives, these tools amplify an attorney's ability to present their case clearly and persuasively. However, with these benefits come challenges, including the potential for technical mishaps, unequal access to resources, and the risk of overemphasizing visuals at the expense of substance.

Ultimately, the successful integration of technology into the courtroom hinges on balancing innovation with ethical considerations and a deep understanding of each trial's unique demands. By staying informed, rehearsing diligently, and maintaining a commitment to fairness, legal practitioners can ensure that technology enhances—not hinders—their pursuit of justice.

Review Questions

1. What is the role of the trial technician, and why is it compared to a stage manager?
2. List three best practices for integrating a trial technician into the trial team.
3. Describe an example of how visuals can simplify complex evidence.
4. What is a "tech inventory," and why should it be included in trial preparation?
5. What is the difference between "extended desktop" and "duplicate desktop" and why is the former recommended for trials?
6. What are aspect ratio and resolution, and why are they important for courtroom presentation?
7. How does trial presentation software differ from general presentation software like PowerPoint?
8. Discuss some challenges associated with video conferencing technology in court.
9. How can courts mitigate the potential prejudicial effects of technologically advanced demonstratives?

Glossary

ABA (American Bar Association): The national organization that sets professional and ethical standards for lawyers in the United States. See also: Model Rules of Professional Conduct (MRPC).

Adobe Acrobat: A software program used to create, edit, secure, and manage PDF documents, including OCR, redaction, and Bates numbering. See also: Document Metadata Removal, Bates Numbering.

ALU (Arithmetic Logic Unit): The part of a CPU that performs arithmetic and logical operations, such as addition, subtraction, and comparisons. See also: CPU, Control Unit.

ASCII (American Standard Code for Information Interchange): A character encoding standard that represents text in computers as numbers. See also: Binary Code.

Bandwidth: The maximum rate at which data can be transmitted over a network, often compared to the width of lanes on a highway. See also: Router, ISP.

Bates Numbering: A method of assigning unique, sequential numbers to documents for identification in legal proceedings. See also: Adobe Acrobat, Chain of Custody.

BIOS (Basic Input/Output System): Firmware stored on a chip on the motherboard that initializes hardware and loads the operating system. See also: Motherboard.

Binary Code: The base-2 system of ones and zeros that computers use to process and store information. See also: ASCII, CPU.

Blockchain: A decentralized, tamper-resistant ledger used to securely record transactions or data across multiple computers. See also: Smart Contracts, Chain of Custody.

Cache Memory: A small, high-speed memory located near the CPU that stores frequently used data for quick access. See also: CPU, RAM, Registers.

Casetext Co-Counsel: A generative AI legal research and drafting assistant developed for attorneys. See also: Lexis+ AI, Generative AI.

Chain of Custody: The documented process that tracks the handling and transfer of evidence to maintain its integrity. See also:eDiscovery, Bates Numbering, Blockchain.

Chipset: The set of electronic components on a motherboard that manages data flow between the CPU, memory, and peripherals. See also: Motherboard, CPU.

Comment 8 (Technology Competence): The ABA rule interpretation requiring lawyers to stay up to date with the benefits and risks of relevant technology. See also: Duty of Technological Competence, Rule 1.1 (Competence).

Confidentiality, Integrity, Availability (CIA Triad): A foundational cybersecurity model ensuring data is kept private, accurate, and accessible. See also: Encryption, Cryptography.

Control Unit (CU): The part of a CPU that directs the flow of data and instructions between components. See also: ALU, CPU.

CPU (Central Processing Unit): The main processing unit of a computer, often described as its "brain." See also: Cache Memory, Registers, Control Unit, ALU.

Cryptography: The science of securing information through encryption and decryption techniques. See also: Encryption, Blockchain.

Deep Learning: A subset of machine learning that utilizes neural networks with multiple layers to identify patterns in large datasets. See also: Machine Learning, Artificial Intelligence.

DNS (Domain Name System): The Internet's "phone book" that translates domain names (like google.com) into IP addresses. See also: IP Address, Router.

Document Metadata Removal: The process of stripping hidden information (like authorship or edits) from documents to protect confidentiality. See also: Adobe Acrobat, Metadata.

Driver: A piece of software that allows an operating system to communicate with a hardware device. See also: Peripheral Devices.

Duty of Technological Competence: The ethical obligation for lawyers to understand and use technology appropriately in their legal practice. See also: Comment 8, Rule 1.1 (Competence).

eDiscovery: The process of identifying, collecting, and producing electronically stored information (ESI) for legal cases. See also: Metadata, Chain of Custody.

Encryption: The process of converting information into a coded form to prevent unauthorized access. See also: Cryptography and the CIA Triad.

Ethernet: A standard method of connecting computers in a local area network using cables. See also: LAN, Router.

Form Factor: The size and layout specification of computer hardware, such as a motherboard. See also: Motherboard.

Generative AI: A form of artificial intelligence that creates new content, such as text or images, based on patterns in training data. See also: Lexis+ AI, Casetext Co-Counsel.

Gigabyte (GB): A unit of digital information equal to 1,024 megabytes (roughly one billion bytes). See also: Kilobyte, Megabyte, Terabyte.

Hard Disk Drive (HDD): A data storage device that uses spinning magnetic disks to store information. See also: Solid State Drive (SSD).

IP Address (Internet Protocol Address): A unique numeric identifier assigned to every device connected to the Internet. See also: IPv4, IPv6, DNS.

IPv4: The older Internet addressing system using 32-bit numbers, supporting about 4.3 billion unique addresses. See also: IPv6.

IPv6: The newer Internet addressing system using 128-bit numbers, supporting vastly more unique addresses. See also: IPv4.

ISP (Internet Service Provider): A company that provides users access to the Internet (e.g., Comcast, Verizon). See also: Router, Bandwidth.

Kibibyte (KiB): A unit of digital storage equal to 1,024 bytes, preferred for technical accuracy over kilobyte. See also: Kilobyte.

Kilobyte (KB): A unit of digital storage equal to 1,024 bytes, commonly used to measure small files. See also: Megabyte, Gigabyte.

LAN (Local Area Network): A network connecting devices within a small geographic area, like an office or building. See also: Ethernet, MAN, WAN.

Lexis+ AI: A generative AI tool integrated into the Lexis legal research platform. See also: Casetext Co-Counsel, Generative AI.

Machine Learning (ML): A type of artificial intelligence that enables systems to enhance their performance through experience and data. See also: Deep Learning, Artificial Intelligence.

MAN (Metropolitan Area Network): A network that spans a city or large campus, connecting multiple LANs. See also: LAN, WAN.

Megabyte (MB): A unit of digital storage equal to 1,024 kilobytes, used for medium-sized files. See also: Kilobyte, Gigabyte.

Metadata: Hidden data embedded in a file, such as the author, edit history, or file path. See also: Document Metadata Removal, eDiscovery.

Model Rules of Professional Conduct (MRPC): A set of ethical guidelines for lawyers published by the ABA. See also: Rule 1.1 (Competence), Comment 8.

Motherboard: The main circuit board in a computer that connects and allows communication among all components. See also: Chipset, Form Factor, BIOS.

NSLT (National Society of Legal Technology): An organization that provides training modules in legal technology tools. See also: Procertas Legal Technology Assessment.

OSI Model (Open Systems Interconnection Model): A conceptual seven-layer model describing how data is transmitted across networks. See also: TCP/IP Model.

PAN (Personal Area Network): A small network organized around a single user, such as connecting a laptop, printer, and mouse at home. See also: LAN, WAN.

Peering Agreements: Arrangements between ISPs to allow data to flow across each other's networks without fees. See also: ISP, Router.

Peripheral Devices: External devices, such as keyboards, printers, and scanners, that connect to a computer. See also: Driver.

Petabyte (PB): A unit of digital storage equal to 1,024 terabytes, often used for large-scale data centers. See also: Terabyte.

Procertas Legal Technology Assessment: A training and certification tool focused on Microsoft Office and Adobe Acrobat skills for lawyers. See also: NSLT, Adobe Acrobat.

Quantum Teleportation: An experimental communication method using quantum entanglement to transmit information instantly.

RAM (Random Access Memory): Volatile memory that temporarily stores data for quick access while a computer is running. See also: CPU, Cache Memory, Registers.

Registers: Small, high-speed storage locations inside the CPU that hold data temporarily during processing. See also: Cache Memory, RAM.

Router: A device that directs data packets between networks, ensuring they reach the correct destination. See also: Bandwidth, DNS, ISP.

Rule 1.1 (Competence): The ABA ethical rule requiring lawyers to provide competent representation to clients. See also: Duty of Technological Competence, Comment 8.

Smart Contracts: Self-executing digital agreements stored on a blockchain, triggered automatically by predefined conditions. See also: Blockchain.

Solid State Drive (SSD): A faster, more durable storage device that uses flash memory instead of moving parts. See also: Hard Disk Drive (HDD).

Styles (Microsoft Word): Predefined formatting sets that ensure consistency in headings, text, and documents. See also: Table of Contents (ToC).

Table of Contents (ToC): A navigational aid in a document that lists sections and page numbers, which can be generated automatically in Word. See also: Styles.

TCP/IP Model: A practical four-layer framework used to implement data transmission across the Internet. See also: OSI Model.

Terabyte (TB): A unit of digital storage equal to 1,024 gigabytes, commonly used for large hard drives and other storage devices. See also: Gigabyte, Petabyte.

WAN (Wide Area Network): An extensive network covering a wide geographic area, such as the Internet. See also: LAN, MAN, PAN.

Index